DATE DUE

Game Changer

The publisher gratefully acknowledges the generous support of the General Endowment Fund of the University of California Press Foundation.

Game Changer

Animal Rights and the
Fate of Africa's Wildlife

Glen Martin

UNIVERSITY OF CALIFORNIA PRESS
Berkeley · Los Angeles · London

University of California Press, one of the most distin-
guished university presses in the United States, enriches
lives around the world by advancing scholarship in the
humanities, social sciences, and natural sciences. Its activities are supported by the UC Press Foundation and by
philanthropic contributions from individuals and institutions. For more information, visit www.ucpress.edu.

University of California Press
Berkeley and Los Angeles, California

University of California Press, Ltd.
London, England

Library of Congress Cataloging-in-Publication Data

Martin, Glen, 1949–
    Game changer : animal rights and the fate of Africa's
wildlife / Glen Martin. — 1st ed.
        p.   cm.
    Includes bibliographical references and index.
    ISBN 978-0-520-26626-1 (hardback)
    1. Animal welfare—Africa.   2. Animal rights—Africa.
3. Animal rights—Environmental aspects—Africa.
4. Wildlife conservation—Africa.   5. Animal rights
activists—Africa.   6. Animal rights movement—Africa.
I. Title.
    HV4877.A3M37   2012
    179'.3096—dc23   2011035059

Manufactured in the United States of America

21 20 19 18 17 16 15 14 13. 12
10 9 8 7 6 5 4 3 2 1

In keeping with a commitment to support environmentally responsible and sustainable printing practices,
UC Press has printed this book on Rolland Enviro100,
a 100% post-consumer fiber paper that is FSC certified,
deinked, processed chlorine-free, and manufactured with
renewable biogas energy. It is acid-free and EcoLogo
certified.

To Tess and Kimo

Contents

Illustrations

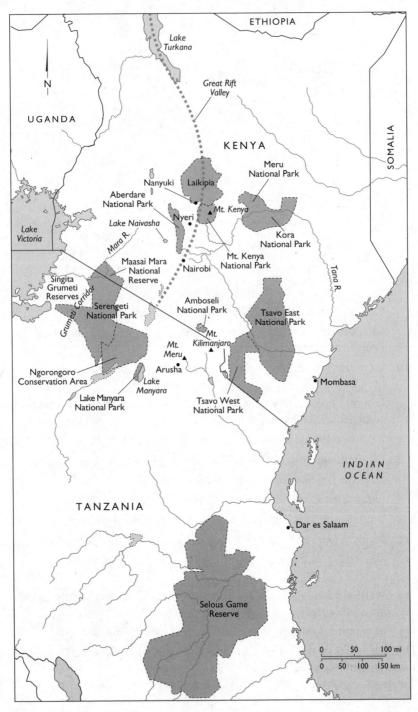

ETHIOPIA

Lake Turkana

Great Rift Valley

UGANDA

KENYA

Nanyuki
Laikipia
Meru National Park

Aberdare National Park
Mt. Kenya
Kora National Park

Lake Naivasha
Nyeri

Mara R.
Maasai Mara National Reserve
Mt. Kenya National Park

SOMALIA

Singita Grumeti Reserves
Nairobi

Grumeti Corridor
Serengeti National Park
Amboseli National Park
Mt. Kilimanjaro
Tana R.
Tsavo East National Park

Ngorongoro Conservation Area
Mt. Meru
Arusha
Lake Manyara

Lake Manyara National Park
Tsavo West National Park

Mombasa

Lake Victoria

TANZANIA

INDIAN OCEAN

Dar es Salaam

Selous Game Reserve

N

0   50   100 mi
0   50   100 150 km

Kenya and northern Tanzania

Namibia

CHAPTER I

Never an Eden

For anyone who has traveled the developing world, Nairobi is instantly recognizable. It is the doppelganger of Manila, Mexico City, Lagos, Bangkok—a dynamic conurbation of immense size, swelling almost visibly, with a core of decayed high-rises surrounded by concentric rings of slums and gridlocked roadways. The only clues that this is the capital of Kenya, the heart of East Africa, are the marabou storks perched disconsolately on the fever trees along Uhuru Highway, the city's primary thoroughfare. Somehow, they still evoke the veldt and the bush, the teeming game.

Fifty years ago, lions hunted and black rhinos browsed in the acacia scrub on the very outskirts of town. Today, the only sizable expanse of open land near the city is Nairobi National Park, a partly fenced thirty-thousand-acre reserve that is adjacent to Kenyatta International Airport and still contains fairly robust populations of plains game. It is not unusual to see the bloated carcass of a zebra or impala that somehow broke through the wire next to the airport's service road, only to be struck by a cab shuttling passengers to and from the city.

The park, however, is a mere remnant of what was. More (or less) than that, it is hardly representative of an intact and functioning East African ecosystem. Rather, it is a de facto landscape-scale zoo that exists because of the fences. Nor is it inviolate. Poaching, poisoning, and encroachment by livestock herders and squatters all go on here, reflecting in microcosm the processes that are degrading game populations and habitat throughout the region.

Not far from the park is the bosky suburb of Langata. This exceedingly pleasant purlieu is characterized by large tree-covered lots, well-appointed homes, and a pervasive tranquility that contrasts markedly with the chaos of central Nairobi just to the north. Songbirds throng the trees, and leopards still occasionally drift through, subsisting on rats, cats—and especially dogs, a highly favored prey item. Leopards remain the one charismatic predator in Africa that has held its own. Like coyotes in North America, they are fecund and flexible, able to adapt to a variety of habitats, including suburbs and slums. They are as happy to den in a culvert or abandoned building as in a cave or in an inselberg or a baobab trunk cavity. In Langata, as throughout all of Kenya save the very heart of Nairobi and Mombasa, dog-lovers still secure their pets at night.

Kenyans in the professions or government service live in Langata. Among them is a smattering of white citizens, mostly elderly and retired from government, farming, or both. Their status is ambiguous, their very existence a reminder of the colonial period, a time fraught with strife and blood. Still, they are Kenyans, and their love of country typically is profound. They have endured many vicissitudes, and both age and experience have made them philosophical. Ian Parker belongs to this cohort.

I came here one morning to interview him as part of an investigative project on East African conservation issues. Many of the people I had talked to earlier had emphasized the necessity of meeting with him: Parker, they said, had perspective. He understood the history of game management—more to the point, he had contributed to that history; he was part of it. He was unsentimental and science oriented. He could see and explain the Big Picture. After some effort, my cabbie found his home—a small house set well back from the road in a grove of large trees. Parker answered the door at my knock. We sat down, drank hot beverages—tea for him, coffee for me—and talked into the afternoon.

Now in his seventies, Parker is spare and fit, his erect posture a testament to his military background. His movements are precise, his demeanor reserved, his eyes cool and calculating. But he is no martinet. Humor is integral to his personality, as dry as the Laikipia bushlands north of Nanyuki. His long face, seamed and florid from a lifetime of brutal sun, is often illuminated by a wintry smile as he relates self-deprecating and mordant anecdotes that typically involve unexpected or inexplicable violence—hallmarks of many conversations in Africa.

As a commander of a platoon of the Kikuyu Tribal Police, Parker fought the Mau-Mau on the slopes of Mount Kenya and the Aberdares. Later, he spent decades as a game ranger and warden, ultimately responsible for wildlife management in a district that covered thousands of square kilometers. He shot hundreds of elephants in culling operations aimed at protecting the rangelands and killed a comparable number of Cape buffalo that threatened tribal and colonial cattle with bovine diseases. He battled Somali *shifta* (bandits) who were terrorizing pastoral herders, and he implacably persecuted poachers. He consulted on game management and traded in ivory. He is one of a remaining handful of professional hunters and wardens who experienced East Africa at a time when it was a wilderness surrounding a few islands of human habitation, unlike the current obverse.

Parker has published a couple of memoirs, in which his life seems Brobdingnagian, heroic in scope. Hemingway and Robert Ruark wrote about men like Parker and desperately wished they were like him. Since Parker's early years as a "settler boy" on a Kenyan farm, his life has been defined by the wild creatures of East Africa, from the Daddy Christmas swallowtails he netted as a toddler to the elephants he both hunted and protected as a man.

Nor is his life one of contemplative rustication today. A couple of years ago, he and his wife circumnavigated the shoreline of Lake Turkana by canoe. This huge Rift Valley lake is located in the no-man's-land of Kenya's Northern Frontier District, hard on the Ethiopian border. It is situated in one of the hottest, driest places on earth. Its alkaline waters teem with crocodiles, and *shifta* haunt the sere shores. It is wild in every sense and dangerous in the extreme; roads are both rough and rare, and civil authority and medical care are wholly absent. Get in trouble around Lake Turkana, and no help will be forthcoming. Yet Parker recalls the trip as a pleasant idyll, a sojourn marked by incomparable vistas, pleasant days of fishing for huge Nile perch, nights spent under skies gaudy with stars.

"It was marvelous," he recalls. "If you've lived an active life, you really can't spend your later years sitting around doing nothing. Inaction is a depressing prospect." Lately, Parker has taken up sailboat racing. "I'd never done it before, and I'm enjoying it tremendously," he says. "It's a thrilling pastime."

But as Parker looks back on his life, he has no illusions of overarching accomplishment. All the years he spent as a game warden, diligently enforcing regulations and apprehending malefactors, now seem to him, in large degree, wasted effort. Kenya's megafauna continue to decline despite the best efforts of game wardens, wildlife biologists, animal enthusiasts, and a 1977 hunting ban that was originally hailed as a template for the salvation of the continent's wildlife.

"The one thing I had a real chance to do in my career was stop the spread of the Indian crow," Parker muses, "and we didn't pursue it." Corvids from the Indian subcontinent, Indian house crows are large, slim birds that first showed up on the Kenyan coast in the 1970s. "I was working the coast at that time, and there was only one small colony of them. If we had put some effort into it, we could have eliminated them," Parker says. "But the powers-that-be had other ideas about where our energy should be expended."

The house crows quickly spread from their small redoubt and now are wreaking havoc on native birds throughout coastal Kenya and Tanzania. Like English sparrows, they thrive in disturbed habitats, including suburbs and farmlands—areas that are spreading rapidly throughout East Africa at the expense of pristine woodland and savanna. And like English sparrows, house crows use roads and railways as convenient paths from one potential habitat to another. "They represented my one real opportunity for effecting beneficial change," Parker says with a wry smile. "And I wasn't able to take it."

Parker is thus less than optimistic about the future for Africa's wildlife. He acknowledges that many well-meaning and well-funded efforts by people of good conscience are under way to stem and reverse the decline of the game. But, he says, it probably won't be enough. It's not just the poaching, the government corruption, the ongoing implacable conversion of habitat to cropland and grazing commons; those trends, he says, are mere symptoms. The real problem, the only problem in his eyes, is shifting trends in biomass.

"In the past decade, Africa's human population has grown by, oh, something like one hundred million people," Parker says from a chair in the cool, shadowed interior of his Langata cottage. He sips tea between sentences. Two small terriers lie at his feet, occasionally jumping up to patrol the room, gnaw at skin irritations, or beg for a caress. "So with a little basic math, you arrive at something like fifty billion kilos of biomass added to the continent. And that's vertebrate, omnivorous biomass, mind you—human beings. More than that, modern humans consume disproportionately more resources than other vertebrates, including earlier humans who had simpler lifestyles. They require not just a subsistence diet; if possible, they'll secure a surfeit of food, of many varieties. And things like cars, air-conditioning, televisions [consume even more resources]. So they—we—represent a tremendous demand on any resource base."

To the newcomer, East Africa is vast, seemingly endless. The Serengeti stretches to the horizon, speckled with plains game. The hills and gorges of Laikipia and the Northern Frontier in Kenya, bordered by the eastern Rift Valley, form a gigantic fractal landscape that defies normal conventions of space and boundary. But Parker has patrolled this land for fifty years, from Uganda through Tanzania. To him, it is familiar, discrete, comprehensible—and finite. And it is not large enough, rich enough, to respond to the demands now made on it. Something has to get the short end of the stick. And that, says Parker, is the megafauna—and the people who historically depended on the megafauna, such as the Wata, a near-extinct Kenyan tribe whose members specialized in hunting elephants with powerful longbows and poisoned arrows. All have been supplanted, he says, with the "strange form" of human being: modern, technologically savvy, urbanized primates whose social status depends on the accumulation of wealth, namely, the conversion of natural resources into goods and money.

As is the case with many people, elephants in particular engage Parker. But unlike most pachyderm fans, he does not romanticize them. He acknowledges their deep intelligence and complex social order. But for him, they are, more than anything else, the emblem of wild Africa—more accurately, the wild Africa that was but now exists merely in tourist brochures. Wild Africa was largely doomed, Parker says, when it started getting chopped up into nation-states. "The large fauna, particularly elephants, had evolved with few geographic constraints," he says. "They literally had the continent at their disposal, and they ultimately came to require resources on a continental scale to survive."

Parker explains that East Africa's great elephant herds originally traversed thousands of miles in their migrations, traveling from Ethiopia to Zambia and back in stately, seasonal rounds as they sought forage and water. And wherever they went, they shaped ecosystems. "They were one of the great evolutionary engines on the continent. An area that contained too many elephants was ultimately stripped of forest. Then the elephants declined in number or moved on and plains game moved in, until the forest came back. Then the elephants returned, and on and on." This dynamic resulted in a rich tapestry of habitats, with many "edges": mature and secondary forest, brushlands, savanna, transition zones of every permutation. This varied habitat in turn supported a tremendous diversity of wildlife.

"The problems start when an area has too many elephants that can't go anywhere," Parker says. "And elephants started running into real obstacles when Africa began the transition from a series of tribal home-lands to nation-states that supported greater numbers of people with accompanying infrastructure—more and larger farms, cities, roadways. Elephants had evolved to need a continent, and then the continent was denied them."

East Africa's national parks were conceived to provide elephants and other megafauna with an option to extinction, but in Parker's view, they have merely delayed an inevitable collapse. "Within ten years of creation, virtually every national park had elephant problems," Parker recalls of the early days of his career. "They flattened landscapes, utterly disrupted local ecosystems, drove the decline of many species. They could not be allowed open-ended population growth in circumscribed areas. Ultimately their populations would grow beyond the means of the available habitat and finally collapse—but not before they had destroyed everything."

That led to culling—a practice that Parker and a handful of other wardens refined to a science. It was not a business for the faint-hearted, he acknowledges. Given the complexity of elephant society, tremen-dous stress can be generated in a herd if certain members are selectively killed, particularly older female members, who act as *askaris* (guards) and instructors of younger elephants. "It is much more humane and much less disruptive to the larger population if entire family groups are killed quickly," Parker says. "If you shoot the matriarch, the remaining elephants cluster around her, and you are able to take them down in very short order. Ultimately, we got it down to where a few of us could kill an entire herd in fifty seconds." Culling also had other benefits, in Parker's view. Local villages were given the meat, highly esteemed food on a continent where protein shortages are endemic. That created a cer-tain tolerance for elephants among farmers who cultivated lands on the margins of the parks, where the animals sometimes foraged: "They felt there was something in it for them."

Too, ivory from the culled elephants both contributed to communal tribal wealth and supported the conservation efforts of Kenya's early wildlife services. Ultimately, of course, the ivory trade generated its own dynamic, one that led to the cessation of legalized hunting in Kenya. Parker acknowledges that poaching for ivory played a significant role in the reduction and even the elimination of local elephant populations, but he insists the African elephant was doomed as a populous, free-ranging species long before the Ivory Wars of the late twentieth century.

"Human beings evolved with elephants," he says, "and we were adapted to them. We shared this continent with them for millions of years and were able to exploit the same habitats." But then, says Parker, the "strange form" of humans returned to the continent after hundreds of thousands of years of global peregrination and evolution. They brought with them technologies and cultural imperatives that allowed them to reshape the land—demanded it of them. Since this strange form invaded, wildlife habitat in Africa has steadily diminished.

"As a game warden, I was brought up with the idea that conservation is a growing thing, an idea that would only gain power with time," says Parker. To a certain extent, he says, the decades have borne out that intimation: conservation and its later permutation, environmentalism, have never been more voguish. But the reality shows that where it counts, real conservation is declining. As a percentage of government expenditures, the greatest amount of money put into Kenyan conservation was around 1900. Also, in 1900, 23 percent of Kenya's land was game reserve—absolutely inviolate sanctuary where hunting was proscribed. Today, only 4 percent of Kenya's land has reserve status." Driving the land conversion, Parker observes, is population growth; Kenya's human numbers have shot up from eight million people at the declaration of the country's independence in 1963 to thirty million today. Since 1977, the year the hunting ban was introduced, wildlife populations have fallen by 70 percent.

Still, a fraction—even a significant portion—of the game could be preserved, says Parker, if it had real value for the people who live with and around it. But public policy in Kenya, he claims, has reduced its value. The hunting ban ultimately has come to mean that wildlife cannot be utilized in any way and hence has no value to rural residents. Ecotourism benefits the wealthy lodge owner and the tour company operator but not the pastoral herdsman caring for a herd of goats or the freehold farmer scratching a subsistence living from a hectare of maize and pumpkins. For them, wildlife is at best a neutral entity, although seldom even that: elephants raid the maize, lions and hyenas eat the goats. Tribal people can't, legally, take an elephant or eland for food or sell a permit to a wealthy trophy hunter for a lion. So it makes more sense to poach the elephant, poison the lion, and subsequently raise the goats and maize in peace.

Simultaneous with the surge in Kenya's human population was the emergence of modern environmentalism. This has not necessarily benefited African wildlife, says Parker. "It was most unfortunate when conservation transformed into environmentalism. The -*ism* is the problem. When you start creating -*isms,* you're creating systems of belief and faith rather than pursuing science-based courses of action." In East Africa, Parker says, conservation started off as something that was "as emotionless as agriculture. It was obviously in the public interest to pursue it, so we looked at the most effective ways to implement it. Then, over the course of the past fifty years, it has become a cause, a platform for charismatic personalities and heated philosophy."

The upshot, he says, is that scientists and game managers can no longer implement effective conservation policies, because that can produce images repulsive to African wildlife's largest fan base—tourists and animal lovers from the developed world. For these people, megafauna is a highly valued commodity—but also a highly romanticized one, a commodity that can be appreciated only while alive. If a lion is killed for a trophy or an elephant culled to preserve habitat, it is transformed from an object that inspires near religious reverence to an object whose death inspires utter disgust. Never mind, says Parker, that regular rations of meat from the regulated culling of elephants and buffalo would provide subsistence farmers with real incentives for keeping game around or that pastoral tribes would tolerate predators more readily if they were to derive some income from trophy hunting concessions. The mere prospect of the sanctioned killing of wild animals is too horrific for many environmentalists to contemplate, even though it could actually work to preserve wildlife on a large scale. To a significant degree, Parker says, the lives of individual animals have come to mean more to many environmentalists-cum-animal-lovers than wild ecosystems and the complex assemblages of species they support.

Part of the problem is simple emotional accessibility, Parker acknowledges: a dewy-eyed Thomson's gazelle, lolling lion, or cute-as-a-button elephant calf is more immediately comprehensible to the layperson than a long treatise on predator-prey relationships in acacia parklands. Still, he says, "the 'environmental ethic' in Kenya is pernicious, because it has become heavily invested with dogma. It is a doctrine now, a belief system, having nothing to do with the reality of ecosystems, real wildlife in real situations, the preservation of habitat. The idea of trade-offs or compromises that could result in some real progress on the ground— forget it. Ideological purity is what counts."

Parker is particularly incensed by what he terms a faulty sense of history about Kenya—the idea that it was a stable and pristine wilderness burgeoning with wildlife until white settlement began in the late nineteenth century. He notes the evidence is solid that game populations in Kenya have always been in flux and generally pegged to shifts in human population. "When human populations were high, game was scarce. The opposite was true when situations reversed. Yes, Kenya was teeming with game at the end of the 1890s, when the central highlands started seeing significant [European] settlement. But that situation followed severe declines in tribal populations."

In the 1880s, Kenya's cattle herds were almost extirpated by successive waves of rinderpest and bovine pleuropneumonia; that catastrophe culminated in the great famine of 1897–98, which depopulated vast regions of countryside. The absence of cattle resulted in abundant forage for grazing and browsing wildlife, increasing the prey base for predators. Encounters with human beings were minimal. "Basically, the wildlife had a great deal of scope for expansion simply because the number of human beings was low," Parker says.

In earlier decades and centuries, the reverse was true: human populations were relatively high in what is now Kenya, much of the land was used for grazing and farming, and wildlife conflicts with herders and cultivators were common. More people, in short, meant reduced options for wild animals. "Basically, it's the situation we're seeing these days," Parker says, "though obviously the scale [of the pressures on game] is now on a much larger order."

Misconceptions by the lay public about Africa and its wildlife are thus driving unrealistic policies, particularly in Kenya, says Parker—policies that seem high-flown and virtuous but are utterly unrealistic and unworkable, inflicting harm rather than ameliorating it. "There's this message going out that East Africa used to be a Garden of Eden," Parker says. "Nonsense. It's never been a bloody Eden; it has always been a very, very rough place. Man evolved here, and so did a multitude of microorganisms that controlled human numbers—think malaria, sleeping sickness. People were just part of the shifting mix of fauna. It was always easy for people to succumb to disease, to get eaten, gored, or stomped here, to die in any number of unpleasant ways. When wildlife thrived it was at the expense of human beings and the other way around. Elephants inhibited agriculture until enough people picked up enough sticks to inhibit the elephants. That's still how it works in the bush. So if you want people to change—out where it counts, where the animals still live—you have to give them a palpable reason, one based on self-interest, *not* to pick up the stick. Simply passing a hunting ban and issuing pious statements from Nairobi about the sanctity of wildlife isn't going to cut it."

Parker thinks often of the Wata, an elephant-hunting tribe of east-ern Kenya that has now been reduced to a remnant population. He is deeply familiar with many of Kenya's forty-plus tribes, but he par-ticularly admires the Wata for their honesty, gentleness, great hunting prowess, and encyclopedic knowledge of wildlife. In 1960, Parker origi-nated the Galana Scheme, the goal of which was to provide an exclu-sive province for the Wata—a reserve of three thousand square miles along the eastern border of Tsavo National Park, which allowed them to practice their traditional elephant-hunting culture in a sustainable fashion. Under the plan, ivory taken by the Wata was sold by the gov-ernment through legal channels. The Galana Scheme was implemented with great hope and was managed first by the colonial government, later through a private enterprise. But administrative problems plagued the program until it was finally curtailed in 1976. Ultimately, the Galana Scheme was an attempt to fuse conservation with programs designed to meet the exigent needs of local people, and though it didn't work, Parker still feels it was on the right track.

Like the Wata, Parker knows the megafauna on their own terms; he respects Africa's large wild animals; he hunted them, fought fiercely to maintain the habitats they require for survival. He can still remem-ber a time when the great beasts dominated the landscape. Parker once roamed the East African bush as freely as both the elephants on their endless migrations and the Wata who trailed along their spoor, poi-soned arrows nocked to their bowstrings. Like them, his movements have been circumscribed by the modern world. Langata is by no means an unpleasant place, but seeing Parker at his repose, you get the sense of an old, tough bull elephant at Aberdare National Park in central Kenya, a fenced reserve of montane forest surrounded by agricultural land, safe from rapine and ruin only because of the barriers. Parker is backed up against the wire, facing into the forest, looking at an Africa that exists only in his mind, in the memories of a few peers, and in some shrinking islands of functional habitat.

But he is hardly morose. He has a profound talent for inhabiting and enjoying the moment, and comparisons of the past to the present don't vitiate his pleasure in contemplating both. "I've enjoyed all of it, enjoyed it tremendously," Parker says, recalling his years as a soldier, warden, game cropper, and man of letters. "But I was never emotion-ally invested in it. Most people who know me say that was probably my weakness, but it was really my greatest strength. I never felt that things had to be a certain way, that I could or should fight trends that were beyond the power of anyone to reasonably affect. I certainly didn't enjoy all the developments I've witnessed, but I didn't let them depress me. I only had one life to live, and depression wouldn't have made me more effective in my work in any event."

As to the future, Parker admits to deep pessimism: "There is already famine in the Northern Frontier District. People are foraging in the bush for whatever they can eat, some are dying. And that's with fewer than forty million people in the country. Twenty years from now, it will be seventy million people. Again, that growth will come at the expense of wildlife and wildlife habitat."

Nor does Parker think effective policies will be implemented to sustain the wildlife that remains. The trend in conservationist thinking continues to emphasize the warm, cuddly fuzziness of individual animals over habitat management. "As an example, take my specialty, elephants," Parker observes. "Anyone who knows anything at all about these issues knows that for maximum biodiversity in forest ecosystems, you have to control elephant numbers. There is no alternative, given that migration options for elephants have now been eliminated. But the chances for a sustained rational program [of elephant culling] in this country are nil."

The current zeitgeist, in short, supports anthropomorphism. Africa once seemed isolated from this trend, but no longer. Indeed, the modern apotheosis of the individual wild animal actually began in Kenya about sixty years ago, and the man who started it all—George Adamson—was one of Parker's contemporaries and colleagues.

CHAPTER 2

The Man Who Hated Hyenas

The syrupy strains and the histrionic lyrics will still be recalled by people of a certain age. But despite their schmaltz, they created a beatific vision, one evoking a time and place central to the human dream, if not human reality:

> Born free, as free as the wind blows
> As free as the grass grows
> Born free to follow your hear-r-r-rt.

The song, the eponymous theme for the film *Born Free,* won an Oscar in 1966 and hit number seven on the charts. It was inescapable that year, blaring from every car radio and home stereo, whistled or hummed on the streets. And the film—a loose interpretation of the efforts of the Kenya Game Department warden George Adamson and his wife, Joy, to rehabilitate and release lions to the wild—enraptured the public. Unlike all other Africa-themed popular movies to that date, *Born Free* wasn't about safaris, parlous interactions with wildlife and tribal people, or intrepid white explorers slogging through jungles and across savannas. It portrayed the African lion as a complex animal capable of receiving and reciprocating human affection. Lions, the film implied, warranted preservation simply because of their sentience and the role they have played in Africa's ecosystems. In essence, *Born Free* was the first environmentally themed movie. It got people in Europe and North America thinking about Africa's wildlife as something other than a potential head on a wall or rug on a floor.

The Adamsons, of course, were not the primary protagonists of *Born Free*. That distinction belonged to Elsa, the lioness whom the couple raised from a cub and ultimately released to the wild. Their efforts with Elsa and other lions were seminal, marking the first real attempt at establishing a protocol for the rehabilitation of African predators. Their vision has since grown into a large and discrete segment of the general environmental movement. Wildlife rehabilitation is now pursued on a very large scale, involving everything from pachyderms to pinnipeds. When practiced as part of species recovery, it is a valuable adjunct subsumed into a larger mission. In other instances, it is a goal in its own right, one devoted to alleviating suffering and maximizing survival opportunities for individual animals. The thirty-two-million-dollar Marine Mammal Center in Sausalito, California, for example, devotes much of its funds and a good deal of the energy of its large staff of professionals and volunteers to saving injured, ill, or starving California sea lions, a species that numbers around three hundred thousand individuals off the state's coast and is hardly in imminent danger of extinction. For the supporters of the Marine Mammal Center, each sea lion is precious and deserving of extraordinary effort to succor. Adamson helped inculcate modern society with this way of thinking through his early efforts with Elsa, Boy, and his other leonine charges.

Today, Born Free, an organization founded on the Adamsons' vision, is one of the world's foremost conservation-cum-animal-rights groups; George Adamson has been canonized as its founding saint. Both his life and his demise work toward this end: he drew international attention with his efforts to return captive lions to the wild, and he died a hero's death fighting Somali *shifta* in 1989. And without doubt he looked the part. He was spare and sunburnt, with thick white hair that hung to his shoulders, and a trimmed white goatee; a big briar pipe was omnipresent in his teeth. Yet he did not start off as a doting, charismatic animal lover—and indeed, his affections were selective throughout his life.

He was born in 1906 in Cheltenham, England, and by 1938 he was in Kenya, where he took a job with the colony's game department. He was assigned to patrol the Northern Game Reserve, a huge swath of wild forest and bush that constituted much of northern Kenya, including the Laikipia Plateau, the Aberdares, and Mount Kenya. He served briefly in the British military during the early years of World War II. After returning from the war, he was provided with a contingent of

FIGURE 1. George Adamson in a contemplative moment. Adamson looked like central casting's idea of a Kenyan ranger and warden. Highly idiosyncratic in his approach to his job, he was often at odds with his bosses and mainline conservationists. No one could dispute his personal ethics or courage. He died at the age of eighty-three at the Kora Reserve fighting Somali bandits who had attacked a tourist. (© Bill Travers/ www.bornfree.org.uk)

game scouts from local tribes and ultimately given jurisdiction over the wildlife that inhabited an eighty-five-thousand-square-mile chunk of territory that ran east from Lake Turkana and north from the Tana River to the Somali border—somewhat less than half of Kenya.

Adamson's job throughout his association with Kenya's game agencies was to protect the wildlife, but he also was required to protect human beings, livestock, and property from the depredations of wildlife. As a consequence, he was required to kill quite a few animals. According to records obtained by Ian Parker (who served with Adamson in the Game Department, knew him well, and considered him likable and charismatic if quixotic), he reported killing fifty lions, fifty-two elephants, three rhinos, four leopards, and five buffalo from 1938 through 1949. The beasts were dispatched for various reasons, including killing or menacing human beings.

Adamson also recorded dispatching two African wild dogs, not because they threatened people or livestock, but because he considered their mode of killing prey brutal and found them somewhat repugnant. But if he disliked wild dogs—now threatened throughout their range and the object of massive attention from conservation biologists and animal lovers alike—he absolutely loathed spotted hyenas. Indeed, says Parker, Adamson's wildlife casualty reports are wholly inadequate, because Adamson preferred poison, primarily strychnine, to the gun when it came to eliminating bothersome predators, and he spread it with a particularly liberal hand wherever he found hyenas. "As a poisoner George Adamson had no rival in the Game Department," Parker wrote in his memoir, *What I Tell You Three Times Is True*. "He used [strychnine] routinely on hyenas[,] for which he had a pathological dislike. No one with experience in Kenya's Northern Frontier District will deny that hyenas do a lot of damage, but George's attitude was extreme."

In the *Monthly Report to the Game Warden* for February 1939, Adamson noted: "There are certainly far too many [hyenas] in many places, wherever I find them troublesome I always put down poison." Adamson also issued strychnine to his subalterns to distribute to local livestock herders. According to Parker, the usual method of poisoning predators at that time was simple, nondiscriminatory, and highly effective: chunks of meat dosed with large quantities of strychnine were tossed about wherever problems had been reported. One night's work could result in as many as twenty dead hyenas, plus ancillary casualties—lions, leopards, lesser cats such as caracals and servals, wild dogs, jackals, and bat-eared foxes. As was the case for most other game wardens, Adamson also shot antelope for food and killed elephants on license; he then sold the ivory he obtained, which bolstered his income considerably.

Adamson's techniques were standard for the 1940s; indeed, his predator control efforts were based on the "best available science" of the time. As for killing elephants and selling their ivory, elephants were plentiful, and the trade was utterly licit. Indeed, according to Parker, selling ivory was essential to a warden's survival: the pay was abysmally low. "It was how you made ends meet," Parker observed during an interview in his Langata home. "Money problems were part of the job."

But Adamson's ultimate career, of course, wasn't as a Game Department ranger. His real vocation began in 1956 in Meru, when he was forced to shoot a charging lioness. He subsequently discovered that she had been protecting her cubs, which were hidden in the bush nearby. Joy Adamson undertook the task of raising the cubs, which prospered under her care. The two largest, Lustica and the Big One, were ultimately sent to a zoo in Rotterdam. But the couple had become inordinately attached to Elsa, the runt of the litter; they decided to keep her.

Domesticating wildlife was something of a tradition among white colonials in Kenya. Colobus monkeys, bush babies, hornbills, even kudu, warthogs, and bush pigs—all had been drafted as pets by settlers at one time or another. In Laikipia, tales are still told of settlers who domesticated spotted hyenas: highly intelligent and sociable by nature, they supposedly were as faithful, friendly, and eager to please as border collies.

Lions, of course, were another matter. Even the most ardent field researcher would be hard pressed to describe them as highly acute. Laurence Frank, a conservation biologist who works in Kenya and who specializes in large predators, describes lions as "the big dumb blondes of the veldt." With some notable exceptions they are completely unpredictable, generally focused on obtaining and consuming prey. And the Adamsons, no tyros in the bush, were aware of the danger inherent in keeping lions around a camp; they decided to return Elsa to the wild. At this point, they were on their own, their actions unsanctioned by the Game Department. They trained Elsa to hunt, released her, and were gratified when the lioness had cubs of her own. In 1961, Elsa died from babesiosis, a parasitic disease, and her cubs—named Jespah, Gopa, and Little Elsa—became local menaces, killing livestock and threatening people. So George Adamson trapped them and transported them to Tanzania, where they were released in the Serengeti.

Joy wrote about Elsa's training and release to the wild and published the account as *Born Free* in 1960. *Living Free,* the story of Elsa and her cubs, followed in 1961. The two books launched the Adamsons as international celebrities—and laid the groundwork for the conflation of conservation, modern media, and anthropomorphic obsession. The Adamsons changed the way the developed world viewed wild Africa. But did the change serve a larger and better end? Was conservation actually advanced?

Adamson's supporters maintain conservation was not simply advanced by his efforts; it was transformed and supercharged, changed from a stodgy academic backwater to an international cause célèbre. Will Travers, the executive director of Born Free, the conservation group that grew out of the Adamsons' work, is the son of Bill Travers, the British actor who played George Adamson in the movie *Born Free*. As a young child, Will Travers met Adamson on the Kenyan set of the film, where the erstwhile warden served as technical consultant. Adamson became a close friend of the Travers family, and Will Travers visited Adamson's camp in the Northern Frontier District several times through the 1970s; Adamson and Bill Travers ultimately collaborated on a book, the last book Adamson produced before his death in 1989.

Will Travers recalls Adamson as a man who was not necessarily reserved but quiet, measured—in a word, calm. "He never felt the need to be overly demonstrative, to attract attention," Travers recalls. "And that only added to his charisma. People sensed George had found what he was looking for, and that made them want a piece of it."

In virtually any situation, Adamson was unflappable. Travers recalls a time in the 1980s when Adamson visited the Travers family in London. He came to the house in a brown tweed suit, his pipe clenched between his teeth. "It was the first time he had visited the U.K. in twenty years," Travers says. "My dad got him a drink and then asked him if he wanted to watch some television—George mentioned he had never seen color TV. So we turned it on, and there was this British entertainer, Matt Monro, and another fellow singing a duet of 'Born Free.' The coincidence just floored us, but George merely showed polite, somewhat detached interest and sipped his whiskey."

Still, Travers says, Adamson was passionate about his work. And it was passion based on compassion—for the individual lions in his charge. Anthropomorphism? Yes, avers Travers. But that was what made the message effective. "I'm not an enemy of anthropomorphism," Travers says. "We can only see and interpret the world as human beings—it's an urge that can't be eradicated. George knew that, he didn't resist it, and that's why the world responded the way it did to his work. You can treat your dog in the cold, scientific way many researchers use with wildlife, but who does that? To connect people to dogs, anthropomorphism *must* be involved."

Travers acknowledges that Adamson did his share of killing, including elephants. But, he emphasizes, Adamson was a work in progress, not a hypocrite. "Like all of us, George was on a journey," Travers says. "His opinions evolved as he aged. By the time I really got to know him, his views on wildlife, particularly elephants, had changed completely. Their intelligence, their social relationships, deeply moved him. He once told me that he thought the killing of an elephant should be a capital crime."

During an interview with Travers, I related a story of a colloquy that occurred between Laurence Frank, a lion and hyena researcher, and Rosie Woodroffe, a biologist who specializes in African wild dogs. The duo had been working together, fitting telemetry devices to predators in Laikipia, south of Kenya's Northern Frontier District. They had found a cheetah in one of their snares—a rare occurrence, since cheetahs don't normally come to bait. After tranquilizing the animal they took tissue specimens and placed a telemetry collar around its neck. Woodroffe was clearly enraptured by the cat. "Oh, Laurence," she cooed, "it's so cute and fuzzy!" Frank looked up from his work, an irritated expression on his face. "Not so," he snapped. "It's a superbly adapted predator!"

Travers laughs at the anecdote. "The thing is, they were both right," he says. "Of course a cheetah is a superbly adapted predator, but it's also extremely cute and fuzzy. And it's the cute and fuzzy aspects that capture the public, that can actually translate into effective conservation initiatives on the ground. If you don't have 'cute and fuzzy,' only a small subset of human beings will be interested in conservation."

Travers views Adamson as the first of a cadre of conservationists who unabashedly and unapologetically invested individual wild species with qualities that human beings find sympathetic. "After George, you had Jane Goodall with chimpanzees, Hugo van Lawick with wild dogs, Dian Fossey with mountain gorillas, Iain Douglas-Hamilton with elephants," says Travers. All, he observes, advanced the conservation of threatened species by emphasizing the charisma of the individual animals. "And emphasizing that charisma ultimately delivers real benefits in terms of habitat conservation," he continues. "I use George's work as a perfect example. The Kora Reserve [in central Kenya] was changed to a national park because of the attention George generated for Elsa and lions in general. So now you have Kora at five hundred square kilometers situated adjacent to Meru National Park at eight hundred square kilometers; basically, you've encompassed an entire ecosystem, preserved a major chunk of critical habitat, not just for lions, but for a wide array of African wildlife."

But other conservationists and most scientists view Adamson's contribution differently. Tom McShane, a former director of the World Wildlife Fund's Central Africa program and the principal investigator for Advancing Conservation in a Social Context, a program headquartered at the Global Institute of Sustainability at Arizona State University, thinks that Adamson represents a major shift in the culture and politics of conservation: the practice of naming individual animals. "It changed the debate in many ways," says McShane. "It first gained currency with Adamson and was later amplified by Goodall, Fossey, and Douglas-Hamilton. A kind of 'animalism' came out of that impulse: it moved conservation from broad-based ecological approaches to an obsession with individual animals."

Such animalism hasn't served wildlife well in terms of achieving real progress on the ground, McShane says; indeed, it has subverted the real mission, drawing attention away from the essential issues of integrating local people into conservation initiatives and preserving critical habitat to apotheosizing cute critters. On the other hand, McShane admits, the kind of conservation promulgated by Born Free, the International Fund for Animal Welfare, and like-minded groups has demonstrated that their approach is extremely efficient at getting people to open up their wallets: "If you want to raise lots of money, you need species that possess perceived humanlike qualities, such as chimps and elephants, have big soulful eyes, like seals, or are fuzzy and noble-looking, such as the large cats, wolves, and bears. You see it in all the wildlife documentaries; they draw you in with these predictable cues. But that kind of approach doesn't work for spiders, lizards, or crocodiles, though they may be just as important from the perspectives of ecological integrity and conservation. It's worrisome."

I mentioned to McShane a conversation I had overheard during a reception at Mpala Research Centre in Laikipia. Mpala, a forty-eight-thousand-acre tract of scrub and grassland maintained in part by the Smithsonian Institution and Princeton University, supports a variety of conservation initiatives. During the fete, a man I later identified through photographs as Fritz Vollrath, a director of Save the Elephants, was talking pachyderms with a local rancher. Dressed in a polo shirt that bore the Save the Elephants logo, Vollrath, white-haired and sharp-featured, was highly animated. "Bees," he said. "They have a word for bees!" He explained that elephants can communicate the presence of disturbed bees to one another through—for lack of a better word—language. The rancher, though amiable, seemed dubious. Later research revealed that Vollrath has published a paper opining that the sound of disturbed bees might be deployed to keep elephants at bay; one of the coauthors is Iain Douglas-Hamilton.

McShane seemed less than charmed by the story. "That kind of thinking can be very dangerous in a place like Laikipia," he said. "On the one hand, you have very large mammals running around causing a good deal of trouble for local residents, and on the other you have a great many people studying the animals and naming them, claiming they have language, arguing that every single one must be preserved. Then the guys who were studying the elephants get back on planes for Europe or the United States, well-pleased with their efforts, while the people who have to deal with elephants eating their maize or stomping their cows are stuck in Laikipia. It impacts the hard management decisions that have to be made to ensure that both elephants and people thrive in Laikipia. It skews public opinion, it influences the Kenyan government, and ultimately it affects national [Kenyan] policy."

Some wildlife researchers hold a more indulgent view of Adamson and the role he played in combining wildlife conservation and animal rights. John Robinson, the director of the Wildlife Conservation Society—the oldest conservation group in the United States and the owner of the Bronx Zoo and the New York Aquarium—feels Adamson was first and foremost a devotee of wild Africa; his work with Elsa and his other lions was therefore a manifestation of a larger passion. "Adamson clearly identified with nature, and the way he expressed that was through engagement with individual animals," Robinson said. And that, he added, was not necessarily a bad thing. "I grew up with Joy Adamson's books, and I aspired to the life and the ethic they portrayed. Many conservationists and scientists will say the same thing."

Robinson feels animal rights and wildlife conservation grow out of the same impulse, though they are not the same things. "There are superficial similarities," he says, "and there are points where they converge. There are other points, of course, where they diverge. That can cause problems, deep disagreements. But for Adamson, concern for his lions and conservation were the same thing."

It isn't difficult to understand Adamson's motivations, Robinson says; identifying with wildlife—particularly species that are large, attractive, or intelligent—is a natural impulse for human beings. "It's easier to do it with, say, a lion or an elephant than a nematode," he says. "From the animal advocacy perspective, lions and elephants seem particularly valuable, deeply worthy of effort and love. [WCS] manages thousands of animals in our zoos, and I see this expressed every day. Our curators who work with the animals, particularly certain charismatic mammals, develop deep bonds of affection for them. From the standpoint of true conservation, however, lions and elephants may not be more significant than a nematode, particularly if we consider the nematode in the context of the ecosystem it inhabits. That raises the sticky issue of evaluating the value of different species. How do you do it objectively? Clearly, it's complicated by animal rights issues."

Although Adamson can be credited with popularizing a philosophy that is changing the course of conservation in Africa, it is unlikely he saw himself as a revolutionary. Adamson, says Parker, was first and foremost a romantic, someone who was so caught up in his solipsistic dream that—from the view of Game Department professionals, at least—he went utterly rogue. "He had a magnificent delusion," Parker says. In his Langata home, he rummages in his files and extracts a yellowed memo dated November 22, 1958, written by Adamson and sent to the secretary of the East African Professional Hunters' Association in Nairobi:

Dear Sir,
    This is to inform you that I have recently released my tame lioness "Elsa" on the Ura River in Isiolo area No. 6, at a large rock outcrop called Dungie Akaite, about 34 miles from the Kinna Duka, along the Kinna-Tharaka track.
    Would you therefore please warn any of your members who may have booked the area during the coming hunting season, to avoid, if possible, making camp on the Ura.
    Elsa being a particularly friendly animal, might walk into a tent and with the best of intentions, cause alarm to the nervous.
    Few safaris visit the Ura, as there is little to attract them there.
    Yours faithfully,
    G. A. G. Adamson
    Senior Game Warden
    Northern Province

As a matter of fact, Elsa wasn't so friendly, says Parker: she bit one hunter on the arm, whether or not her intentions were benign. More to

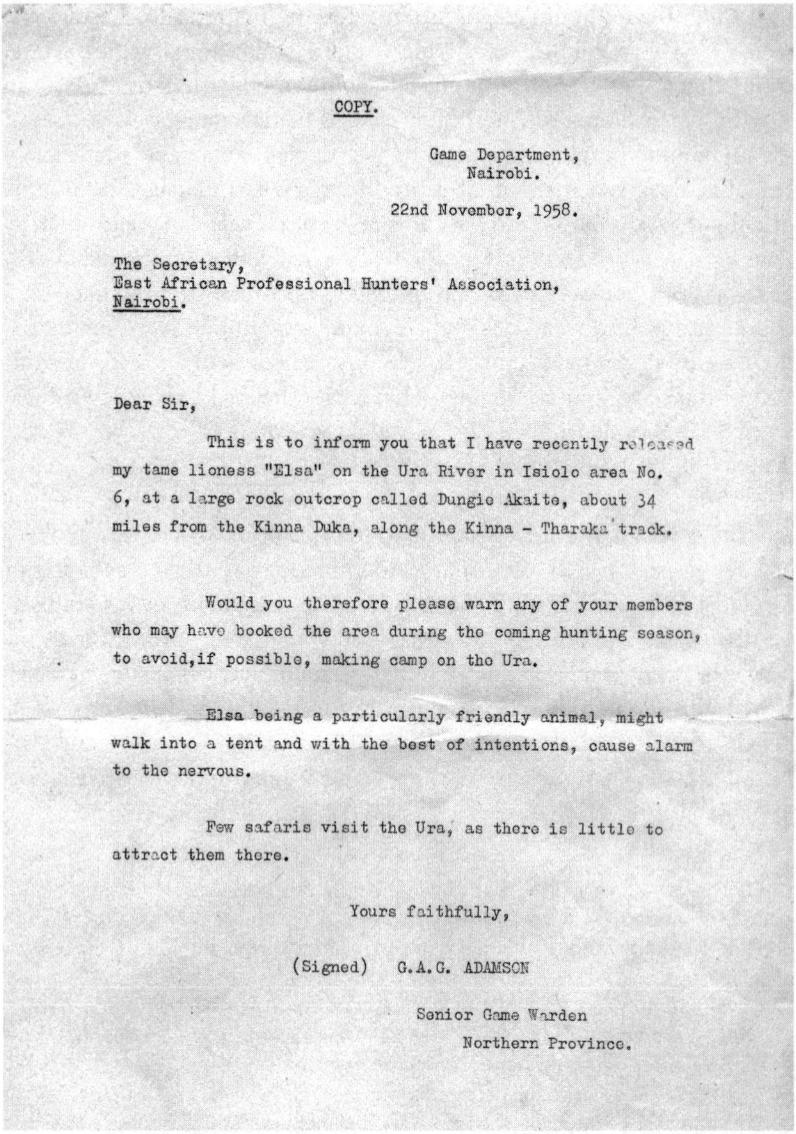

Game Department,
Nairobi.

22nd November, 1958.

The Secretary,
East African Professional Hunters' Association,
Nairobi.

Dear Sir,

This is to inform you that I have recently released my tame lioness "Elsa" on the Ura River in Isiolo area No. 6, at a large rock outcrop called Dungie Akaite, about 34 miles from the Kinna Duka, along the Kinna – Tharaka track.

Would you therefore please warn any of your members who may have booked the area during the coming hunting season, to avoid, if possible, making camp on the Ura.

Elsa being a particularly friendly animal, might walk into a tent and with the best of intentions, cause alarm to the nervous.

Few safaris visit the Ura, as there is little to attract them there.

Yours faithfully,

(Signed)   G.A.G. ADAMSON

Senior Game Warden
Northern Province.

FIGURE 2. A memo from George Adamson to the secretary of the East African Professional Hunters' Association announcing the release of his lioness Elsa to the wild and requesting forbearance from hunters and wardens alike. Despite Adamson's assurances that Elsa was a friendly beast, she later bit a hunter on the arm. (Courtesy of Glen Martin)

the point, Parker continues, Adamson's work militated against true conservation, because it elevated essentially tame animals over the preservation of wild animals and the habitat that supports them. Further, Parker
says, Adamson "committed crimes for which he should have been jailed.
He killed lions in Meru National Park to save Boy [a rehabilitated lion
that had been released], and he was caught shooting antelope to feed
his lions in Serengeti National Park. At a certain point, [Kenya's chief
warden] Willie Hale had a talk with George and told him, 'George, this
can't go on—you've become a lion-keeper.' And George had to leave the
department."

By that time, of course, it hardly mattered. George and Joy Adamson
had become stars in the conservation firmament, and they had turned
their tame lions, paradoxically, into ambassadors for wild Africa. Parker
found this a delicious irony. "He created the myth about himself within
the Game Department through his reports and writing," Parker wrote
in his 2004 book, *What I Tell You Three Times Is True.* "Outside the
Department others added to it. His delightful nature predisposed people
to believe the best of him. . . . From the purely conservation standpoint,
his records prove an ineffectual career. Though this is indisputable, it
is neither what the public wished to hear nor makes him a lesser man."

By the late 1980s, the Adamsons' cathected, highly subjective view
of African wildlife was ascendant. In a very real way, they gave their
lives for their vision, which only served to reinforce it. Joy was stabbed
to death in early January 1980 at Shaba Game Reserve in northern
Kenya, where she had been studying leopards. A former camp worker,
Paul Ekai, was convicted of the murder, though he claimed he had been
tortured by Kenyan police into confessing—a story that cannot be dismissed out of hand, given the poor reputation of the country's police
agencies among both Kenyan citizens and NGOs. (In a 2004 prison
cell interview, Ekai recanted and said he had killed Adamson, but only
because she shot him in the leg after he complained about not being
paid.)

There is little mystery to George Adamson's demise, however. He died
at the age of eighty-three in 1989 when he engaged three Somali bandits who were attacking a tourist visiting his remote camp in Kenya's
Northern Frontier District. Adamson charged the *shifta* in his vehicle,
and they opened fire, killing him and two of his assistants. The brutal
martyrdom of the Adamsons was a tragedy for all who knew them, yet
it served their cause greatly, casting the issue of conservation irrevoca-

bly into a chiaroscuro of black and white from which all shadings of gray were drained.

Anthropologist Desmond Morris (author of *The Naked Ape*) credited *Born Free* with changing the way an entire generation viewed wildlife. Never again would Africa's animals be seen as "game" by the world at large. Never again would their conservation be a dispassionate process. Adamson shifted the preservation of the continent's wildlife from an issue for the mind to one of the heart.

CHAPTER 3

Dreaming the Peaceable Kingdom

As Desmond Morris noted, Adamson's philosophy resonated with younger conservationists and researchers. Iain Douglas-Hamilton, the founder of Save the Elephants, said he was led to his life's work by *Born Free*, and this, perhaps, is the greatest legacy of the Adamsons. Douglas-Hamilton's efforts took the inchoate philosophy of the Adamsons, transferred it to a species even more appealing than lions, and gave it some solid scientific underpinnings.

Douglas-Hamilton took his doctorate in zoology from Oxford and at the age of twenty-three conducted a study on elephant behavior in Tanzania's Lake Manyara National Park. The arc of his career spanned the African elephant's greatest crisis to date—the Ivory Wars of the 1970s and 1980s. He chronicled the decline of elephants during this period, a decline that was precipitated in large part by poaching and secondarily by habitat loss. More to the point, he helped make this decline an international media event; he brought the graphic images of elephant poaching to the world, and the world was repulsed. Perhaps more than any other single human being, Douglas-Hamilton helped make the 1989 trade ban on ivory by the Convention on International Trade in Endangered Species of Wild Flora and Fauna (CITES) a reality.

The success of the ivory ban has been significant, but its effect may be waning. In the first ten to fifteen years following its implementation, poaching seemed checked, if not scotched. Elephants made significant recoveries in various regions of East Africa. But recent indications are that poaching is once again on the rise—stimulated, in no small part, by Chinese development projects in East Africa. Demand for wildlife products—particularly ivory—among Chinese engineers, construction supervisors, and consultants is high and is being vigorously accommodated. (Ivory objets d'art are still greatly valued by Asian consumers, despite—or perhaps even because of—the CITES strictures.)

In 2006, more than 25,000 kilograms of African ivory were confiscated throughout the world. In March 2008, Chinese authorities seized 709 kilograms of illegal ivory, worth an estimated $6,500 a kilogram. And in 2009, a six-ton consignment of Tanzanian ivory was seized in Vietnam, which has emerged as a major processing center for ivory ultimately destined for China. According to an article by Samuel K. Wasser, Bill Clark, and Cathy Laurie published in *Scientific American* in 2009, the current death rate of African elephants surpasses their annual reproductive rate.

Certainly, the 1989 ivory ban stands in opposition to history. Ivory has never been a commodity in Africa; it has always been, literally, a currency, one that sometimes has exceeded even gold as a store of value. African elephant ivory was esteemed and traded in Hellenic Greece and was a primary symbol of wealth and prestige in Rome. By the late fifteenth century, it constituted a bulwark of the robust trade between the Portuguese and Indians, commerce that also included spices, silk, and gold. Various East African tribes—the Kamba, Boran, Orma, and, later, Kikuyu—were active participants in the trade, jockeying with one another for dominant positions as wholesalers of ivory and as procurers of slaves for the caravans that hauled the tusks from the interior to the coast. There were no routes suitable for wheeled transport between the ports and the elephant lands, tsetse flies would have decimated oxen and draft horses had such roads existed, and ivory was both bulky and heavy. The only practical way to move the stuff across the rugged landscape of East Africa was to have human beings carry it and travel by shank's mare.

Most of the ivory was provided by hunting-and-gathering tribes, some of whom specialized in large dangerous game, such as the Wata. Researchers have noted that such highly skilled subsistence hunters often preferred to expend their energy on elephants, which could yield a ton or more of meat with one poisoned arrow, rather than on smaller and more abundant game such as zebras. The ivory was also an incentive, providing a means of exchange for iron, flour, salt, beans, and other goods impossible to obtain in the bush. In South Africa, the quest for ivory drove both exploration and settlement. In 1736, a group of elephant hunters forded the Great Fish River and became the first Europeans to investigate the Transkei. Jacobus Coetsee, also in quest of ivory, was the first Caucasian to cross the Orange River.

Though the emphasis in the ivory trade was on obtaining tusks and moving them to markets, there is evidence that the necessity of protecting the source of the product was acknowledged early on. Strict game conservation statutes were enforced in South Africa by Dutch governors in the mid-seventeenth century. (Those initial policies, however, were not maintained. Thomas McShane and coauthor Jonathan Adams note in *The Myth of Wild Africa* that virtually all large game had been eliminated from South Africa by the early twentieth century.)

As observed in a thesis by Nora Kelly on the history of game preservation in Kenya, conservationist impulses were particularly strong in the British colonial holdings. By 1888, the Imperial British East African Company, chartered by the British government after the partition of Africa into European estates in 1884–85, established control over the game lands of Kenya, declaring itself a monopoly in the commerce of ivory. It decreed specific measures for the trade, including rigorous conservation measures for elephants. Indeed, the depletion of megafauna in general was a significant concern for the IBEAC's principals. In an attempt to effect control over the unregulated taking of large game, the company announced to the British Foreign Office in 1891 that it would charge license fees to sport hunters entering its domain: "For regulating the hunting of elephants, and for their preservation, for the purpose of providing military and other transport in our Indian Empire or elsewhere, the Company may, notwithstanding anything hereinfore contained, impose and levy within any territories administered by them, other than their Zanzibar territory, a licence duty and may grant licences to take or kill elephants, or to export elephants' tusks or ivory."

Ultimately, the IBEAC failed as both a business and a force for conservation, falling into bankruptcy after seven years because it could not turn a sufficient profit. But the company's basic commitment to conservation was by no means an outlier's sentiment at the time. The colonial government, confirming the necessity of tight hunting strictures, assumed control of Kenya's wildlife after the company dissolved. An international conference on preserving African wildlife in the British capital in 1900 resulted in the London Convention for the Preservation of Wild Animals, Birds and Fish in Africa. The accord was ratified by few European powers and hence had little real authority, but it nevertheless signaled general agreement among the colonizing nations that their purview included the preservation of wild fauna as well as the governance of native people and the utilization of natural resources.

The preservation of game remained a top priority of the British colonial government until Kenya's independence in 1963, though "preservation" was viewed within a context that placed equal emphasis on a thriving agricultural sector; in other words, if elephants ravaged sisal or lions killed cattle outside the national parks or established reserves, they were eliminated. Similarly, vast numbers of buffalo were shot to reduce tsetse threats, and hundreds of thousands of fecund and voracious Burchell's zebras were expunged to preserve rangeland forage during dry years. Indeed, the difficulty of maintaining, as Ian Parker has put it, "Pleistocene wildlife amongst Holocene people (and) their agricultural land," became increasingly evident to colonial administrators through the early decades of the twentieth century. In 1945, the Royal National Parks of Kenya Ordinance was passed, creating a national park system that immediately established itself as a world standard for the preservation of megafauna. Kenya was known for its big game before the ordinance, but the parks transformed the colony into a living metaphor for wild Africa. With the parks, Kenya became more than a European colony, an exotic locale, a place to shoot large, dangerous animals. It became an ideal.

And through it all, big game hunting remained both a cherished Kenyan tradition and a significant source of revenue: wildlife was a profit center as well as a public trust. The parks were acknowledged as proper and inviolate refuges, but hunting, it was felt, also had its place. The concept that individual animals warranted extraordinary effort to protect, that they were worth the expenditure of public funds and labor to nurture at the expense of other conservation priorities, simply did not exist.

Ivory, in particular, continued as the ne plus ultra of both legitimate hunting trophies and illegal wildlife commodities. Indeed, ivory supported Kenya's drive for independence. Jomo Kenyatta, a Mau-Mau leader and the first president of sovereign Kenya, sustained his fighters in the field by killing elephants for both their meat and tusks. Muthoni-Kirima, a Mau-Mau combatant, noted in interviews that she secured a permit to deal in ivory from Kenyatta once he attained the presidency. She remembered the sites in the forests where the Mau-Mau had buried ivory against future need; returning to them, she exhumed the tusks and legally traded in ivory for some time following independence. Ultimately, Kenyatta issued such collecting permits to a number of favored ex–freedom fighters and allies. There was a good deal of ivory in the bush, mostly from elephants that had died of natural causes, and the permits were a cheap and easy way to generate goodwill and return favors. But the permits also provided a conduit for illicit ivory to the legal market; some collectors killed elephants for their tusks or paid others to do so. Ultimately, these permits created a situation that was to play out tragically.

Meanwhile, conditions were rapidly changing on the lands where the elephants lived. Drought hammered Kenya in 1960 and 1961, particularly in the region that contained Tsavo National Park, a huge protectorate that had been established in 1948. The effective management of Tsavo was problematic from the start. The region was generally sere and poor; indeed, the reason the park had been established was that the land was unsuitable for intensive grazing or cropping. The elephants quickly expanded their numbers past the range's ability to support them. This was especially the case in the eastern portion of Tsavo. Confined within the park's borders, elephants monopolized the forage, ultimately destroying the woodlands. Thousands of animals died in the drought of the early 1960s, particularly black rhinos; scant water was one cause, but the lack of vegetation due to excessive browsing by elephants was the primary reason.

And though the rains ultimately returned, the wooded cover at Tsavo East never fully recovered, because elephants were being driven into the park by the growing populations of farmers and pastoralists who lived outside the sanctuary lands. Tsavo's elephants were increasing but for the wrong reasons; Kenya's population of elephants was at best stable and possibly declining during this period. Their population was dramatically increasing only in the parks, where the already meager carrying capacity of the land was stretched past the limit. Census flights over Tsavo East, West, and adjacent areas during 1961 indicated the elephant population was at least ten thousand. By 1968, that number had grown to forty thousand. Parker, who was working in the Tsavo area at that time for the Game Department, reported the woodlands "were melting away" as the numbers of elephants expanded. Both game managers and conservationists were split on an appropriate course of action. One camp favored aggressive culling. The opposition, fearing that the abundant tusks resulting from so many dead elephants would prove a corrupting influence and create a boom in the illegal ivory trade, opposed thinning the herds. David Sheldrick, the first warden for Tsavo East, ultimately sided with those opposing culling.

In 1971, drought returned to Kenya—indeed, a good portion of East Africa. The elephants in Tsavo East, overpopulous and already stressed by inadequate forage, died wholesale. Their tusks, representing millions of dollars, littered the park. By this time, an extensive shadow network of illicit ivory collectors and dealers had been established in Kenya, the ultimate result of the ivory permits handed out by Kenyatta seven years earlier.

This army of ivory hunters descended on Tsavo East en masse, spiriting the tusks past the park's borders to lands controlled by the Kamba, a tribe that was active in the ivory trade. The rains returned to Tsavo in 1972, and the supply of ivory from elephants that had succumbed to natural causes was quickly exhausted by the ivory seekers. But the trade, fueled now by high demand and serviced by a large professional cadre that moved ivory from the field to markets quickly and efficaciously, did not stop. The ivory takers simply shifted from salvaging downed tusks to killing elephants. The Kamba, located hard by Tsavo East's borders, had always resented the creation of the park on lands that they had traditionally used for subsistence hunting and seasonal grazing. Their transition from ivory gathering to elephant hunting seemed to them natural, a serendipitous economic opportunity and a matter of appropriate recompense for past wrongs. Gangs of Somalis, armed with modern automatic rifles, also intruded from the north and began working over Tsavo's remaining elephants with dispatch. Nor were government employees exempt from ivory lust. In the late 1970s, staffers from the Wildlife Conservation and Management Department—which had been created by the merging of the Game Department and the National Parks Department in 1976—were implicated in the slaughter of scores of elephants.

By 1975, David Sheldrick's meager force of rangers was utterly overwhelmed by ivory hunters. Hundreds of poachers were entering Tsavo East every month, and their take of tusks and rhino horn became industrial in scale. In 1975, Sheldrick's rangers arrested 212 men and recovered 1,055 tusks and 147 rhino horns—products that represented a fraction of the presumed total kill. But their efforts were utterly inadequate to the holocaust that had enveloped them. The great Ivory Wars had begun.

The liquidation of Tsavo's elephants coincided with the maturation of electronic media. By the final spasm of the Ivory Wars in the 1980s, video images were widely transmitted by satellite, delivered to virtually every TV set in the world. A regional issue that once would have interested only game managers, trophy hunters, and hard-core conservationists became a global story of mass appeal. The video footage of bloated elephant carcasses, of piles of illicit ivory, of heroic wardens with disreputable-looking poachers in coffle, bypassed the intellectual processes and engaged people from the developed world on a visceral level. Intelligence was now widely understood as a salient quality of elephants. Millions of people all around the planet found themselves in instinctive concord with George Adamson: the killing of elephants was tantamount to a capital crime.

The Ivory Wars ultimately drove Kenyatta to declare a total ban on all big game hunting. The 1977 Wildlife Conservation and Management Act must be considered a leap of faith, a last-straw decision made to check an unfolding catastrophe. It was based on anxiety over civil chaos, international pressure from outraged animal lovers, and worries that one of the country's major economic underpinnings—wildlife-based tourism—was on the verge of collapse. It was not based on science. Indeed, the prevailing view of game managers was that regulated hunting discouraged poaching; armed professional hunters and their clients not only provided essential information to rangers about poaching activity in their blocks but were also significantly more intimidating to poaching gangs than unarmed ecotourists. The emphasis, many wildlife professionals felt, should have been on beefing up the ranger cadre while rooting out the corrupt officials who were part and parcel of the illegal wildlife trade. According to some authorities, Kenyatta considered the act a temporary fix, a measure designed to provide some breathing room until government control could be exerted on the ground. But his long-term strategy remains unknown; he died in 1978, well before any amendment to the ban could be contemplated. And under his successor, Daniel arap Moi, the 1977 act was established as the permanent wildlife policy of the nation. Indeed, the act was hailed as a template for the future by animal lovers—a guidepost for a new, enlightened policy for wildlife management, one that didn't involve guns or killing.

Enforcement of the hunting ban ultimately fell to Richard Leakey, designated by Moi in 1989 as the head of the newly formed Kenya Wildlife Service. It was no coincidence that Leakey's elevation occurred in the same year as the CITES ivory strictures. (The convention declared that the African elephant was threatened with extinction and listed it as an Appendix 1, or most endangered, species; a complete ban on the international trade in ivory followed in 1990.) Leakey pursued his mandate with vigor, particularly in regard to elephants. He was tireless, widely considered incorruptible, an able administrator—and his rangers had official imprimatur to shoot-to-kill poachers engaged in the field. Shortly after his appointment, Leakey arranged a dramatic public relations coup by convincing Moi to publicly burn twelve tons of captured ivory—the yield of about two thousand elephants. Kenya's elephant population, which by most estimates had fallen from around 175,000 in 1973 to 16,000 by the late 1980s, stabilized and began a long, though ultimately modest, recovery.

Leakey's success in temporarily stemming the ivory trade was real; more than that it was necessary, an effective response to an emergency situation. But in a larger sense, it signaled the waxing power of animal advocacy over traditional conservation biology. No African nation had ever attempted a move as bold as a total hunting ban. In the eyes of the world, Kenyatta's ad hoc response to elephant poaching was transformed into visionary permanent policy by Moi and was justified, given real world credence, by Leakey.

Still, the 1977 wildlife act didn't accomplish its primary goal: the preservation of wildlife in Kenya. By any analysis, the decline of most game species in the country has accelerated. During the past twenty-five years, there has been a 70 percent decrease in game in the country. Today, no more than 30 percent of Kenya's wildlife is found in the national parks and the Maasai Mara National Reserve; the remaining 60 to 70 percent subsists on private ranchlands. The hope that ecotourism would provide a revenue stream to compensate for the loss of trophy hunting—and, as a consequence, create strong incentives for wildlife preservation—hasn't materialized. In some cases, tourism is now the problem. In 1977, the same year the wildlife act was passed, Kenya closed its border with Tanzania. For many Kenyan visitors, the previously unimpeded ecosafari loop of the Maasai Mara, the Serengeti, and Ngorongoro Crater now started and stopped at the Mara. As noted by Martha Honey in her book *Ecotourism and Sustainable Development,* the spike in visitors to the Mara resulted in a helter-skelter rush to provide lodges, roads, food, and recreational amenities such as balloon rides. The resulting development, driven in large part by Kenyan politicians who profited directly from the ventures, was pursued with little if any thought given to the requirements of migratory game. The visitor boom in turn stimulated additional pressures to expand local agriculture; today, vast wheat fields produce grain where plains game cropped wild grasses a few years ago. The result is that the Mara is in crisis, a fact easily confirmed by the decline in species emblematic of the ecosystem. From 1977 to 1997, the Loita Plains wildebeest herd, which ranges mostly in Kenya and doesn't penetrate the Serengeti, has dropped from about 120,000 to 20,000 animals. The Nairobi-based International Livestock Research Institute has found that the Mara's populations of giraffes, warthogs, topi, waterbuck, and impalas have also dwindled dramatically.

Nor has the act truly stemmed the trade in wildlife commodities. As of this writing, the poaching of elephants and rhinos is again on the rise. Field biologists report that trade in rhino horn, ivory, and lion teeth and claws is brisk in the Mara and adjoining lands. Still, it would be erroneous to assume this latest commerce in wildlife parts is a recent trend; rather, it is a continuation of business as usual after a modest downward blip.

The road from Nairobi to Nyeri is one of Kenya's primary thoroughfares, leading through rich farmland long cultivated by the Kikuyu. The Kikuyu are a populous tribe, and this is their heartland; small, meticulously cultivated farms dominate the hills and valleys, producing an abundance of provender for the nation. There is no wildlife habitat to speak of; as in Langata, though, the opportunistic leopard is by no means unknown. Businesses of every description dot the highway, from simple eateries to vulcanizing shops. (The names of Kenya's roadside businesses often have a certain skewed or macabre charm: the Mount Kenya Pork Den; the Gender Equity Bar and Restaurant; the Manson Hotel.)

I recently visited one of these enterprises, a curio store, with Rian and Lorna Labuschagne, managers of a large private game reserve in Tanzania. South African by birth, the Labuschagnes have batted about southern and eastern Africa all their lives. For many years, they managed the Ngorongoro Conservation Area. Their interests are catholic and include the collection of African art. Rian had heard this particular shop contained some good masks, and he was anxious to evaluate the wares. "There's always a lot of junk in these places," he said as we entered the cool, shadowed interior, a welcome relief from the heat and white glare of the road. "But sometimes you can find some real gems. They tend to pile it all together, and you have to take your time going through it all."

Rian's initial take was accurate; most of the items in the shop were pure schlock produced for the tourist trade: *rungus* (fighting sticks) hastily hacked out of acacia limbs, inexpertly forged *pangas* (machetes) stuck into uncured leather scabbards, spurious Maasai spears extruded by commercial foundries in Nairobi or Dar es Salaam, carved wood giraffes so alarmingly attenuated they looked like the hack work of a Giacometti understudy. But among the brummagem were a few genuine articles—specifically, several West African masks of great elegance, with the stains of the years on them. There was also something else: a kind of homunculus-like statue, a small, aged, crudely carved manikin that had been fitted with a chimpanzee skull. One arm was raised in a minatory fashion, and the jaws gaped wide. It was an object that seemed to pulse with malevolent force. The Labuschagnes regarded the fetish with neutral expressions. "The only thing remarkable about it is that it isn't at all remarkable," said Lorna. "You can find objects like this at shops all over East Africa. The use of animal parts from endangered species never stopped—it never even slowed down."

In other words, while CITES proscriptions on wildlife products may carry quite a bit of weight in Europe, North America, and other regions of the developed world, they are not much of an issue in Kenya. The trade continues in tusks, lion claws, leopard skins, ape skulls—it's simply illegal. And that is hardly a deterrent in Africa, Rian observes, given that game law enforcement remains nonexistent to spotty at best and is usually checked by bribery when it does occur. The average Kenyan gains nothing by obeying wildlife regulations, because he or she derives no benefit from observing such laws—a significant issue when annual per capita income is around sixteen hundred dollars. On the other hand, a tusk or serval pelt sold on the black market can provide a significant boost to family income, and a snared impala or speared warthog can represent something of equal value—meat, still a great luxury in protein-poor East Africa.

The 1977 Kenya Wildlife Conservation and Management Act and the 1989 CITES ivory ban were noble in intent, promising a modern retread of the Peaceable Kingdom: not just the lion lying down with the lamb, but also modern human beings lying down with the lion—and the elephant and rhino as well. Kenya, it seemed, could become the place where conservation would transcend itself, become something finer and higher, something rarefied and beautiful. It would become the place where wild animals wouldn't simply be observed and appreciated; they would be *loved*.

But a critical component was not addressed in this equation: the people who actually share the land with the animals. In colonial times, conservation laws in East Africa tended to exclude tribal people. To a significant degree, not much has changed; ecotourism in Kenya caters to a wealthy foreign elite, with most of the revenues flowing to the tour companies and political cadres influential enough to seize a part of the action. The people who live with the game—the rural hoi polloi, the average pastoral tribal members who count their wealth in cows and goats—receive little or no recompense. In such a situation, it is no surprise that game regulations are viewed with suspicion, even disdain.

And yet, as Adams and McShane point out in *The Myth of Wild Africa,* many Africans cherish their wildlife heritage. Tanzania, one of the world's poorest nations, has devoted almost 15 percent of its land to wildlife parks and reserves; that compares to less than 4 percent of land set aside for the same purpose in the United States. Julius Nyerere, the founder of modern Tanzania, established conservation as a priority in a 1961 speech presented at a conference on natural resources held in Arusha, a town that served as the main entrepôt for safari companies and hunters in the lands surrounding the Serengeti. Nyerere's presentation became known as the Arusha Declaration of Wildlife Protection, and it set the tone for things to come in the emergent Tanzanian state: "The survival of our wildlife is a matter of grave concern to all of us in Africa. These wild creatures [and] the wild places they inhabit are not only important as a source of wonder and inspiration but are an integral part of our natural resources and our future livelihood and well-being. In accepting the trusteeship of our wildlife we solemnly declare that we will do everything in our power to make sure that our children's grandchildren will be able to enjoy this rich and precious inheritance."

It must be noted that Nyerere made a subtle distinction between conservation and animal advocacy. Wildlife, he observed, was something that warranted admiration; the game was beautiful, he implied, and deserved protection simply because beauty makes the world endurable. But he also emphasized that wildlife is a natural resource and a renewable one at that. In a country as poor as Tanzania, a resource so rich, so abundant, could not go unexploited. Just as Tanzanians had an obligation to protect wildlife, they also had a right to utilize it. And therein lies the difference between Tanzania and Kenya; in Kenya, the obligation to protect wildlife is acknowledged, but there is no option for legitimately utilizing it.

As of this writing, drought has again blighted northern Kenya. The forage has withered, and the herds that sustain the region's pastoral tribes have been decimated. People are dying of hunger. Hit particularly hard are the Turkana, a herding tribe with ancestral lands in the northwest corner of the nation. For a Turkana pastoralist whose cattle have perished, whose children are wasting away before his eyes, who lives in a brushwood *banda* and has no nearby source of water or fuel, the idea of an inviolate wildlife refuge seems an absurdity. On the other hand, this same man likely would support a reserve that would accommodate regulated grazing and firewood collecting, furnish small stipends derived from tourists or hunters, or even provide occasional rations of meat from wildlife culls. To abide in the Peaceable Kingdom, after all, one must have a full belly; otherwise, the lion will be killed and the lamb devoured.

CHAPTER 4

From Automata
to Sentient Beings

The animal rights movement originated in western Europe and its colonies, reaching back to the seventeenth century. In 1635, an ordinance was passed in Ireland that prohibited pulling the wool off sheep or attaching plows to horses' tails, deeming such activities unnecessarily cruel. In 1641, the Massachusetts Bay Colony prohibited "Tirrany or Cruelty toward any bruite Creature which are usually kept for man's use." Under Oliver Cromwell, laws were passed in England that discouraged the blood sports dearly loved by the hoi polloi, including cockfights, dogfights and bullbaiting.

Such initial attempts to imbue animals with certain rights may seem tepid by today's standards; indeed, these regulations mostly dealt with domesticated animals, creatures generally considered essential to human welfare. Wildlife, as a whole, was still considered vermin or proper subjects for hunting, either for the larder or as a gentleman's pursuit. Still, tentative as these initial forays may seem, they were revolutionary in their own quiet way, in that they ran against the prevailing philosophical mode of the era. By habit, the common ruck viewed animals as property, food, or objects for amusement, scorn, or ire. Intellectuals generally accorded with Descartes, whose rigorous mechanism excluded animals as reasoning beings, categorizing them as biological automata.

But the nascent concept of animal rights gained credence when Rousseau published his *Discourse on Inequality* in 1754. Here, he argued that animals are integral to natural law—and hence have inherent rights—because they are sentient; they are capable of perception, of emotional response, and, most pertinently, of suffering. To Rousseau, the power of ratiocination doesn't even enter into the argument. For Cartesians, to think is to be. For Rousseau, to *feel* is sufficient to establish a claim to the rights inherent to existence: "For it is clear that, being destitute of intelligence and liberty, [animals] cannot recognize . . . [natural] law: as they partake, however, in some measure of our nature, in consequence of the sensibility with which they are endowed, they ought to partake of natural right; so that mankind is subjected to a kind of obligation even toward the brutes . . . this is less because they are rational than because they are sentient beings."

Rousseau notwithstanding, the English and Irish established themselves as the most ardent champions of animal rights. Attempts in Parliament to pass laws forbidding bullbaiting and wanton cruelty to cattle and horses were quashed with much attending ridicule in the first two decades of the nineteenth century, but in 1822, Richard "Humanity Dick" Martin, the MP for Galway in Ireland, gained passage of the Ill Treatment of Horses and Cattle Bill, which forbade wanton cruelty to these large domesticated beasts. The act was strengthened by an amendment in 1835, which extended the cruelty ban to dogs, bears, and sheep and also proscribed bearbaiting and cockfighting; by another amendment in 1849, which increased the fines for animal abuse; and by a final adjustment in 1876, which placed limits on animal experimentation. Following the British lead, France and the United States also passed laws forbidding cruelty to animals.

But these early laws were hardly enforced with zealotry or obeyed with punctilio by the general population. In 1824, the Society for the Prevention of Cruelty to Animals was formed, which became the Royal Society for the Prevention of Cruelty to Animals in 1840 under a charter granted by Queen Victoria. The goal was to enforce prosecution of violators of the animal cruelty laws and promote even tighter strictures. Since then, the animal rights movement has only waxed in power, spreading to all countries in the developed world. It sometimes took some bizarre turns: Animal rights, for example, were part of the Third Reich agenda in the years leading up to World War II. In 1934, tough hunting bans were passed in Nazi Germany, followed by laws regulating animal transport and restricting vivisection.

From the beginning, animal rights advocates generated fierce opposition. The RSPCA, in particular, has been vilified by its opponents since its earliest meetings. The rancor increased as the society made its influence felt, however nominally, in Britain's colonies, including those in Africa. That most accomplished of satirists, Evelyn Waugh, savagely lampooned animal rights advocates in his acrid 1932 novel, *Black Mischief*. At one point in the book, Dame Mildred Porch, a leading light of the RSPCA, decides to investigate reports of animal cruelty in Anzania, an island nation that is a pastiche of Zanzibar, Kenya, Somalia, and Ethiopia.

Waugh portrays Dame Mildred as an arrant snob and a feckless, irredeemable busybody who cares far more about animals than human suffering. On arriving in country, she writes a letter to her husband, noting, "I have heard very disagreeable accounts of the hunting here. Apparently the natives dig deep pits into which the poor animals fall; they are then left in these traps for several days without food or water (imagine what that means in the jungle) and are then mercilessly butchered in cold blood." Later, she notes in her dairy: "Condition of mules and dogs appalling, also children." And still later: "Road to station blocked [due to] broken motor lorry. Natives living in it. Also two goats. Seemed well but cannot be healthy for them so near natives."

Dame Mildred makes her way to the Anzanian capital of Debra-Dowa, where she is feted by the country's young emperor, Seth. Determined to demonstrate Anzania's modernity, Seth throws a banquet for Dame Mildred. But he misapprehends the name of her sponsoring organization, interpreting it as the English Society for Cruelty to Animals—an understandable mistake, given that animal cruelty is a fact of Anzanian life. He prints gilt-edged menus for the occasion, which include such offerings as Small Roasted Suckling Porks and Hot Sheep and Onions—dishes calculated to appeal to anyone with a predilection for hurting animals. Needless to say, Dame Mildred is deeply offended, and the scene dissolves into typical Waughian farce.

Of course, the RSPCA's attempts at influencing animal welfare policy in Africa have hardly been so ham-handed; for the most part, their efforts are focused on programs aimed at improving conditions for domestic animals. One campaign involves the promotion of humane methods for dealing with dogs infected with rabies, a perennial threat to both canids and humans in Africa. As regards cattle, the organization implies that the situation is better in some ways in Africa than in Europe and the United States, noting with approval that pastoral lifestyles provide cattle with "a good standard of welfare." In other words, the animals get to roam around almost at will on the range, enjoying the fresh air and sunshine—in virtually all ways, an existence superior to that of cattle consigned to the feedlots and factory dairies in the developed world. Still, the RSPCA notes African cows, sheep, camels, and goats suffer greatly in other ways, specifically when it comes to their transport and slaughter. The group is now prodding African nations to enforce the World Organization for Animal Health guidelines in their livestock sectors.

An exception to this general focus on domestic animals is the RSPCA's work in Zambia, where it is attempting to reduce conflicts between elephants and villagers in the areas surrounding national parks. Working in partnership with the French NGO Awely, the RSPCA is promoting an "animal friendly" approach that involves crushing powerful chili peppers and macerating them in motor oil. This highly irritating admixture is then slathered on fence posts bordering the reserve lands—a highly effective means for keeping elephants in the parks and out of maize patches on adjacent private lands, claims the RSPCA. As part of the program, about two hundred farmers have been contracted to grow the requisite chilies.

(As an aside, anyone who has seen elephants interacting with fences in Africa must be excused if they take such rosy reportage with a grain of salt. Even fences constructed of structural steel posts and high-tensile, highly charged electrical wire are not proof against determined elephants, which typically drop large branches or even whole trees onto electric barriers to short them out. Chili pepper concentrate could certainly irritate them and may even confound them for a period of time, but effectively exclude them from lush maize and pumpkin patches? No.)

Like all promoters of significant social causes, the animal rights movement presents a broad spectrum of doctrines as well as an evolutionary trend: the newer groups tend to espouse a more activist agenda than the older groups. If the Royal and American Societies for the Prevention of Cruelty to Animals represent the conservative roots of the movement, groups such the Animal Liberation Front in the United States and Hunt Saboteurs in Britain are the more (depending on perspective) radical or progressive, advocating direct confrontation and even the destruction of private property to save individual animals. The animal rights cause is both more established and more influential in the United States and Europe than in Africa, but it is growing robustly on the African continent, particularly in Kenya and South Africa.

As in Europe and the United States, the melding of animal rights with conservation is a hallmark of these newer African environmental groups. Earthlife Africa, based in Johannesburg, is a typical example. It casts a very large net, supporting campaigns for animal rights, biodiversity, the reduction of toxics, carbon mitigation, the treatment of acid mine drainage, and the production of sustainable energy.

The most influential groups are more focused but still hew to a doctrine that equates animal liberation with conservation. The International Fund for Animal Welfare and Born Free are certainly the best known of these organizations, but despite the complaints of their critics, they are hardly the most aggressive. That claim would properly go to Animal Rights Africa, a South African group founded in 2008. Animal Rights Africa uses a logo of a lion's paw print superimposed on a clenched fist and espouses a "total liberation" philosophy for animals that, while familiar to activists in the developed world, is new in Africa—and distinctly disturbing to the continent's old-school conservationists.

The keynote speaker to the Animal Rights Africa inaugural event was Steven Best, an associate professor of humanities and philosophy at the University of Texas at El Paso and a leader in the animal rights movement. Best combines animal liberation, environmentalism, and social progress into a syncretic philosophy that essentially demands equal rights for all living creatures. In his keynote speech, Best declaimed,

> The interests of one species *(Homo sapiens)* are represented as millions go unrecognized except as resources to be preserved for human use. But in the last three decades a new social movement has emerged—animal liberation. Its power and potential has yet to be recognized, but it deserves equal representation in the politics of the twenty-first century.... Every year alone humans butcher seventy billion land and marine animals for food; millions more die in experimental laboratories, fur farms, hunting preserves, and countless other killing zones.... On a strategic level, the animal liberation movement is essential for the human and earth liberation movements. In numerous key ways, the domination of humans over animals underlies the domination of human over human and propels the environmental crisis. Moreover, the animal liberation movement is the most dynamic and fastest growing social movement of the day, and other liberation movements ignore, mock, or trivialize it at their peril.

In the coda to his speech, Best urges animal liberationists to link up with—and dominate—other progressive movements and intimates that Africa is ripe for such engagement: "The kind of alliance politics one finds in South Africa remains weak and abstract so long as animal liberation and vegan interests are excluded.... The animal liberation movement can no longer afford to be single-issue and isolationist but must link to other social justice and environmental movements. Each movement has much to learn from the other, and no movement can achieve its goals apart from the other. It is truly one struggle, one fight."

But is it, in fact, *truly* one fight? From the perspective of traditional conservationists, vertebrate biologists, and habitat ecologists, clearly it is not: to these people, wildlife preservation and animal liberation are two distinct, even inimically opposed, issues. And there is also the matter of simple pragmatism: the disparity between what is "right" and what can work can be profound, particularly in Africa. For example, should the rights of elephants trump the rights of other wildlife species? This is a pressing question wherever elephants are found in Africa but particularly in South Africa's Kruger National Park, a reserve that has been profoundly influenced by the continent's nascent animal rights movement.

At more than seventy-three hundred square miles, Kruger is one of the largest game reserves in the world. It has more mammalian species than any other protected area in Africa, including the so-called Big Five: elephant, rhino (both species), lion, leopard, and Cape buffalo. But as vast as it is, Kruger is still limited in terms of its wildlife carrying capacity, especially in regard to elephants. If there are too many elephants—in Kruger or anywhere else—the land takes a beating. First, the trees are damaged from excessive browsing, and finally they disappear. The habitat literally changes, from forest to parkland and then to grassy savanna. The topsoil erodes. All the species that relied on these transitional habitats—from birds and forest antelopes to arboreal primates—disappear. An excessive number of elephants will eat everything, including themselves, out of a home.

As with most other African parks, Kruger is an island; the migration routes that had supported the region's megafauna since the late Pleistocene are severed now, and the park is largely fenced. Progressively managed hunting preserves and tribal properties along Kruger's borders have resulted in the removal of the wire in some areas, expanding available habitat to a degree. More significantly, a transfrontier pact has allowed fence removal between Kruger and Mozambique's Limpopo National Park, essentially doubling the size of the protected habitat. Still, in general terms, Kruger's elephants aren't going anywhere. They have to stay in the Kruger-Limpopo biome; they have been denied those corridors that once allowed them to roam the continent as hunger, thirst, and will dictated. These strictures imply enforced limits on elephant numbers. The general consensus among biologists and game managers is that no more than eight thousand elephants should inhabit

Kruger proper, and much of the park's budget and management efforts over the past two decades have been devoted to trying to keep the herd to this figure.

In the past, the solution was easy: cull to the desired population. As previously discussed, experienced sharpshooters, mostly professional hunters and the game scouts they had personally trained, would identify family groups appropriate for removal and take them out in a minute or two of concentrated gunfire. It wasn't pretty, nor was it even hunting; it was killing, and it sometimes emotionally damaged the men who had to do it. But culling was a long-established tradition in South Africa, and it worked. Eliminating entire family units rather than targeting individual animals from different groups kept the essential social structure of Kruger's elephants intact, because it minimized stress on the population as a whole. Elephant herds are matriarchies. Each herd is controlled by a dominant cow, and each member has a place within the group. Killing individual animals (particularly the dominant matriarch) within a group invariably traumatizes the group as a whole, commonly resulting in the phenomenon of pachyderm "juvenile delinquents": young males that act aggressively toward other elephants and are often inclined to attack humans or livestock.

But Kruger severely restricted culling beginning in 1989 as a result of international pressure—more from people enamored of elephants as a charismatic species than from scientists or mainline conservationists. In other words, animal rights advocates drove the change in policy. By 1995, culling was no longer actively pursued.

(As an aside, it should be noted that Kruger's history of unexpected consequences in wildlife management is not dissimilar to other reserves on other continents where ambitious tinkering with the native fauna has been attempted. Gray wolves were mostly eliminated from Yellowstone National Park in the United States by the 1900s. As a result, the region's elk population exploded, ultimately destroying much of the riparian vegetation and harming many species associated with Rocky Mountain riverine environments. But the elk population dropped after wolves were reintroduced to the park in the late twentieth century. Riparian flora rebounded, and with it beavers returned. These large aquatic rodents created extensive systems of dams and pools that attracted nesting waterfowl and other birds. In short, Yellowstone's ecology was significantly enriched by reintroducing an apex predator long absent from the region.)

Unfortunately, all efforts to control Kruger's elephants since the cessation of general culling have failed. Relocation and contraceptives have been tried. Both are expensive, extremely stressful on the animals, and, in the final analysis, ineffective. The elephant population swelled to almost 12,000 by 2004 and then to 15,500 by 2006. A new plan was refined between 2008 and 2010, dividing the park into discrete blocks. The scheme is, frankly, complicated. The basic idea is to manage each block separately for vegetative cycles—that is, to allow habitats to "degrade" or "recover" from elephant impacts at varying levels. This, ideally, will result in a wide range of niche habitats for varying species and minimize the need for elephant culling. But the plan may well be doomed simply because it has so many variables. Complex wildlife management schemes are difficult to implement successfully anywhere, all the more so on a huge preserve in Africa—even South Africa, which has well-developed infrastructure and a relatively responsive political system. Critics of the scheme abound. Some of the most incisive writing on the issue comes from Ron Thomson, a legendary former game warden.

Thomson worked as a ranger and warden in colonial Rhodesia (now Zimbabwe) for twenty-four years. During his duties, he killed five thousand elephants, eight hundred buffaloes, more than fifty lions—including six man-eaters—and two hundred hippos. He supervised a culling team that killed twenty-five hundred elephants at Gonarezhou National Park in the 1970s. These kinds of credentials, of course, don't necessarily impress animal rights advocates. But Thomson's work with black rhinos would certainly earn their plaudits. Thomson was an early pioneer in the live capture and translocation of rhinos. Over a seven-year period in the 1960s and 1970s, he led Rhodesia's black rhino capture team, tranquilizing and moving 140 of the great beasts. Because a rhino stalk usually requires absolute silence, Thomson usually worked alone, armed only with a tranquilizer dart gun. Animal rightists may well disparage Thomson's CV, but no one can dispute his deep and intimate knowledge of Africa's game and the habitats they require to survive.

At this point, Thomson is thoroughly disenchanted with conservation policy across Africa. CITES, he feels, is an abject failure, especially when it comes to preventing the trade in elephant and rhino products. Poaching, he says, is driven by poverty—specifically the poverty in the communities surrounding the great parks. To stop poaching, the poverty must be alleviated, and that inevitably will involve the regulated taking of "surplus" animals within the parks.

Kruger's new management plan is thus unworkable for a number of reasons, says Thomson. It treats elephants as discrete quanta—entities separate from elephants in other blocks, from the park as a whole, and from the surrounding countryside, including the villages full of poor hungry people on the border of the park. The idea that you can effectively manage Kruger's elephants and improve biodiversity by juggling vegetative canopies—allowing elephants to devastate some blocks while culling to prescribed numbers in others—looks good on paper, Thomson avers on a Web site devoted to African game management and hunting issues, but applying the plan effectively will be next to impossible. Parts cannot be substituted for the whole; the forest cannot be ignored for the trees. And by the way, a lot of elephants will still be killed under the new plan:

> In the new Kruger elephant management model it has already been decided that the northern and southern elephant management blocks will initially have their elephant populations reduced at the same rate at which they are now expanding. This will entail reducing each year's standing population by 14 percent. The first 7 percent will take off the annual increment. The second 7 percent will represent the reduction. The number making up the 14 percent, therefore, will get smaller and smaller as the population size diminishes by 7 percent each year.
>
> In those populations that are being culled, therefore, the population will be halved—and halved again repeatedly—every ten years. And in those populations that are not subject to culling, the populations will double their numbers every ten years. Ironically, the new elephant management plan for Kruger National Park—although it came about because of animal rights objections to the culling of elephants—will probably end up killing more elephants every year than was the case before.

The hard reality, then, is that elephants must be somehow controlled if Kruger is to maintain its biological richness. As Ian Parker noted, elephants are engines superbly designed for changing landscapes. If allowed to reproduce freely, they would change Kruger's landscape right down to the hardpan, leveling every standing tree. And despite its threatened status, the African elephant is hardly a shy breeder: when not subject to culling, Kruger's elephant population typically grows at 6 to 7 percent a year. Contraception and translocation, it is now known, are ineffective. Creating transnational parks to accommodate more elephants, as the International Fund for Animal Welfare and other groups advocate, is certainly a good idea, but opportunities are limited. Ultimately, effective elephant management must rely on a bullet. As Thomson observes, lethal force will remain the cornerstone of Kruger's new elephant policy—a policy that was developed in direct and sincere response to protests from animal rights advocates. There is simply no alternative, except for a complete cessation to all culling and trophy hunting, habitat degradation notwithstanding. And this may well happen. For many people of good conscience, including some with extensive backgrounds in wildlife issues, the specter of shooting any elephant for any reason is too horrible to countenance—to contemplate, even. To them, the elephant is sentient—more than that, intelligent—and killing sentient and intelligent creatures is murder. Better, perhaps, that there are fewer elephants, worse habitat, less biodiversity, as long as there is no murder. It is thus not a matter of conservation; it is a matter of essential morality, of civilized behavior.

Certainly, organized resistance to hunting is growing, particularly in the United States and Europe. Trophy hunting, especially, is drawing concentrated fire. A 2004 white paper titled *The Myth of Trophy Hunting as Conservation,* submitted to the British environment minister Elliott Morley by the League against Cruel Sports, limns the battle lines in no uncertain terms. The report inveighs thunderously against sport hunting, dismissing as lies any claims that hunting can be effectively employed as a conservation tool. And while the paper acknowledges that trophy hunting inevitably will continue in Africa for the foreseeable future, it suggests another strategy—depriving hunters of a major incentive for killing charismatic game: "While it may not be possible in the short term to prevent hunters from travelling around the globe to kill endangered animals, it is possible to deny them the perverse pleasure of bringing back a stuffed, mounted trophy of their kill."

Further, the report casts the argument as a conflict between good and evil, as a struggle between wealthy "pale males" (white hunters) and poor disenfranchised people of color who are the natural beneficiaries of ecotourism. Nor can there be any compromise, the report warns: "It is virtually impossible for these two groups to co-exist. The hunting industry, and the governments they have wooed, are battling against eco-tourism operators and local communities for control over the planet's endangered species—and are often winning."

At a certain point, vetting the arguments of both the pro- and anti-hunting camps feels utterly futile; to paraphrase Mark Twain, it becomes a matter of trying to separate the lies, the damn lies, and the statistics. More charitably, both groups can make compelling arguments for their respective positions on the consumptive use of game in Africa and elsewhere.

Only one group, however, can claim ascendance. Just as the hunting ethic was considered an integral component of the social contract in the nineteenth and early twentieth centuries, so its obverse is now true. A general opposition to hunting now prevails in the urban centers of the developed world. This anti-hunting sentiment has combined with a larger sense that cruelty to animals in general, including simple neglect, is anathema to civilized people. According to the U.S. Fish and Wildlife Service, between 1975 and 2006 the number of hunters in the United States (e.g., people who had purchased hunting licenses) declined from 19.1 million to 12.5 million. That figure is expected to plummet to 9.1 million by 2025. Some states—most notably those with large rural populations—have shown relatively slight drops, but the decline in others has been profound. In California, the decline was 38 percent; in Rhode Island, 59 percent. Some of this is due to expense (hunting is a relatively pricey activity), the loss of public-land hunting opportunities, and habitat loss. But the biggest driver appears to be a shift in the zeitgeist. Hunting is not considered au courant, especially among younger people. This is glaringly apparent in the American media. There are a great many TV shows dedicated to alternative and extreme sports—surfing, snowboarding, motocross, even street luge racing. The participants are young, fit, and attractive. And while there are some hunting and fishing shows on television—there's even a channel or two devoted wholly to field sports—their presentation and production values are stodgy by comparison, and the hosts and participants are generally middle-aged, paunchy, and anything but sexy. In the most basic terms, the culture that really counts in America—youth culture—has moved decisively against hunting.

The same holds true for urban Africa. As the League against Cruel Sports claims, compromise of any significant degree is probably impossible for anti-hunting and pro-hunting groups. But the organization is wrong when it maintains hunters are winning. The hunters are *not* winning, including those in Africa. In Nairobi and Johannesburg, hunting is viewed as a colonial relic, something pursued by wealthy white men besotted with delusional fantasies of Hemingway, Ruark, and the Golden Age of the Safari. Even in countries where the hunting tradition is still relatively strong—Tanzania and Namibia, for example—the activity is viewed as a somewhat atavistic rural pursuit and, at best, a source of foreign currency. Hunting big game is not an aspiration of the people who really count in Africa—educated, upwardly mobile, professional urbanites. Thanks to the Internet and cellular technology, Africa is now integrated into world culture in a way that was unthinkable even a few years ago. By way of illustration: I visited Kenya's Laikipia highlands in 2001. At that time, standard hardwired telephony had just made it to the region. Up to that point, ranchers had communicated by CB radio—or more often, by driving or flying to one another's homes. I observed that the ranchers seemed somewhat flummoxed by the technology, which was then more than a century old, of course. When they picked up the phone, they had a tendency to say "over" after finishing their part of the conversation, as they would on a two-way radio.

Flash forward eight years. Cell phones are now ubiquitous across East Africa, including in Laikipia and the Maasai Mara. Everyone—city dwellers, ranchers, pastoralists—has at least one cell phone. They are calling, texting, Googling, reading news feeds. They are as exposed to the world—and to global popular culture—as anyone in Paris, London, or New York. Just as it has in the United States, this vastly enhanced access to media hasn't necessarily raised the level of discourse: a lot of attention seems concentrated on scandal, sex, and crime.

Still, matters of more elevated import percolate through the new African media, including those related to wildlife conservation. The debate in Kenya over reintroducing big game hunting has drawn particular attention. In the countryside, the issue is strictly a matter of shillings and security: conversations with any pastoralist or farmer revolve around protection of livestock from predators, excluding elephants from crops, or the return in meat or money that game animals may yield. In Nairobi, however, the issue is both more complicated and familiar: it sounds a lot like the heated point and counterpoint you'd hear in any American or European city. In 2007, a Kenyan journalist opposed to hunting described it as bored and wealthy Arab royals and Americans potting away at big game while starving children looked on from mud-and-wattle huts. While the issue is certainly more nuanced than that, this image contains enough truth to make for a powerful self-propagating message—an idea that is simple, clear, and easy to understand and communicate. Indeed, this portrayal of hunters as callous and blood-crazed neocolonials trying to insinuate themselves back into a country from which they were properly ejected during a war of liberation has resonated dramatically in urban Kenya. Kenyans may not be deeply invested in the doctrine of animal rights, but the injustices of white colonialism still rancor, and big game hunting remains the preeminent symbol of the colonial era.

Thus, the basic conversation on African conservation is changing, driven by new media and reflecting the changing concepts of environmentalism in the world at large. The "old" science-based approach to conservation—dispassionate, data-driven, focused on habitat and suites of species rather than on narratives that anthropomorphize individual animals—is under dire threat. Its adversary is a New Environmentalism founded on the "deep ecology" philosophy articulated a generation ago by the Norwegian mountaineer Arne Naess, but it diverges from Naess's original doctrine of planetary health in that it focuses on a single component of ecological well-being—the inherent rights of the individual animal—to an inordinate degree. The New Environmentalism is thus more about social, even religious, trends than it is about science. This invests it with a power that science alone will never have, because it is grounded in the heart more than in the mind.

Africa is the ultimate battleground for these dueling conservation concepts. It still has enough wildlife to make the stakes worthwhile. Alaska and the Canadian Arctic, the only other regions with large populations of megafauna, are generally not in this battle. Animal rights groups maintain a presence there, but wildlife management is rigorously codified under federal, state, and provincial law and based on data, not morality. Though good cases can be made that wildlife policies in Alaska and Canada are significantly influenced by political pressure, nothing is likely to shift the argument decisively in favor of animal rights advocates. True, the clubbing of harp seal pups has diminished as a result of international outrage. But all the major terrestrial species—including brown bears, wolves, caribou, musk oxen, Dall sheep, mountain goats, even polar bears—are still hunted. The support for consumptive wildlife management is broad and deep. Hunting in Alaska and the Canadian North is largely considered a birthright.

But Africa is in a state of flux, and new doctrines are not reflexively spurned. Big game hunting has never been a favored activity for most indigenous Africans, with the exception of tribes such as the Wata and the San. Moreover, since it carries the indelible stain of white colonialism, hunting will always be controversial, even in situations in which it is a proven and effective conservation tool. Ecotourism, on the other hand, is appealing for the opposite reason: it has no ties to an oppressive past. In many cases—as will be discussed later—ecotourism can exert deleterious impacts on land and wildlife. And the revenues of many ecotourism enterprises are monopolized by foreign owners and government officials, with few benefits trickling down to local villagers. But as a brand, ecotourism is ascendant. It is allied with the New

Environmentalism, with animal rights, with all that is modern, young, and appealing. Hunting labors under an onus imposed by its own name, by a history that appears drear and cruel, by the whiteness and age of its primary practitioners. In the future, poaching will continue in the African game lands; the same can't be said of legal hunting.

CHAPTER 5

My Cow Trumps Your Lion

The road north from Nanyuki into the rangelands of Laikipia starts out as macadam but quickly turns to dirt. After about twenty miles or so, a side road joins the main highway from the west—a track, really, gouged out of the rock and bush long ago by a small grader or perhaps a gang of men wielding shovels and picks. From the looks of it, the road seems used more by wildlife than motor vehicles; animal tracks are everywhere in the buff-colored dust on the shoulders. Taking even a four-wheel-drive rig down this route is a rough go. Deep gullies and big rocks allow a top speed of perhaps fifteen miles an hour, slower still on the innumerable curves and steep little pitches and grades. The topography here is like a sea abruptly fossilized during a squall: dips and bumps and declivities, hills, scarps, plateaus, abrupt drop-offs, all covered with the ubiquitous thorn-wood scrub that blankets the soil from the slopes of Mount Kenya north through the Horn of Africa.

The game is abundant—more than a layperson would expect for such an arid and spare landscape. Thomson's and Grant's gazelles bound away from the road at the approach of a car. Dik-diks seek the shade of every low-hanging shrub. Panicked wart hogs sprint through the bush, their tails erect as semaphores. Hartebeests and oryx graze singly or in small groups. Giraffes extend their necks above the thorn-wood canopy. As the road winds down a slope to a bridge crossing the sluggish Ewaso Nyiro River, waterbucks can be discerned drifting between the fever trees, and troops of baboons forage for grubs and grasses, monitored by alpha males squatting on their haunches. In the deep, stagnant pools, hippos abide. At night, spotted hyenas, bat-eared foxes, and leopards are often startled by the headlights of approaching vehicles. Everywhere are piles of soccer ball–sized turds—elephant dung.

After crossing the river, the track wends along a small flat, where brilliantly hued lilac-breasted rollers preen on acacia branches. The road then veers up a steep hill, skirts a ridge, and terminates abruptly at Sungelai, the home of Laurence Frank—a research associate of the Museum of Vertebrate Zoology at the University of California and one of East Africa's foremost predator researchers.

The structure is literally built into a cliff: a sprawling assemblage of native stone and lumber, with great plate glass windows that overlook the Ewaso Nyiro gorge. It is easy to spend an entire day on the deck beyond the windows, glassing the river course and miles and miles of surrounding hills for game. Nor do you have to look far. Hyraxes have established themselves in the rocks below the house and often lounge on the deck's railing, importuning handouts. Elephants drift in front of the home almost daily, their utter silence both eerie and intimidating as they pad across the rough, scrubby land. And a small herd of Cape buffalo forages in the immediate area; one old lone bull, with a gigantic boss and wicked, majestically curved horns, typically beds down about a hundred yards from Frank's bedroom door. At twilight, several hundred white-winged bats stream into the sky from the rafters of the house for their nightly round of foraging, providing a dramatic spectacle for guests enjoying preprandial cocktails.

Sometimes the wildlife does more than display itself in picturesque fashion beyond the plate glass. A few years ago, Alayne Cotterill, a biologist who works with Frank on his predator projects, was sleeping in a bedroom with her two children and her dog. As she often did, Cotterill had left her sliding glass door open to access the cool night breeze that sweeps down the Ewaso Nyiro gorge. She was awakened in the early morning by the frenzied barking of her dog. Turning on the light, she found a large leopard contemplating the family tableau from the foot of the bed. After a moment, the cat turned and walked back out the bedroom door. Because African leopards seldom attack human beings without provocation, Cotterill feels the cat was drawn by her dog. In any event, she now sleeps with her bedroom doors closed.

This is Frank's headquarters, though he is often away for days or weeks at a time, overseeing predator conservation projects across Kenya. It is his redoubt, the place he uses to work up data, recharge, perhaps even relax a little. Now past sixty, Frank is six feet tall and big-boned, and he still carries a lot of muscle. He has tangled, thinning hair, large eyes that stare fixedly from behind thick spectacles, blunt features, and a prognathous jaw that creates an impression of latent aggression. And indeed, he can be aggressive, a quality that doesn't necessarily ill-serve him in Africa. Most of the people who know Frank highly respect him, and a few fear him, including some of his own research associates. Normally low-key, even diffident, he quickly gets his back up when encountering stupidity or ineptitude. On more than one occasion, he has not shied from physical confrontation. He characterizes himself as "a putz, a puppy dog, somebody who is all thumbs." But anyone who has seen him at work—setting snares for lions, engrossed in laboratory procedures, tearing apart a Land Rover transmission, repairing a handgun—can only consider his self-evaluations false modesty. By any consideration, he would seem one of the most competent people on the planet.

In predilection, Frank seems a man from another age. His diction is precise, and he speaks in complete thoughts; his conversation somehow seems meticulously punctuated, down to semicolons, hyphens, and parentheses. Though he is not Scottish, he deeply enjoys the bagpipes and the smokiest, most phenolic of single malt scotches. His manners are almost courtly, though he also is capable of blithely interjecting rude, shocking, or scabrous comments into genteel conversations. He is a lifelong insomniac, a great fan of British spy fiction, an avid duck hunter with indifferent shooting skills, a man who is capable of bivouacking in the bush over his snares for days at a time, augmenting his meager diet with meat salvaged from his "bait"—carcasses of zebras, elands, or camels that have been dispatched by lions or hyenas.

Many things disturb Laurence Frank. He is upset when forced to spend long periods of time away from his five daughters because of his work; the red tape involved in transporting animal specimens from Kenya to the Museum of Vertebrate Zoology in Berkeley; his intense chronic lower back pain induced from four decades of pounding around East Africa in Land Rovers; the Byzantine politics of Kenya; the opinions of both opponents and friends; and the general vagaries of fate. But perhaps nothing upsets him more than the decline of his beloved predators.

Frank made his academic bones through seminal research on spotted hyenas, focusing largely on social organization and the role masculinizing hormones play in female development and group dynamics.

He is a cofounder of a captive spotted hyena project at the University of California, Berkeley, initiated to investigate their endocrinology and behavior at close range. The project is ongoing, with the animals housed in spacious compounds at a site in the Berkeley hills; on still nights, their hoots and gibbering resound down the slopes and vales. Spotted hyenas, Frank avers, are among the most intelligent and socially sophisticated of animals. Some of the animals that reside at the Berkeley compound he has raised from cubs. It is an alarming experience to see him casually clamber into a compound with a large dominant female hyena and playfully wrestle her, knowing her jaws could snap his femur with a casual twitch of her masseter muscles. He bars visitors from sharing his fun. "She knows me," he said when I asked one time if I could join him with one of the animals. "She grew up with me. Her reaction to you would be—unpredictable." Frank's eyes glow when he's with his animals. A man who inveighs against anthropomorphism, he nevertheless loves— deeply loves—hyenas.

Over the course of the past three decades, Frank's professional emphasis has shifted from ethology to conservation biology, a change he credits as a logical response to empirical observation. "When the world around you is dying, you can't simply accept it," he says, referring to Kenya's wildlife crash. "You have to act, whether or not it makes a difference."

Frank has established several predator projects in Kenya, all roughly based on the same template: monitoring the number of lions and hyenas through tracking, telemetry, and local contacts; minimizing depredation of livestock through the promotion of *boma* (thorn-wood corral) construction and other intensive husbandry methods; and hiring local *moran* (young warriors) to serve as trackers, community liaisons, and educators. Frank would characterize his success as moderate at best, but others are more generous, particularly in Laikipia, where his work with ranchers on private holdings and with Maasai elders on communal tribal homelands has resulted in a generally stable population of lions and spotted hyenas. On Mugie, a forty-nine-thousand-acre ranch that combines cattle and sheep production with ecotourism on the northern Laikipia Plateau, lions have become a profit center; not coincidentally, Mugie's ranchers are active participants in Frank's program. Mugie supports about ten to fifteen lions along with its rich assortment of other wildlife species, and the interaction of the big cats with their prey is a major attraction for visitors. It's easy to see why: observing lions is a much more intimate experience at Mugie than it is on the Serengeti or Maasai Mara, where you have to jockey with ten to twenty minivans

FIGURE 3. Laurence Frank takes tissue samples from an anesthetized lion at Mugie Ranch, Laikipia. Note the firearms: attacks are always a possibility during fieldwork with lions. (Glen Martin)

to catch a glimpse of a pride. During one trip to Kenya, I passed a couple of days with Frank on Mugie, and much of the time was spent with the lions. On one occasion we observed them, at close quarters, gorging on a zebra kill; on another, we darted a young male and fitted him with a telemetry collar. Besides Frank and me, there were just a couple of his associate researchers, the ranch manager Claus Mortensen, and the wildlife. The experience is an indelible and treasured memory.

Still, frustration is part of Frank's job description. A few ranchers continue to evaluate lions, hyenas, and leopards according to the old Game Department definition of "vermin" and eliminate them remorselessly. And in southern Kenya among the Maasai, the fierce opposition to predator conservation has been daunting. But even while trying to change hearts and minds in Maasailand, Frank says he understands their position. "The Maasai are a deeply conservative people," he says. "Their resistance to change has allowed them to maintain cultural cohesion. And the focal point, the node of Maasai culture, is cattle. They believe God has delivered all the world's cattle to their care. They love them, sing to them. Cattle aren't just a store of wealth, a symbol of wealth— they *are* wealth, the best of all possible currencies. The Kenyan shilling is considered a poor if sometimes acceptable substitute for a cow."

To the Maasai, a lion that kills a cow or goat thus strikes at the very heart of social order and must be eliminated. Moreover, observes Frank, lions remain a means for *moran* to demonstrate their courage and prowess; though technically proscribed by the governments of both Kenya and Tanzania (where most Maasai live), communal lion hunts conducted by *moran* equipped only with shields and spears remain commonplace. The tail is kept as a trophy and is considered a great status symbol. "In the past, it wasn't much of an issue, because there were plenty of lions and relatively few Maasai," Frank observes. "But the Maasai population has exploded. Currently, you have too many guys poking too few lions with spears. Lions are disappearing wholesale from Maasai territory."

Exacerbating the situation is the use of the insecticide Furadan as a predator poison throughout East Africa. For years, Frank observes, Furadan has been available at every trading post and small store in rural Kenya and Tanzania, where it sells for less than a dollar a packet. "Everyone knew it isn't being used for insects," he says. "It's an extremely effective predicide. Put it on a kill, and it wipes out lions, hyenas, and leopards very efficiently. Also vultures, jackals—anything else that comes into the carcass." Furadan availability has only lately been reduced, thanks mainly to CBS's *60 Minutes,* which featured a segment on Frank.

Despite the efforts of Frank and other conservation biologists, lions are in free fall across East Africa, particularly—and ironically, given the *Born Free* saga—in Kenya (Laikipia being the notable exception). By best estimates, continental populations have plummeted from roughly two hundred thousand two decades ago to perhaps thirty thousand today. Retaliatory killings by pastoralists are the primary cause; a subsidiary but growing threat is the Chinese traditional medicine market. "Tiger bone is a favored remedy, but with tigers disappearing, the Chinese are turning increasingly to lion bone," Frank observes.

But the underlying reason for the lion decline, says Frank, is even more basic: lions have no value in modern Kenya. Mugie and a few other private ranches that maintain tourist lodges, the national parks, the Maasai Mara National Reserve—these are exceptions to the general rule, places where lions are hanging on because they have a constituency: wealthy tourists and the businesses that cater to them. But across the rest of the country, across most of Africa, lions are liabilities, potential threats to property and human life.

"It's all very well to admire lions from the safety of a minivan," observes Ian Parker. "But if you're a pastoralist living in a little *manyatta* [semipermanent camp] deep in the bush with nothing to your name but a few cows, it's another matter altogether. You're not just worrying about lions taking your stock and depriving you of your livelihood, though that's a constant concern; you're also worried they'll kill you or your family members outright."

Frank thus measures his success to the degree that he has been able to reinvest lions with value. On Mugie and other Laikipia ranches that support his work, the lions are part of the tourist draw. And in Amboseli National Park and surrounding lands, the Lion Guardians project, which employs Maasai *moran* to track and protect lions, is yielding positive results, not because the Maasai have abruptly changed their general view of lions, but because they derive considerable benefit from the program. Initiated by two of Frank's associates, Leela Hazzah and Stephanie Dolrenry, the Lion Guardians program has proved so successful at Amboseli that the researchers plan to extend it to the Maasai Mara.

Lion Guardian participants receive a salary and are given cell phones—tremendous incentives in Maasailand. Jobs that pay hard currency are exceedingly difficult to come by in the region, and though the Maasai generally are disdainful of modern technology, they have taken to cell phones enthusiastically; the devices allow tribal members to stay in close touch with far-flung relatives and, even more critically, allow them to track cattle prices in local markets. Before the advent of cellular coverage in Maasailand—placing an international call from a mobile phone is now as easy in the middle of the Serengeti as in Manhattan—tribal members had to take whatever price was offered when they brought their stock to market. Typically, they were low-balled. Now they can monitor prices at various markets throughout Kenya and Tanzania, delivering their animals only when given a quote that suits them.

But the Lion Guardian program also provides Maasai *moran* with something they value far more than money or advanced technology: prestige. Though the Maasai will typically exterminate any predators they encounter, lions are inextricably intertwined with their lives, culture, and mythos. Lions are the supreme test of a *moran* and hence help define what it means to be Maasai. "When a Maasai man attains elder status, usually in his early forties, he is expected to spend his days advising, drinking beer, and telling tales of past deeds," says Rian Labuschagne. "It is considered the appropriate progression for a man who has spent a dangerous youth and early adulthood caring for livestock and defending the tribe." And the stories that confer the highest status to the teller, says Labuschagne, are those that concern successful cattle raids against enemies—and lion hunts.

The Lion Guardian program accommodates this almost reflexive need of young Maasai males to interact with lions, says Frank: "It keeps them associated with lions, which ultimately gains them great respect from other tribal members. They're out in the field, tracking lions, informing locals when lions are in the area, helping herders build *bomas* to protect their stock. The fact that we offer paying jobs is a tremendous incentive, but the opportunity to interact with lions on an ongoing basis, allowing the *moran* to gain the admiration of their relatives and friends, is also a real attraction." The *moran* of the Lion Guardian corps are thus able to collect their own heroic tales of lion encounters, to be told when they are elders—but tales with a crucial difference from those of earlier Maasai culture. In these stories, the lions have been transformed from the killer, the despoiler, the implacable enemy of the people, to something of inherent value.

That, at least, is the hope; no one is less certain of positive results from any conservation initiative than Frank, who has spent more than forty years adjusting the ideals of his youth to the hard realities of Africa. But if he is not certain of success, he is most certainly convinced of failure if innovative programs are not instituted to preserve predators; and the Lion Guardians, he emphasizes, is just such a program. It works. "It has been successful beyond anyone's wildest hopes," he says. "It has totally halted lion killings in the areas where it's implemented. The aftermath of the [2009–10] drought shows this. In a four-month period, eighteen lions were killed in one small area [five hundred square kilometers] that had no Guardians—and *none* were killed in a thirty-five-hundred-square-kilometer area patrolled by Guardians. That's a stunning achievement."

Frank also maintains that successful lion conservation programs paradoxically must involve the elimination of selected animals, specifically chronic livestock killers. If a particular lion develops a taste for beef or mutton—something that often occurs when injury or age renders an animal unfit to take wild game—then it must be killed, Frank says. There can be no alternative: once a lion keys into livestock as primary prey, rehabilitation is almost impossible—and, in the larger scheme of species conservation, hardly worth the time and money required for even a successful attempt. Too, Frank's initiatives depend on the goodwill of the people who live in lion country.

"Candidly, cattle killers are usually created by bad livestock practices," he observes. "When people construct good *bomas* and really
watch their animals, there's usually no problem—the lions never learn
to kill stock. But when a lion does go bad, we'll work with the affected
rancher or pastoralist and the Kenya Wildlife Service to eliminate it.
It's very rare that it comes to that, but we have to be willing to help
out when it does. If we didn't, we wouldn't have any credibility. We're
good at tracking and snaring, and we've put telemetry collars on a lot of
predators, so sometimes we can locate the problem animal right away."

Frank, in fact, has become a kind of de facto troubleshooter for
ranchers and pastoralists with predator problems. On one occasion, I
accompanied him to a Laikipia ranch that reportedly supported a rabid
spotted hyena. Rabies is endemic among East Africa's predators and
sometimes poses as much of a threat to local hyena populations as poisoning does; Frank is anxious to do what he can to control the disease
at any opportunity. On arriving at the ranch, Frank conferred with the
owner, who directed him to a brushy river course. It didn't take long to
find the hyena—a relatively young male; we approached it easily as it
staggered along the riverbank, shivering and whining, before disappearing into thick brush. Frank loaded his short-barreled 12-gauge pump
shotgun with rifled slugs and set off in pursuit; I was timorous at the
prospect of encountering a rabid hyena in heavy vegetation, so elected
to stay behind. In short order there was a single shot. I investigated, to
find Frank standing over the dead hyena, which he had dispatched with
a slug placed behind the shoulder. He seemed deeply saddened. "I hate
killing these guys," he said as he prepared to drag the carcass to his
Land Rover and ultimately to his lab for the usual battery of samples
and tests. "It makes me feel incredibly bad when I have to do it. They
are such wonderful animals." He sighed deeply. "Sometimes there's simply no alternative."

On another occasion, Frank was called to a ranch to pick up a leopard. The couple who owned the property—amiable quasi New Agers
who combined modest cattle production with some low-key ecotourism—had captured the animal in a box trap after it had eaten their
favorite dog. They didn't want to kill the cat; they simply wanted it
gone. Frank and I arrived, and we bent down and looked into the box
trap. The leopard, which had been crouched in the gloom at the far
end of the trap, made an enormous leap and slammed against the gate,
claws extended, teeth bared, spittle flying, eyes lambent with green fire.
The entire trap shook with the impact, and a snarl that sounded like an

FIGURE 4. Laikipia Predator Project researchers take measurements and tissue samples from an anesthetized leopard that had been killing dogs. It was captured in a box trap by local ranchers. (Glen Martin)

overrevving F-15 split the air. The charge was so abrupt and frightening that I felt any number of internal organs loosening, but Frank merely evinced mild interest. "Aw, poor guy," he said. "Look—he broke off a canine. They get into these box traps, and they tear themselves up trying to get out. Box traps are really a terrible way of dealing with predators; our snares are much more effective and humane. The animals can't damage themselves, and you can anesthetize them and release them easily."

After considerable effort, Frank managed to inject the animal with an anesthetic. Once the leopard conked out, Frank took tissue samples and buckled a telemetry collar around its neck, then loaded the limp, drooling, and utterly unconscious animal into the back of the Land Rover. We drove over rutted tracks through the bush for about an hour, to a site Frank felt was far enough away from human habitation to give the leopard a chance at staying out of trouble.

"Of course, we're releasing it in another leopard's territory—every place around here is a leopard's territory—so he could get killed," Frank said. "But what are you going to do?" Just as he was unhitching the tailgate to the Land Rover, a truck drove up. It was an acquaintance of Frank's, a local cattle rancher who loathed predators and disapproved of efforts aimed at their preservation but was nevertheless on good terms with the biologist. They stood and talked for a while—too long, as it turned out.

After an extended palaver, Frank scooped up the leopard in his arms, still chatting with the rancher. A low, deep snarl emanated from the cat. Frank looked down, and the leopard looked up at him peevishly. The anesthetic was wearing off. "Um—I think we have a situation here," Frank said. The cat abruptly voided its bladder, soaking Frank's shirt with pungent urine. Its snarl waxed in volume and rose in timbre.

The rancher almost did a back flip as he vaulted behind Frank's Land Rover. He pulled a compact semiautomatic pistol from a holster at the small of his back and shakily pointed it at Frank and the leopard. Along with their taste for dogs, African leopards are known for unmitigated ferocity if cornered or wounded. It is not uncommon to hear of multiple maulings—leopards chewing and clawing through a group of people, one after another, before escaping, rather than taking the most direct and expeditious route for egress.

The leopard's flanks had begun twitching now; its lips pulled back from its teeth, and its yowls grew louder. Its eyes seemed to bulge from their sockets. Frank, meanwhile, kept the ninety-pound animal nestled securely in his arms. He walked calmly around the truck and proceeded

FIGURE 5. Laurence Frank prepares to release the aforementioned leopard to the wild. The cat was regaining consciousness when this shot was taken, and worries were growing that it would begin mauling people. (Glen Martin)

fifty yards or so into the bush, where he gently placed the leopard on the ground at the edge of a small clearing. The rancher muttered imprecations and holstered his pistol. Frank rejoined us; he stank abominably of cat urine. We watched as the leopard got shakily to its feet, glanced darkly at us, and skulked off into the bush.

"Gee," said Frank. "That went well, didn't it?"

By any measure, Frank has accomplished real things on the ground in Kenya. He has built good relations with tribal people, white ranchers, and lodge owners. He has had great success in eliminating the Furadan poisonings that were wiping out predators across the country. As a persistent, though never didactic, advocate for conservation, he is changing human reactions to lions and hyenas one person at a time. Pessimistic by nature, he is quick to characterize his life's work as bootless and unproductive, but there is no doubt Kenya's predators would be in even worst straits if he had not been in their corner for the past forty years.

Still, he feels his greatest problem isn't Furadan or Maasai lion hunts or rancher bias against anything that might eat a cow. Rather, it's the growing disconnect between the ideal and the real—the sense that "loving animals" is the same as saving wildlife. As animal rights advocates gain influence in East Africa, he says, it becomes harder to implement effective conservation programs, because some of those programs may involve killing animals. Frank has a negative and immediate reaction to the "Disneyization" of wildlife, as he puts it. A few years ago, he was greatly pleased when an Austrian pilot who had heard of his work volunteered to fly a small plane to Kenya to aid him in telemetry research for his initial program, the Laikipia Predator Project. Frank met the pilot at the Nanyuki airstrip with high hopes, but his optimism was checked when he saw what had been painted on the side of the plane: characters from Disney's *Lion King* mugging around a Laikipia Predator Project logo. Not only was it an illegal copyright infringement—hardly a pressing concern for Frank—but it invoked his darkest, his most dire enemy.

"No, no, no, NO!" he screamed. The pilot was nonplussed, all the more so when Frank insisted on the removal of the Disney figures. The pilot stayed in Laikipia for several months and proved a great help in Frank's work, but the two men never became very close; petty disagreements ultimately grew into major complaints, and they parted company on something other than the best of terms.

What it will take to save Kenya's predators, Frank feels—what it will take to save all the country's charismatic wildlife—is the rejection of the Disney ideal. The apotheosis of the individual lion has made the preservation of *Panthera leo* problematic—even doubtful. When the public recoils in horror at the taking of a lion for profit or sport, lions will remain valueless to the people who live with them. Lions will still be killed, because they are significant threats to cattle and human beings. Indeed, any incentive to preserve them disappears.

If the rights to shoot three or four large-maned male lions in Laikipia were auctioned off annually, said Frank, it would generate hundreds of thousands of dollars—big money in Kenya. Care must be taken, he emphasizes, to ensure that hunt proceeds would directly benefit pastoralist settlements: "Not just the chiefs and councilors—the little guys, too." Such revenues would also bolster conservation efforts on the ranches and, most important, demonstrate that lions could be major profit centers for rangeland-based enterprises. "It's important to remember that the lions trophy hunters are interested in—and the only lions they should be allowed to hunt—are the big old males," Frank says. "And those are also the ones, from the point of view of species preservation, that are expendable. They've already passed on their genes. They're getting infirm and rickety and are burdens on their prides. If a hunter doesn't kill them, sooner or later the hyenas will pull them down, or they'll start taking cows and somebody will put a spear through them or poison them. No wild animal dies a peaceful old age."

Frank emphasizes that general big game hunting should currently not be allowed in Kenya, with the possible exception of buffalo and plains game in certain regions. Wildlife populations are simply too depleted to withstand additional pressure. This is especially so for lions because of their rapid disappearance across East Africa. "But the good thing about lions is that they're fecund," he says. "If they have decent habitat and they aren't mercilessly persecuted, they can bounce back rapidly. But for that to happen, people have to have a reason to tolerate lions. There has to be something in it for them. Any wildlife policy that doesn't allow local people direct benefits from lions is doomed."

CHAPTER 6

Death to l'Ancien Régime

So here is a challenge to all of you in the conservation community: stop hiding behind your ultra-thin computer screens in your air-conditioned offices, and stop rushing around in your chrome-spangled 4WDs from one piece of irrelevant Conservation Bling to another. Have the courage to admit that everything you have recommended, supported, funded and implemented over the last 30 years in Kenya has been a failure—or was it your intention to sit idly by while some 70% of the wildlife vanished from under your very noses? For goodness sake, get together and sit down with government and sort this mess out before, literally, all is lost.

—Michael Norton-Griffiths, *Swara* (the journal
   of the East African Wildlife Society), July 2009

Some have likened Michael Norton-Griffiths to Cassandra, a high-strung doom crier who is always quick to find the dark cloud that supports every silver lining. But for many of East Africa's conservation biologists, Norton-Griffiths is an implacable realist who speaks truth to power. If he is quick to inveigh, even to insult (he has been known to refer to opponents as "reptiles"), his essential message, his supporters say, is spot on: conservation has failed utterly in Kenya, and the country's wildlife is in danger of vanishing unless policies are changed radically and soon.

Certainly, Norton-Griffiths's bona fides compel even his critics to take him seriously. He spent five years as the senior ecologist for Tanzania's Serengeti National Park, managed the Eastern Sahel Program for the International Union for the Conservation of Nature (IUCN) and spent four years developing information networks for the United Nations' Environment Program. Born in the United States, he was educated in

England, earning a degree in ethology from Oxford University; he has spent most of the past twenty years in Kenya. No American would take him as a countryman. His accent is a hybrid of the Oxonian and the colonial Kenyan. He is stocky and hirsute, with a big-toothed smile that somehow recalls the British comedian Terry-Thomas. His conversation is fluent and laced with humor even when addressing issues of the gravest import; both bons mots and droplets of the purest venom are distributed throughout.

I met Norton-Griffiths in a small business complex sheltered by a bower of tall trees in Langata. We repaired to an outdoor café and ordered sandwiches and salads. In the trees, weaver birds chattered furiously. Over the food, we discussed the state of wildlife conservation in East Africa generally and in Kenya in particular. I had prepared myself for the interview by reading many of the papers he has written on conservation and habitat management. This was not difficult; though his subject matter is dense, Norton-Griffiths has a provocative, insouciant style of writing that makes an exegesis on cattle-stocking ratios as absorbing as a gossip column.

Norton-Griffiths has become the bête noire for groups such as the International Fund for Animal Welfare and Born Free with his contention that forbidding the consumptive use of wildlife essentially guarantees its extinction. Lately, says Norton-Griffiths, the African conservation movement's "ancien régime"—venerable mainline organizations such as the World Wildlife Fund, the IUCN, and the African Wildlife Foundation—have found their rationales and spheres of influence usurped by "brash upstarts" advocating animal welfare above all else. Further, he maintains that the older established conservancies have accepted this power grab with docile equanimity. In a recent controversy over the Draft Wildlife Bill (which in later iterations authorized tighter strictures on wildlife use in Kenya), Norton-Griffiths notes, old guard conservationists put forth only token resistance to the International Fund for Animal Welfare's proposals—a ban on the killing of *all* wild animals, including birds and fish.

Still, he adds, he understands the diffidence of the old school organizations. "They didn't suddenly change their minds and start seeing the world through IFAW's eyes," Norton-Griffiths says. "They still support the consumptive use of wildlife in the pursuit of conservation. But they knew IFAW had already won the public debate over hunting. If they had vigorously fought [the Draft Wildlife Bill], they would've been branded as people who think 'shooting animals for fun' is a good thing. For the modern environmental movement, that is like being labeled a pedophile. It's the kiss of death."

One of Norton-Griffiths's particular areas of expertise is rangeland management. He says it is on Kenya's private pastoral lands—the vast, semiarid tribal holdings and ranches—that the battle for the country's wildlife will be won or lost. That's because almost three-quarters of the nation's wild animals live on these lands, outside the parks and reserves. So the economic policies that dictate rangeland management will be the ultimate determining factor for Kenya's game. And the outlook, says Norton-Griffiths, is not encouraging.

According to Norton-Griffiths's research, Kenya's wildlife declined about 3.2 percent per annum from the mid-1970s to the mid-1990s. Cultivation—basically, the conversion of rangelands to croplands or other intensive agricultural use—grew at a rate of about 8.6 percent per annum during the same period. Cattle sales at local markets also rose significantly, at 4.4 percent annually (though some of the increased commerce could be due to the sale of cattle brought in from Tanzania, Sudan, Ethiopia, and Somalia). These trends point to more than a shift in Kenya's agricultural sector, says Norton-Griffiths: they mark a titanic cultural change. For thousands of years, the people who inhabited the rangelands of East Africa conformed to a system of nomadic pastoralism, subsisting on cattle and goats that they ceaselessly herded across the landscape, seeking fresh forage. In such a system, the land dictated the carrying capacity for both livestock and people. In periods of lush rainfall, the numbers of both increased; during drought, they would fall.

In this pastoral system, there was also a place for wildlife. The people, cattle, and game could share the land to a significant degree. But it was never, as Ian Parker observed, an Eden. In one of his studies, Norton-Griffiths surveyed about a hundred thousand square miles of East African rangeland and found that more than 93 percent of the wild animals tallied were in areas where no human beings or livestock existed at the time of counting. The game could sometimes be found in relatively close proximity to people and their domestic animals, but they did not mix with one another, as various species of plains game will do. Grant's gazelles, impalas, topi, and zebras can often be found grazing placidly together, but all these ungulates take care to avoid propinquity with cattle. In other words, the doctrine of the Maasai, the Samburu, and other pastoral tribes living in pleasant harmony with wildlife is spurious; they cannot inhabit the same area simultaneously.

They *can*, however, inhabit the same general range, utilizing specific areas at different times. As long as the people and cattle are not too many, wildlife can subsist, even thrive, on land exploited by pastoral tribes. The difficulties emerge when pastoral populations outstrip the carrying capacity of the land, as is now happening in certain portions of Maasailand, or, even worse, when rangelands are converted to more intensive uses.

Land conversion, says Norton-Griffiths, is driven mainly by land rents: the net economic returns of land to landowners or users. Land rents can be derived through any number of processes—grazing, vegetable production, ecotourism, sport or subsistence hunting, or a mix of multiple uses. In some instances—specifically, those involving relatively low levels of conversion—biodiversity can actually increase. But at higher levels of conversion—say, turning rangelands into extensive hothouse flower operations, as is happening throughout much of Kenya—biodiversity dips and ultimately tanks. In this situation, natural vegetation and charismatic megafauna suffer most.

Land conversion is particularly problematic in areas of relatively high rainfall, such as the Mount Kenya region and lands surrounding the Aberdares. The abundant precipitation constitutes a goad for development, promising high cash returns for vegetables, coffee, tea, and flowers. The land rents that could be derived from conservation-based activities—tourism and hunting, specifically—could not compete. In high rainfall regions, then, wildlife conservation may require putting regulatory brakes on land conversions and simultaneously providing significant subsidies to land users. "But in arid or semiarid areas, [the rents] from wildlife operations—both consumptive and nonconsumptive—could exceed those realized from converting the land to more intensive agricultural uses," Norton-Griffiths says. "By encouraging those uses, you could provide significant incentives for preserving rangeland habitat and wildlife."

It is essential that these incentives are aggressively promoted now, says Norton-Griffiths, given the accelerating rate of land conversion in Kenya. And consumptive use doesn't necessarily trump nonconsumptive use, he emphasizes. In areas of low rainfall—that is, those areas where habitat preservation is still practical in Kenya—Norton-Griffiths's research shows that ecotourism can sometimes return more cash than hunting: "While one thousand people can observe a herd of twelve hundred buffalos, only five people can (reasonably) hunt them," he says. On lands with three hundred millimeters of precipitation annually, the return for tourism is about $1.80 a hectare per year, while the return for hunting is about $1.30. Cultivated crops yield about $2.30 per hectare per year, while livestock comes in last at about $.50.

These figures belie certain facts not immediately evident, however. Norton-Griffiths emphasizes that the numbers for tourism and hunting assume the landowner is managing aggressively for these enterprises and has invested significantly in them. This is feasible, he says, only for well-funded private ranches owned either by ex-colonials or foreigners. Most of Kenya's rangelands are "group ranches" owned by the tribes, who typically don't have money to invest for tourist facilities or hunting concessions. For these group holdings, tourism and hunting invariably remain subsidiary pursuits, with the land mostly dedicated, out of necessity, to subsistence livestock grazing.

But while livestock will continue to dominate pastoral land economies in Kenya, any viable conservation strategy requires providing landowners the option of consumptive wildlife use, Norton-Griffiths insists. That could translate as regulated cropping, sport hunting, or both. Without these incentives, he says, wildlife will continue to disappear from the landscape. "Picture a goat," he muses by way of illustration. "You're the owner of that goat, and you live on a group ranch in northern Kenya. Now, that goat is a significant asset. It eats forage from the tribal common, so it doesn't require any direct expenditure of capital to feed. You can eat it—an extremely important fact, given that food, particularly protein, is so scarce in your region. Or you can sell it and get cash, which is also difficult to obtain. If it's a female, you can get milk, another extremely valuable food. Or you can breed it and get more goats, increasing your wealth. The fact that you can utilize that goat in any number of ways makes it something you're more than willing to preserve and protect. The goat has palpable value for you."

But then assume you are forbidden by law to eat, sell, milk, or breed the goat, Norton-Griffiths continues: "In fact, the only thing you're allowed to do is let the goat be photographed by people who drive by in tourist buses. They don't pay you for the privilege, however; any money they spend goes to the tour operators and the owners of the lodges where they stay. You own the goat, but you can't use it directly, and any ancillary money generated by its existence goes to other people. Do you think there would be any goats left in Kenya if that was the situation? Not bloody likely."

And that's analogous to the current state of wildlife on private rangelands in Kenya, Norton-Griffiths says. The landowners are responsible for the wildlife, but they can't utilize it; the animals have become the unproductive wards of land managers who must protect them but cannot derive any income from them. Quite the opposite, in fact: predators consume valuable domestic animals, and wild ungulates compete with livestock for forage. Wildlife is thus not even a neutral entity on Kenya's private rangelands; it is a negative force, draining away scant resources from people who need them desperately for basic survival.

Exacerbating the condition is the country's exploding population growth and the rapid evolution of landownership patterns in Kenya. A strong entrepreneurial impulse is manifest in modern Kenyan society, and this is driving the breakup of large communal properties—tribal holdings—into smaller individually owned plots. Such subdivisions fragment ecosystems in two ways. First, subdividing land destroys traditional pastoral culture: the practice of people and livestock moving across large expanses of open land. Subdivision encourages permanent settlements, creating landscape barriers—fences, homes, roads—all the infrastructure associated with nonpastoral people.

Second, private landownership encourages intensive land use, either agricultural or commercial. A citizen who obtains a hectare of land in Laikipia will starve if he or she attempts to raise cattle on it as a sole means of income. But if a well is sunk, the land could be used to grow produce, or perhaps it would support a store or small restaurant. Subdivision makes it possible for such ventures to proceed. Dividing land invariably increases its value, making it easier to raise capital for its development. In either event, the land has lost its ecological significance to the wider biome. Fences keep out antelope; predators are harried away by dogs and irate people. Norton-Griffiths's research limns a grim consequence for land subdivision in rural Kenya: for every percentile decrease in the size of a given landholding, wildlife diversity shrinks by 0.4 percent, and wildlife density declines by 2 percent.

These figures impose a merciless calculus on the land, one that conservationists ignore at their peril. If the benefits to be derived from converting rangeland into cultivated or developed land are greater than the benefits that can be derived by livestock or ecotourism, land conversion in Kenya will continue; indeed, it will accelerate in lockstep with the country's extremely high birth rate. Today, this is most evident in the Maasai Mara, the vast game reserve contiguous to Tanzania's Serengeti National Park; the two preserves support East Africa's great wildebeest migration, the most dramatic cyclical movement of megafauna on the planet. Currently, the Serengeti-Mara wildebeest population stands at somewhat fewer than 1.5 million animals—a heartening figure, given that the number was about 250,000 wildebeest in the 1980s. The population climbs some in wet years and declines in dry ones, but the range has remained within a couple of hundred thousand animals for the past two decades. Conservation is never about a snapshot of the present, though; in its purest sense, it is about preserving the greatest possible complexity in a given natural system—forever. Obviously, this makes long-range planning paramount. But that is something that is always difficult in Africa—and is beginning to seem impossible in the Maasai Mara.

It is not that the Mara's basic economic engine, ecotourism, has changed. It continues to draw hundreds of thousands of visitors, providing millions of dollars in foreign exchange. But ecotourism is, paradoxically, the Mara's biggest problem. It has resulted in a mushrooming accretion of infrastructure—lodges, roads, restaurants, boutiques. In the last few years, tourist camps have proliferated near the Mara River, the better to accommodate the burgeoning number of visitors who want to see the migrating wildebeest herds run the crocodile gauntlet. In 2010, the Mara Conservancy tabulated fifty lodges and camps with 1,151 beds in Narok (a district in the northern portion of the reserve). This is more than double the number of beds reported by the district's chief warden, an indication that development in the region remains wholly unregulated.

Even more alarmingly, tourism is driving the conversion of adjoining rangelands to villages and croplands. The people who visit the lodges—and who provide tourist services—must be housed and fed. The Narok and adjoining Trans Mara districts have become breadbaskets for the region and nation: where there was grass to the horizon a decade ago there are now vast fields of wheat, worked by large tractors and combines.

So the current robust number of wildebeest in the Serengeti-Mara system must therefore be considered only as a snapshot. Given the trends in human population, infrastructure expansion, and rangeland conversion, the wildebeest herd *must* decline, perhaps by 30 percent. From the point of view of Kenyan policy makers, this isn't necessarily a bad thing—as long as the incentives that drive the wildlife reductions are sufficiently compensatory. Indeed, from a purely pragmatic perspective—the only perspective most Kenyans can afford—a reduced herd associated with a booming tourist sector could well be preferable to a much larger herd and a smaller development footprint. It raises a very pertinent question, writes Norton-Griffiths in an essay on the issue:

"How many wildebeest do you need, given that tourists probably only need to see some three hundred thousand to experience the raw majesty of the migration? Kenya will balance the benefits to be gained from developing agriculture on what was previously pastoral land against any possible tourism losses."

The trope thus promoted by many environmentalists—that ecotourism can save wildlife—is deeply flawed. Ecotourism, as Norton-Griffiths points out, can very easily work to wildlife's detriment. It's not simply that pastoral land of little interest to tourists will inevitably be converted to other uses in Kenya; the Maasai Mara also demonstrates that ecotourism can actually drive wildlife declines.

This unpleasant fact is beginning to register in the conservation community. It is addressed most pointedly by the initiative called Advancing Conservation in a Social Context, a subsidiary project of the Global Institute of Sustainability, as mentioned earlier. Funded by the MacArthur Foundation, ACSC is investigating whether ambitious conservation projects can accomplish their goals in concert with development. The group's members have found that they generally cannot: a deeply disturbing discovery, given that "win-win" thinking has become established doctrine for both conservation funders and practitioners. Rather, it seems that any conservation initiative will involve trade-offs and hard choices; in other words, there will be winners and losers. Any development entails diminution of a resource base; if that base is eroded by even a modest degree, it can redound negatively on conservation goals. In this light, says Tom McShane, the principal investigator for ACSC, the benefits of any conservation project must be weighed against the benefits development brings to local people. ACSC's work will be examined in greater detail later in this book, but McShane provides an example of the kind of trade-offs he studies:

> One region we investigated was in Tanzania, a place characterized both by great biodiversity and significant gold deposits. Placer mining for the gold is polluting waterways and degrading biodiversity. On the other hand, it is improving the lives of local people; they have more money, so they're building better houses, eating more food and putting their kids through school. The choices here are obvious: if we want to preserve biodiversity, we're going to have to pay for it; we can't legitimately ask the local communities to embrace poverty simply so the developed world can feel good that an area rich in wildlife was "saved."

Some projects may thus require compromise—and a subsequent contraction of conservation goals—to achieve anything at all. At the same time, McShane notes, conservationists must determine what positions are not negotiable. It could be the Arctic National Wildlife Refuge; it could be the Serengeti; it could be the great whales. One thing is certain, however: difficult choices will be embedded in each decision. There is not, in the very real world of conservation, any true win-win situation.

Norton-Griffiths shares this perspective and says Kenyan wildlife policy embraces the most egregious example of the win-win canard: the ban on consumptive wildlife use. He is deeply resentful of the failure of the 2008 version of the Draft Wildlife Bill that would have allowed some hunting and cropping of game on private land, viewing the aborted legislation as a first baby step to a rational policy that would have restored incentives for preserving wildlife among tribal communities and ranches. By defeating the bill through intensive lobbying of government officials and the hiring of locals to "demonstrate" against consumptive use, Norton-Griffiths says, IFAW and its allies are promoting the failed notion that forbidding the killing of individual animals can save large populations of wildlife. It's as though the entire nation has constructed a Potemkin village of frolicking animals and happy tribal members to show the world, while behind the façade, the extirpation of the nation's megafauna accelerates.

"When we had this wildlife policy review, there were twelve public meetings across Kenya," Norton-Griffiths recalls. "From the beginning, IFAW did its utmost to sabotage the process. They bused in demonstrators to disrupt the meetings; at a national seminar convened to comment on the draft bill, one [IFAW supporter] screamed for twenty minutes. Didn't really say anything—just—screamed. And I remember a meeting in March 2007 at Kitengela. IFAW and the Kenyan Land Alliance [an ad hoc land reform group sponsored by the international organization Action Aid] had representatives there who said they would arm people to shoot hunters in the field if hunting was introduced. How can you develop a rational wildlife policy in that kind of atmosphere?"

To save Kenya's wildlife, Norton-Griffiths says, the people living on the land have to be given access to the game. If a given community wants to emphasize ecotourism on their land and construct lodges so visitors can take photographs of the animals, that's fine. But if another community wants to eat some animals, crop others for the purveyance of their meat, hides, and horns, and sell trophy hunting permits for others, that must also be countenanced.

Norton-Griffiths's utilitarian approach to wildlife conservation extends to areas even many of his allies fear to tread—most notably, game ranching to provide products now banned by CITES. He argues that the ban on ivory and rhino horn has had only measured success at best and notes that the trade seems to be picking up again. Rather than fight a losing battle, he suggests the market should be used to control the trade, since the market for tusks and horn will always exist, and poor people will always find a way accommodate it from wild venues if there are no alternative sources.

Norton-Griffiths expresses his views on this issue most succinctly on his Web site in a polemic titled "The Kiss of Death—or Does Conservation Work?" In his lead paragraph, he questions the basic strategy of modern conservation:

> We—the public, that is—have been bombarded over the years with appeals from international conservation organizations to save this and fight for that and preserve the absolutely last whatever, each appeal sketching in graphic detail the plight of the remaining few and the deep loss we will all feel and suffer should they vanish. On the other hand, articles in newspapers and magazines and programs on TV and radio tell a different story. Whether it's rain forests, tigers or crested newts, there seem to be fewer and fewer and less and less of everything. God forbid—but are these perhaps connected? If there really *are* fewer tigers now than there were before, is it because we have not given enough in the past? Or would there be even fewer now if we hadn't given what we did give? Or are *they*—and the ICOs and their ilk—not doing the right things? In other words, is conservation working? And how can *we* tell anyway? Or should *we* just go on giving, secure in the knowledge that surely *they* know what's best to do with *our* money?

Norton-Griffiths is particularly concerned with the rare charismatic species that have attracted the most attention—elephants, rhinos, tigers, and the like. For the purpose of illustration, he collectively dubs them "tigophants": "We start, say, with a continent full of tigophants which sport magnificent tusks; but there is a demand for tigophant-based medicines and ornaments so traders purchase tigophant tusks from hunters for onward sale. This reduces the numbers of tigophants so conservation authorities spend more effort in preserving them and in chasing poachers." Meanwhile, he writes, booming populations and rising incomes among people who covet tigophant products spur demand, so prices for the products climb while tigophant numbers spiral downward. All the indicators point to extinction.

The instinct of international conservation groups has been to fight the demand for wildlife products, from forbidding legitimate trade in them to vigorous prosecution of people who kill the animals. But all attempts at outlawing "tigophant" products have merely made the trade illicit—and ultimately, more lucrative. With a few temporary exceptions, markets have remained robust.

And anti-poaching policies largely have failed, claims Norton-Griffiths, because they did nothing to address the supply of the animals that yield the products so much in demand; they merely punished the people who worked to meet that demand. Moreover, it is the most desperate elements of society that must bear the onus of this approach; shoot-to-kill was once the rule in Kenyan reserves for scouts and rangers confronting poachers. "To me, it is quite inexplicable how we can condone the slaughter of destitute peasants in the name of conservation," Norton-Griffiths writes. "Indeed, there is a veritable Pandora's Box of human rights issues to which conservation organizations must one day answer." (Shoot-to-kill is, so to speak, still alive and well. In her recent book, *Nature Crime: How We're Getting Conservation Wrong*, Rosaleen Duffy, a professor of international politics at Manchester University, notes the practice remains de facto policy in Malawi and the Democratic Republic of the Congo for guards protecting endangered wildlife.) Furthermore, only a small percentage of poachers are ever caught or killed. Confiscation of poached tusks, horn, and hides simply raises product prices, requires that more animals must be killed to satisfy demand, and ultimately stimulates greater poaching pressure.

The alternative? Create an equilibrium in which products, demand, and prices are all stable. The only practical way to do this, says Norton-Griffiths, is to increase the number of tigophant products. The very failure of conservationists to scotch the tigophant trade indicates this can't be done through current policies. But by employing other methods, the supply of tigophant products can be increased, driving prices down—and ultimately, eliminating the incentives for poaching charismatic megafauna. Norton-Griffiths suggests that expanding the supply of wildlife products could be accomplished several ways—releasing stocks into the wild, selectively culling, selectively breeding animals for the market, or elephant, rhino, and tiger "farms."

Norton-Griffiths acknowledges that a legal trade in wildlife products could be used as a front for marketing illicit tusks and horns obtained from poached animals or even that the market could place a higher value on "wild" products over "farmed" ones. But, he posits, does Rolex stop making watches simply because its models are counterfeited widely? And can't the market provide tiger penises or rhino horn from "free-ranged" animals as it does now with chicken eggs? Left to follow their entrepreneurial instincts, he says, wildlife farmers will provide what the market demands, and that would ultimately benefit species depleted by commercial trade:

> Clearly, rhino farms which provide horn to the dagger and medicine markets at a price that undercuts the naturally harvested product would have many benefits: parks would be full of rhinos. So extend the idea to tigers (which breed in captivity like rabbits—or vice versa): if there is an annual demand for a thousand dried tiger penises and five thousand kilograms of bones, then for goodness sake farm them as we farm cows, sheep, and pigs for their bits and pieces—else sure as eggs is eggs (battery or free range) the tiger and the rhino will soon be extinct.

Indeed, this approach already is employed for some wild species and has proved successful. Deer products are as esteemed in traditional Asian medicine as body parts from tigers and rhino, and the trade is satisfied almost wholly from farmed sources. Wild deer are numerous—in places, excessively common. And the prices for deer horn in velvet and other cervine products have remained stable for years or have even dropped.

So the international conservation organizations—l'ancien régime—have it all wrong, Norton-Griffiths says. They ask sympathizers for more and more money to protect rare species of megafauna, but their policies are actually driving increased poaching. "It would be far better," he says over sandwiches during our lunch in Langata, "to raise rural incomes to the point that poaching is no longer a pragmatic way to earn a living. Unlike current conservation policies, it would actually be effective, and it would also alleviate a great deal of human misery. But . . . " Here he sighs or, more accurately, issues a subdued snort of anger and frustration and sets his sandwich down on his plate. "That's not really the issue, is it? Effective conservation, I mean. In Kenya, it's about a lunatic doctrine—extreme animal rights—that has been imposed on the nation by foreign NGOs throwing a great deal of money around. And the mainline environmental groups are unwilling to do anything to counter [that doctrine]—you don't hear a peep from them. It's both tragic and absurd."

CHAPTER 7

Reality Check

I am in southern Laikipia in a small Nissan sedan of venerable age, careening down a road that can best be described as a series of gigantic potholes and rock outcroppings conjoined by a roughly graded track. My driver, Matthew, is an impeccably dressed, loquacious, and deeply intelligent young man who provides a running and nuanced commentary on the nutritional requirements of cattle, the economics of charcoal plantations, his girlfriend's varying and puzzling moods, differing tribal mores, and, most especially, birds. (He is an avid birder, and we stop periodically so he can observe one specimen or another with the pair of binoculars he carries on his front seat.)

Our destination is the home of Chris Thouless, a Kenyan economist who lives on a ranch about twenty miles from Nanyuki. There are no signposts; side roads, footpaths, and goat trails veer from the main route regularly. My driver is unsure about the location of the ranch, and the complicated instructions I received earlier from Thouless don't seem to help much. But Matthew drives unerringly to the property, though we sometimes bottom out on rocks and plow through thorn trees that almost obscure the road. There are occasional small habitations along the way, and we pass several pastoralists tending their herds of scrawny cattle and goats among the last wisps of forage; drought has beset northern Kenya for two years by this point, and livestock and herders alike are painfully thin. At one point, we see people gathering at a small corral, where two trucks are offloading large sacks of grain.

"Famine relief," says Matthew. "People are very, very hungry in Laikipia." We drive past an extremely thin man dressed only in ragged shorts and a flip-flop on one foot, pedaling a battered bicycle. As he steers the bike, he balances a bag of grain on his head with one hand.

"That's quite encouraging," Matthew says. "People are actually getting the corn, you see. Usually, it's diverted by corrupt officials, who sell it and pocket the proceeds." He essays a wry smile, in this part of the world a standard response to an embarrassing or lamentable situation: "I am afraid this is business as usual in Kenya."

Farther down the road, we pass a *manyatta* composed of several mud-and-wattle huts surrounding a makeshift *boma*. Several women and children—Laikipia Maasai—squat in the meager shade provided by a copse of scraggly trees. The kids leap up as we approach and sprint alongside the car briefly, extending their arms and clasping and unclasping their hands for alms. When we don't slow down, they pick up rocks and fling them at us, only narrowing missing the rear fender. Looking in the rearview mirror, Matthew clucks his tongue and shakes his head. "Such ill-behaved children," he says. "My own mother would have whipped me severely for doing something like that, I assure you. And my father?" He shakes his head again and whistles in a low tone. "Oh, he would've beaten me—*beaten* me—within an inch of my life." He laughs in a soft and gentle fashion, as though the memory is pleasant.

About two miles farther on, we veer down a track hardly wider than a game trail. Vistas of rolling bush open up briefly before disappearing behind heavy growths of acacia. The road doglegs sharply and suddenly stops at an isolated edifice that is somewhat ramshackle but manorial in dimensions: not unusual for Laikipia, where a few white and South Asian ranchers pursue lives of seigniorial scope. While many are cash strapped, they typically own thousands of acres of magnificent land, much of it teeming with wildlife, and abide in fine old homes lovingly built from native stone and wood. Matthew parks the car in some shade and opens a book, and I walk up to the front door and knock. A fierce barking commences from within, and when the door opens two small terriers tear madly about my ankles, issuing staccato yelps and grinning like runt baboons. Thouless is close behind, halfheartedly berating the dogs. He is tall, unobtrusively fit, and handsome in the kind of patrician fashion you'd associate with the protagonists of Evelyn Waugh novels. We repair to a back veranda to take our tea. Just beyond the backyard of the house, the bush begins. Two hundred yards away is a small reservoir; from the trampled appearance of the muddy banks, it looks heavily frequented by wildlife.

"Oh, there's usually something worth seeing here," says Thouless, though now—on a hot, airless afternoon—there is nothing moving but a go-away-bird perched disconsolately on an acacia limb. "An elephant has been hanging around, and I saw a couple of giraffes this morning. There are quite a few impala and gazelles about."

Indeed, Laikipia is the one place in Kenya, except for a few of the parks and reserves, where the wildlife is more or less holding its own. Well, less, actually—here as elsewhere, there have been declines. But drive around this vast upland plateau, and you'll still see a great deal of game: elephants, impalas, Grant's and Thomson's gazelles, hartebeests, waterbuck, oryx, and in places, large numbers of Cape buffalo. At night, it's not unusual to surprise leopards and hyenas, even the occasional lion or cheetah, in the headlights. The relative abundance of the game is due to one thing, says Thouless: it is valued by the owners. Most of the landholders maintain guest accommodations on their properties and actively court the international ecotourism trade. Laikipia has become known as a welcome alternative to the cookie-cutter mass-marketed tourism of the Mara and Tsavo, where the minivans converge on a single lion or elephant like vultures and jackals on a zebra carcass. Here, visitors can stay in small wilderness lodges or camps, savoring the utter isolation; go on guided horseback tours or treks to find their game; get a sense of the old Kenya, the rhythms and moods of its people and animals.

And yet, it's not enough—not enough for the wildlife *or* the ranchers. "Laikipia is suitable for conservation initiatives precisely because it's a marginal area," observes Thouless. "Along Mount Kenya and the Aberdares, the fringes of the Mara—areas with better soil and more rainfall—conservation isn't really an option. Those areas are basically too productive; given population growth and economic factors, they *must* be used for intensive agriculture of one sort or another."

But Laikipia is dry, and its soils are thin. Raising cattle is the only practical agricultural pursuit, and even that is chancy. Stocking levels necessarily must be low, and during drought years utter catastrophe is always a real possibility. You usually don't have to wander far in the Laikipia bush to discover a desiccated cow carcass or two. In such an area, maintaining wildlife as a means of income becomes a practical option. Hectare for hectare, you won't make as much as growing coffee on Mount Kenya or wheat along the Mara, but you'll make *some* money, as long as you can actually *use* the wildlife.

And that's the catch, says Thouless. True, tourists do come to Laikipia. But compared to the Mara and Tsavo, they are relatively few—not enough, certainly, to sustain the ranches through their commerce alone. Along with renting their lodges, virtually all of the ranchers participating in ecotourism have ambitious livestock programs. Between the two enterprises, most ranchers are able to eke out livings. And a few with particularly large spreads thrive in a modest kind of way—during years when there's adequate rainfall, in any event.

What makes Laikipia unique is that the ranchers and tribal group ranches participating in conservation programs are doing so voluntarily. Neither government fiat nor financial incentives exist to compel them to conserve. To a significant degree, their participation runs counter to their own financial interests. If these private conservation programs are to continue in Laikipia, Thouless says, more incentives are needed: specifically, ranchers and tribal members must be given greater control over the game on their land. They must be able to sell trophy permits to wealthy hunters, crop plains game for meat and hides, cull elephants for meat, and even, perhaps, dispose of the ivory through a licit market. Though the conservation ethic remains strong in Laikipia, not everyone there is a believer, and as the population grows and demand for food and financial return on investment grows with it, the sentiment for preserving wildlife in the region will slacken.

Given this perspective, Thouless is utterly disenchanted with Kenya's anti-hunting laws and recent attempts by animal rights groups to tighten them even more—an impulse he describes as the greatest threat facing the nation's game. In discussing the Draft Wildlife Bill, supported by the International Fund for Animal Welfare, he addresses a permutation of it that will further restrict the consumptive use of wildlife: "It's not even the sections that continue the ban on big game hunting that are the most objectionable," he says. "[Under various drafts], the new bill would make it illegal to pick up a feather or porcupine quill; they'd be considered illegal trophies. And you certainly couldn't hunt birds, which currently is still legal in Kenya. This would be particularly tragic for many of the [tribal] group ranches in northern Kenya, because sport bird hunting brings in considerable revenues for them. For some, it constitutes most of their annual cash income. It could change their lives—basically, their odds for survival—from the merely difficult to the impossible."

More generally, says Thouless, Kenya's game laws are a massive disincentive for preserving wildlife. This is especially significant in political and civic terms, because Kenya is in a unique position when compared to its neighbors, most specifically Tanzania, which has a socialist tradition. "One thing noteworthy about Kenya is that it is a fairly libertarian state," he observes. "The rights of the individual are enshrined. Private property is revered as a concept, and landowners are given a generally free hand in regard to managing their holdings. So to succeed, any conservation initiative must provide incentives and voluntary participation. If IFAW and other groups succeed, anyone with wildlife on their land will have to file detailed and expensive management plans with the Kenya Wildlife Service. That won't preserve wildlife, of course; those plans will do nothing to stop agency corruption or rampant poaching, which will continue. But it will eliminate any reason for people to maintain wildlife on their land."

That's especially so for tribal holdings, Thouless says. He notes that many of the wealthier ranchers—ex-colonials and foreigners—will toe the line, pay for the management plans, and shell out the necessary baksheesh to venal officials; in short, they'll do whatever it takes to stay on the lovely landscapes of Laikipia, surrounded by big sky and ample game. "The people who won't make it are the pastoralists on the group ranches," he says. "The barriers in the legislation that has been proposed are utterly disempowering to local communities. They don't have the money or the political connections to jump through all the hoops; they'll be completely at the mercy of the NGOs and commercial interests. They'll lose whatever autonomy they now have."

Nanyuki is the jumping-off point for the Laikipia hinterlands. Everyone for scores of miles around comes here to buy supplies, and the town always presents an absorbing tableau of Kenya's ethnic diversity: Samburu and Maasai pastoralists bring their goats to sell. Somalis, tall, haughty, and self-contained, stride restlessly among the shops and warehouses, seldom deigning to speak to anyone other than a family or clan member. White ranchers, sweating and red-faced, pull themselves out of their dusty Land Rovers to stand curbside, smoking cigarettes and catching up on gossip. Hindu store owners stand impassively behind their counters, punctilious in their address but ever alert to the security of their goods. Always, there is mutual watchfulness: tribal and ethnic tensions are a fact of life in Kenya, and simple poverty drives crime of its own accord. Nanyuki is a fascinating place, but the milk of human kindness does not flow freely here.

Indeed, on a recent visit to Nanyuki, I found the town was in an uproar over the possible invasion of Mungiki gangs from Nyeri, a

Kikuyu stronghold to the south. The Mungiki are an officially pro-scribed Kikuyu fraternity notorious for extortion, particularly in con-nection with Nairobi's *matatus,* the ubiquitous minivans that are the city's main means of public transport. They pattern themselves after the Mau-Mau; in fact, they're widely considered a neo-Mau-Mau cult, and salacious stories on Mungiki "oathing ceremonies" entailing human sacrifice regularly appear in the country's press.

"Oh, they better not come here," said the Hindu proprietress of one of Nanyuki's larger general stores. Behind the counter, she drummed her fingers, lavishly decorated with gold rings. "I've already talked with the chief-of-police, and he told me, 'If they show up, the officers will be ready for them. They'll be in for a surprise.'"

Two days later, I drove into town and encountered a strange sight: a line of young men, each with one hand on the shoulder of the fellow in front, shuffling down the street. Guarding them were big, grim-faced cops smacking truncheons against their thighs. Passersby stopped to watch the coffle, a few hooting derisively.

"Who are they?" I asked a tall, elderly Somali wearing a tattered sport coat and carrying a *rungu* (fighting stick) in his hand.

"Mungiki," he said. "They came from Nyeri, and the police picked them up at a roadblock."

"Where are they taking them?"

The old man gestured vaguely to the north—to the endless, rolling bush outside town that stretched all the way into Ethiopia and Somalia.

"Out there," he said. "I don't think they'll be coming back." In most other nations, that statement would be melodramatic. In Kenya, with its long history of extrajudicial killings by police, it merely reflects con-ventional wisdom.

But if a rough frontier justice prevails in Nanyuki, the town is also the civil and commercial center for Laikipia. It is where business is done, bills are paid, and people come to enjoy a few amenities—fore-most among them, a good meal in a decent restaurant. Probably the best place to eat in town isn't exactly *in* town but just past the city limits, at the Nanyuki Airport. This is a modest facility, supporting only one short airstrip, but it is heavily used: by local airlines flying Twin Otters from Nairobi, ranchers flying in their small Pipers from the Laikipia inte-rior, and British Army troops, who employ helicopters in the training maneuvers that are regularly conducted throughout northern Kenya. The airport also supports a small office complex and a locally renowned open-air café. Affording a wide vista of the countryside, the café is an exceedingly pleasant place to pass time. A pergola surrounds the dining area, and superb starlings and wagtails strut and fight on an adjacent lawn. The waitresses chafe and charm the clientele and serve delicious pasta al pesto made from basil grown on the premises and steaks carved from steers raised in the nearby bush.

A few steps from the café are the offices of the Laikipia Wildlife Forum, an organization devoted to promoting regional game conservation through private partnerships. The director, Anthony King, is a fair, slim man with wide-set eyes and a mildly harried expression. Like most people in Laikipia, King favors regulations that give landowners wide latitude over the wildlife on their land, as long as basic conservation tenets are followed.

At the airport café, King and I sit over espressos made from locally grown coffee while he explains what he considers Kenya's greatest paradox: "Kenya's international brand is wildlife, but wildlife is not really important in the national psyche," he observes. "With the exception of Laikipia, tourism here exploits wildlife—in a way, 'mines' it—and puts nothing back." From that perspective, King says, actions by IFAW and allied groups can only be seen as unproductive: they do nothing to devise and implement workable programs that will provide local people with incentives for preserving habitat and wild animals. "Instead, they concentrate on lobbying the government to stop any and all policies that might include some consumptive use of wildlife. They act as though an utterly unenforceable ban will stop the poaching, snaring, poisoning, overgrazing, and deforestation. What really seems to tick them off isn't the destruction of Kenya's greatest legacy; it's that somebody might get some pleasure from taking an animal either for meat or a trophy."

In any developed country, continues King, intensive lobbying by NGOs like IFAW wouldn't be a problem; indeed, it could even be salutary, an essential part of the political process. In the United States or Britain, where IFAW is also active, its work is balanced by organizations with opposite points of view. But in Kenya, the government is dysfunctional to a point incomprehensible to most western Europeans and North Americans; in the simplest terms, King says, government policies are determined not so much by government representatives as by the NGOs that influence government representatives. And though it is small potatoes in Washington or London, IFAW is very big in Nairobi.

"Compared to us or any of our allies, they're extremely well-funded," King says. "You have to realize that NGOs are one of the very few means for upward mobility in Africa. The fact that they ossify into the worst kind of bureaucracies once they're established here doesn't matter; bureaucracies are very attractive to Kenyan professionals. By local standards, they provide staff jobs that are extremely well paid. Association with an NGO guarantees status. Ultimately, they have money to spread around, and in Africa even more than elsewhere, successful politics are about wealth and visibility."

Because it is well funded and committed to a presence in Kenya, IFAW has been able to dictate wildlife policy in the country: it is no coincidence that the first things you see on deplaning at Jomo Kenyatta International Airport are IFAW anti-hunting posters of big-eyed lions framed by the cross-hairs of a telescopic rifle sight.

"But once again, simply because they control legislation doesn't mean they control what happens on the ground," King says. "They get the laws they want, they celebrate their victories, press releases are sent out, everyone feels they're fighting the good fight for African wildlife, donations pour in from the U.S. and Europe. Meanwhile, the poaching and snaring continue unabated." King is thus largely disenchanted with NGOs, particularly when it comes to conservation issues. "To accomplish anything in Africa, particularly Kenya, the programs can't come from the top down," he says. "Anything associated with foreign NGOs entails complex and thoroughly compromised bureaucracies. Locals are essentially hired to implement programs devised in London or Washington, programs for which they have no personal investment beyond the next paycheck. It doesn't matter to them if the programs work or not, so invariably the programs *don't* work."

Conservation can succeed in Kenya, insists King, but the efforts must be rooted in local communities; ideally, they will originate there, and any NGO involvement should be restricted to an advisory or a support capacity. Once the NGOs aggressively intrude, once they start dictating policy and hiring staff—once they show up in their chrome-spangled 4WDs, to paraphrase Mike Norton-Griffiths—the program is doomed.

King cites an example: in recent years, elephants and other wildlife came down from the forests of Mount Kenya to raid croplands near the Nanyuki Airport. Officials and NGO representatives dithered about a solution. "Then a local guy named Jackson Mbuthia started putting up a two-strand fence," King says. "Fencing is increasingly used in East Africa as a protective measure for both wildlife and property. At first, he did it all on his own back, raised his own money. And people saw what he was doing and started helping him, contributing time and money and materials. They started building better fencing. Eventually, about thirty thousand hectares was securely fenced, and it has been a great success. Both poaching and crop depredation in the area have declined significantly."

Mbuthia's success—accomplished largely with an idea, personal charisma, sweat equity, and grassroots support—stands in marked contrast to the gaudy and inefficient campaigns of the NGOs, says King. The deeply ironic aspect, he says, is that Kenya continues to be cited by IFAW and other animal rights groups as their greatest success. "And for a fact, Kenya *is* a success—for IFAW. The posters [at Jomo Kenyatta International Airport] say it all. The country is a money machine for IFAW. Animal rights are a huge and flourishing business here. But for the country itself, the failure is complete, and I'm not just talking about the 70 percent decline in wildlife. Ten million people are now starving in Kenya. How is that possible here? Yes, more than 70 percent of the land is arid, the kind of land that's dismissed as 'unproductive.' But it could be teeming with wildlife, and those animals could be utilized as a source of food and money. More to the point, unless you allow people to use the animals, the game will never return."

King's dispute with IFAW seems almost visceral, transcending mere political differences. This is due largely to his sense that they are winning and that one of Kenya's great cultural cornerstones—pastoralism—is at stake. The farming tribes, most specifically the Kikuyu, have constituted Kenya's core polity and held most of the power since the colonial period. But it is the herding tribes who define the regional ethos—the Maasai, Samburu, Turkana, and Pokot, the people who have been moving in seasonal rounds across the region's vast arid scrublands with their cows and goats for millennia. Not only is pastoralism the defining lifestyle of East Africa; it is also the only lifestyle that hints at wildlife sustainability. Game can exist and even thrive in a pastoral culture, as long as human and livestock populations do not exceed the resource limitations imposed by the land. By its very nature, pastoralism implies a minimal human population: arid rangelands can support only a small number of cows. An agrarian society, on the other hand, imposes demands that are absolutely inimical to wildlife: cross-fencing, irrigation, an advanced infrastructure to produce and distribute materials and transport goods to market, and, most pointedly, the destruction of natural habitat, an essential concomitant in the process of transforming rangeland into intensively cultivated cropland.

By demanding tougher hunting strictures, King argues, IFAW is doing nothing to protect Kenya's wildlife. Indeed, such regulations only hasten the decline of the game. Even more to the point, the policy assures the fragmentation of pastoral culture—a human tragedy that is an analogue to the disappearance of the wildlife. "IFAW has gotten a lot of publicity for their posters showing animals lined up in the crosshairs," King observes. "As a media campaign, it has been very effective. But I think we could demonstrate the true situation better if we put out similar posters opposing them—posters that have a profile of a pastoral tribesman in the crosshairs. That's essentially what they're advocating, you see. Preventing East Africans from rationally utilizing the wildlife resources on their land is condemning both a culture and wildlife to extinction."

The road north of Nanyuki cuts across the escarpments, gorges, and swales of the Laikipia Plateau, toward Lake Turkana and the Ethiopian border. About one-and-one-half hours outside town, the road dips down to a rickety bridge. On a recent trip with Steven Ekwanga, Laurence Frank's research assistant, this bridge was guarded by members of the British Army, in full combat kit. Laikipia is a favored training ground for British troops, and the arrangement the British military has struck with the Kenyan government seems to suit everyone: The troops get extended training in a harsh quasi-desert environment—conditions similar to those in Iraq or Afghanistan; the Kenyan exchequer and local ranchers derive tidy returns in a solid foreign currency; and Laikipia residents feel somewhat more secure against marauding *shifta* (nomadic bandits), though the troops technically have no arrest powers and are banned from engaging in active fighting with the locals.

On this occasion, our Land Rover is stopped by a young corporal, who looks thoroughly enervated from fatigue and the heat. He essays a few questions, subjects our vehicle to a cursory inspection, and warns us to drive slowly over the bridge, which is in poor repair. When we tell him we're going to the Mpala Research Centre, a wan smile lights his face. "We're bivouacked not far from the headquarters," he says. "Tell the ladies hello for us." Mpala, a forty-eight-thousand-acre ranch devoted to research in wildlife, ecological dynamics, and sustainable agriculture, always supports a substantial cadre of visiting graduate students and scientists; mutual interest between the young soldiers and academics in their age cohort is reflexive.

Shortly after we drive past Mpala's gate, we spot a small herd of impalas grazing under some fever trees. Nearby, a young boy idly drives a few cattle along with lackadaisical fillips from his herding stick. A few hundred yards farther, we come across a group of graduate students, earnestly examining specimens of one kind or another with hand lenses. The road dips down into a gorge, climbs out again, skirts a hill for about a mile, and then takes a hairpin turn, debouching on a small flat. It is here we almost run into a magnificent bull elephant, which is just in the process of crossing the road. It flares its ears, raises its trunk, and emits a sound that is nothing like the ebullient trumpeting one hears in television nature documentaries. This elephant roars—literally roars, like a maddened bear—and then it charges.

Ekwanga, however, simply downshifts, accelerates, and swerves around the beast, a small smile cracking the mask of imperturbability that is his usual expression. I turn around and look through the rear window. The bull briefly pounds after us, its bulk almost obscured by dust, its enraged bellowing undiminished. I confess to Ekwanga that the encounter has left me a little shaken, and his smile broadens. "Elephants in Laikipia have very short tempers," he says. "In some parks where they haven't been bothered, you can get quite close to them. But in Laikipia, they are always being chased by farmers or ranchers who want them off their land. People throw flash-bangs at them; sometimes they shoot at them. That makes them irritable."

So irritable, in fact, that human casualties from elephant encounters are fairly common in Laikipia. Ekwanga relates a couple of recent examples: A tourist staying at a lodge on a Samburu group ranch decides to take a jog, inserts the earbuds from her iPod, and trots off. She doesn't hear the elephant that has decided to charge her and is stomped almost to death. Also: A Samburu man returning to his home after a late-night party meets an elephant in the dark. He doesn't survive the encounter, and his flattened corpse is discovered in the road the following morning. It occurs to me that these incidents underscore one of Mpala's primary fields of inquiry—wildlife-human conflicts in a working landscape.

Margaret Kinnaird, the executive director of Mpala, seems amused by my breathless recitation of my pachyderm encounter, gives me a drink, and confirms that the incident illustrates one of the core problems facing Mpala: How do you manage land in a profitable fashion while simultaneously pursuing conservation goals? In other words, how do you have both cows and elephants? More to the point—can you have both? Certainly, Kinnaird allows, that's the goal for most landowners and managers in Laikipia. Mpala gets support from a variety of organizations, including the Smithsonian Institution, but it still must pay a significant portion of its own way. That means cattle—for both Mpala and every other ranch on the plateau.

"The problem is that even in good years, even when there's enough forage to get the cattle in good shape, it's pretty tough to make a decent profit on our beef," Kinnaird says. "Not that there's any issue with the product; it's all lean, organic meat, and extremely flavorful." The problem is disease: a variety of maladies, including hoof-and-mouth disease, are endemic in Kenya's cattle herds. And while it is a rarity for tainted meat to reach the marketplace, a more or less permanent quarantine exists in regard to beef exports. "We're restricted to domestic markets," Kinnaird says, "and domestic beef prices are always considerably lower than export prices. Until we can sell abroad, profitable cattle ranching will be difficult for us."

A partial solution has been the leasing of Mpala's lands to the British military for combat maneuvers, but Kinnaird doesn't see that as a long-term solution. "Policies change, military programs lose their funding, and that's that. We need solutions that are long-term and reliable—sustainable, in a word."

For Mpala, that means wildlife utilization. The center has direct experience in this field, Kinnaird notes. About fifteen years ago, the wildlife strictures were somewhat looser than they are today, and cropping— the regulated take of specific numbers of animals of certain species— was allowed. Burchell's zebras were the primary cropping candidate in Laikipia for several reasons: they are fecund, their meat and hides have found a ready market, and they compete with cattle for forage.

"We were instrumental in establishing off-take quotas for zebra, and we showed that it could be done profitably with no deleterious impact on their base populations," says Kinnaird. "It was an extremely successful program, and for many ranchers, it made the difference between a profitable and a nonprofitable year." Now, of course, all is different. No one can touch the zebras—except poachers. The cessation of the cropping program has resulted in a revenue loss that neither cattle nor ecotourism can remedy, Kinnaird observes.

"Tourism, especially, can only take us so far," she says. "And there are real liabilities implicit in the tourist trade." She recalls the recent incident on the nearby Samburu group ranch that resulted in the elephant-stomped jogger. "That woman sued the landowners and won a settlement that's huge by local standards," Kinnaird says. "It's probably going to bankrupt that ranch. We're vulnerable as well. We could be sued here at Mpala if anything happens to any of our visitors. That elephant that charged you? Happens all the time in Laikipia. We have up to six hundred visiting scholars and students a year at Mpala. Now, if we have to increase our insurance, we can do it; it'll be pricey, but we can do it. But the group ranches? There's no way they can afford it. So the idea that you can replace a profitable cropping program with eco-tourism is absolutely false. A zebra quota is reliable; year in and year out, you'll derive at least some food and currency. But tourists are fickle; if they feel there's too much unrest in the country, they won't show up. Or if they do, they can sue you. They can destroy any chance you have of making a living."

CHAPTER 8

The Kenya Model

Two types of enterprises usually boast well-appointed offices in Nairobi: banks and large NGOs. The International Fund for Animal Welfare is no exception to this general rule, maintaining an impressive suite of offices in an elegant, modern, gated, and heavily guarded building on Lenana Road. The address demonstrates IFAW's long-term commitment to its mission in Kenya and to its continuing presence as a political and lobbying force in the country. The organization is not going anywhere, unless it's to other countries on the continent. As the only East African nation that maintains a total ban on all big game hunting, Kenya is ground zero in the global animal rights war, and IFAW has a dug-in position on the high ground, well positioned both to withstand assaults and to initiate effective offensives.

Founded in Canada in 1969 by Brian Davies to oppose the hunting of harp seal pups on the Canadian icepack, IFAW is today one of the world's largest and most influential animal rights groups, with offices in sixteen countries. There is an activist, au courant quality to IFAW that appeals to younger people, a kind of edginess that makes older main-line conservation groups like the Audubon Society and the Sierra Club seem positively stodgy. Endorsements by such celebrities as Leonardo di Caprio and Pierce Brosnan contribute to IFAW's luster.

Even IFAW's foes acknowledge that the organization expresses the present zeitgeist more precisely than old school conservationists. The merging of animal rights with general environmentalism is a fact, and for IFAW supporters, it's also a moral imperative buttressed by science. They point out that the concept of "awareness" as a uniquely human quality is a canard. Increasingly, we are learning that animals are capable of both ratiocination and emotional subtlety: that many species think and feel deeply, that they play, that they love. And not just bonobos and chimps. The other great apes, elephants, cetaceans, wolves, and hyenas, not to mention African gray parrots and other psittacines—ethologists are finding that all these species express a deep and complicated suite of cognitive and emotional responses.

In other words, they are intelligent and sentient, not in precisely the same way humans are, perhaps, but intelligent and sentient nonetheless. Indeed, recent research indicates some animals share certain emotive processes with human beings. Frans de Waal, a renowned ethologist, includes empathy among these qualities. In his recent book, *The Age of Empathy: Nature's Lessons for a Kinder Society*, de Waal argues that basic empathic impulses are shared by all mammals, as evidenced by common concern over the welfare of vulnerable young. And in some species, says de Waal—most notably monkeys, apes, dolphins, elephants, and big-brained birds—empathy is expressed as "targeted helping," a manifestation that mirrors human responses. There are many examples, de Waal and his colleagues note: an elephant in Thailand attempting to push a dying companion into a standing position, and a chimpanzee, obviously grieving over a deceased offspring, subjected to particularly solicitous grooming by her companions. Given these findings, IFAW members ask, can we legitimately kill animals for sport or crop them for their flesh, hides, tusks, and horns? Their response, of course, is no.

IFAW has demonstrated it is more than willing to put a lot of money where its organizational mouth is. It has donated patrol vehicles to the Kenya Wildlife Service, contributed to the David Sheldrick Wildlife Trust to rehabilitate orphaned elephant and black rhino juveniles for later release into Tsavo East National Park, spent $70,000 to rehabilitate a primary school near Tsavo, built housing and drilled wells for park rangers in Uganda, and improved wildlife water sources in the Mkomazi Game Reserve in Tanzania. IFAW also contributed $1.25 million—an immense bequest in cash-strapped Kenya—for conservation efforts in Meru National Park, including the reintroduction of about thirteen hundred animals, among them elephants, black rhinos, white rhinos, leopards, reticulated giraffes, and Grevy's zebras. It is expanding its operations to West Africa, recently establishing programs to protect elephant habitat in Chad, Mali, and Cameroon, emphasizing a "holistic" approach to pachyderm management by creating conjoined megaparks that can accommodate migrating populations. IFAW also is funding elephant DNA testing efforts to track the illicit ivory trade. A program the group supported determined that a 6.5 ton load of ivory seized in Singapore in 2002 came from elephants in Zambia.

Most pertinently, it continues its lobbying in Kenya to maintain the hunting ban. By all accounts, its greatest victory in recent years was the 2007 decision by the Ministry of Tourism to support legislation drafted by an IFAW consultant that not only left Kenya's big game hunting ban in place but also added clauses that could effectively prohibit fishing, bird hunting, and much tourism; according to some interpretations, it could even prohibit the use of antibiotics, given that pathogens can be considered a form of wildlife.

IFAW has long had rocky relations with both mainline conservation groups and many communities of indigenous people. In the mid-1990s, a coalition of Inuit tribes lobbied vigorously against the inclusion of IFAW in the International Union for the Conservation of Nature, perhaps the world's most influential environmental organization and the largest extant NGO. In a statement to the IUCN, the Inuit Tapirisat of Canada and the Inuit Circumpolar Conference declared: "Animal welfare and conservation are manifestly different concepts that need to be kept apart because in some cases, conflicts between animal welfare concerns and ecological concerns might occur. . . . There is substantial evidence to support the view that IFAW policy and campaigns are heavily influenced by animal rights philosophy, although the organization has not clearly outlined the principles and philosophy behind its activities."

The Inuit continued, explaining that IFAW's successful campaign to obtain a European Union ban on young harp seal pelts has been economically devastating to Arctic natives, noting that the annual $6 million subsidy (provided by the Greenland government to traditional hunting communities) constituted 90 percent of the hunters' (already low) annual income. Further, they stated, the furor over the hunt has made sealskins almost worthless: between 1983 and 1986, the sealskins sold in the Canadian Northwest Territories generated Can$889,996; three years later, the revenue was less than a tenth of this amount. Hunting communities that were once self-sufficient have now been reduced to accepting handouts; the basis of their economy has been destroyed. Nor has the impact been one of mere dollars and cents, the Inuit continued:

The majority of Inuit suicides in Greenland and Canada involved young males, but in the Northwest Territories, an alarming increase in suicides among men over 50 was also registered, corresponding with the first crash in the seal market in 1979. When sealskin prices rose for a short period early in 1980, suicides among Inuit men in both age groups fell dramatically. . . . Today [1996], IFAW is heavily involved in the campaign to close the EU market for countries that still use leghold traps. Again, this trade barrier will impose hardships on indigenous peoples.

The IUCN, which supports sustainable hunting, spurned IFAW's application for membership following opposition by the Inuit and has continued to reject periodic efforts by the animal rights group to join. Nevertheless, IFAW continues to grow in membership, funding, power, and prestige.

"The simple fact of the matter is that they're winning," says Chris Thouless, the Kenyan economist who favors regulated hunting and cropping as a means of incentivizing wildlife habitat protection. "They have plenty of money, they spread it around, and they have the ears of the politicians. Their pitch appeals greatly to urbanites in Europe and the United States—people who have the best of intentions and lots of money to donate, if not a solid grounding in wildlife issues. They have the momentum."

Kenya may be the outlier when it comes to the consumptive use of wildlife in East Africa, but that's a point of pride with IFAW. Staffers say being in the minority doesn't make them wrong; besides, they point out, countries that allow hunting—most specifically, Tanzania—are having significant problems of their own in maintaining game populations. If the no hunting policy is uniquely Kenyan, they say, that's not only perfectly legitimate, it's a credit to Kenya, demonstrating a national acknowledgment that wildlife has an innate worth that transcends its value as meat and trophies.

"We have our own wildlife model in Kenya," James Isiche tells me during an interview at IFAW's Nairobi offices. Isiche, IFAW's director for East Africa, is a man of middle stature with a calm, almost placid demeanor. His eyes, however, testify to a strong and redoubtable nature; they lock onto an interlocutor when he is making a point and flash with deep emotion. "We really don't need to look elsewhere," he continues. "It is an attribute to Kenya that this is the only country in Africa that forbids hunting. We constantly hear that Tanzania is doing so well due to their pro-hunting policy. But it's no secret that their wildlife agencies are compromised, that their game populations are falling just as they are here. Is there more wildlife there? Yes, but not because of consumptive use policies. They have twice as much land with roughly the same number of people as Kenya, so the potential for conflicts between humans and wildlife is not as high."

Isiche points out that some facts are ignored by consumptive use advocates when discussing the shortcomings of the 1977 hunting ban, most pertinently that it worked for the species it primarily aimed to protect. "The one species we have a good count for is elephants," he says. "We know that there were about fifteen thousand elephants in Kenya at the time of the ban and that there are now about thirty-five thousand. By any measure, that's a real success."

Isiche also is irritated by the wildlife decline statistics cited by IFAW opponents. The often bruited figure of a 70 percent diminution in game across the country cannot be given credence for a simple reason, he says—it's anecdotal. "Yes, we know there are declines, but we don't know the extent and the localities. Some species are down, others up, some locales are doing worse or better than others. What we need more than anything else is a comprehensive wildlife census, for all species, for the entire country; there can't possibly be any reasonable talk of hunting or consumptive use until we actually know what we have. Perhaps the best thing [in the Draft Wildlife Bill] is the provision for an annual audit of wildlife populations. That will give us the baseline data we need to determine a sound national wildlife policy."

Isiche takes particular umbrage at the notion that Kenyans derive no value from the country's nonconsumptive wildlife policy: "Even as things stand today, wildlife-related activities—essentially, ecotourism— constitute 25 percent of the country's GNP. So the idea that a nonconsumptive policy is utterly unworkable is clearly wrong. It works, and moreover it's a good marketing point. It shows that Kenya *is* different, that we're proud of our difference; the world is aware of that difference and is responding positively."

Isiche freely acknowledges there have been major problems with the implementation of a hunting ban. But he also notes poor governance and inefficient law enforcement are evergreen issues for Africa as a whole, and when it comes to wildlife and land policy, Kenya faces particularly difficult obstacles. "Kenya is overpopulated, conflict between different communities makes wildlife policies difficult to enforce, and deforestation, drought, and poor governance are perennial issues. But simply because there have been wildlife declines in Kenya doesn't mean [the hunting ban] was poor policy. There have been wildlife declines throughout most of East Africa, including those countries that allow hunting."

Isiche notes that in twenty-two public meetings held across the country concerning the Draft Wildlife Bill, support for continuance of the hunting ban was "overwhelming. People opposed to hunting far outnumbered the people who supported it. And they were extremely passionate; they deeply opposed killing animals for sport, and they let their feelings show."

Anthony King recalls those meetings somewhat differently. They were disrupted, he says, by paid agitators hired by IFAW for the specific purpose of shouting down supporters of a revised wildlife policy and short-circuiting rational discussion. "They were loud, obnoxious, and extremely intimidating," King says. "It's an old tradition here in Kenya, hiring people to march or picket or disrupt meetings. It has nothing to do with 'heartfelt feelings'; it has do with pocketing shillings. The fact that IFAW is willing to stoop to such a practice doesn't speak well for their ethics."

Isiche contemptuously scoffs at such criticism. "We've heard all that before," he says, "and it's fabrication. Our opponents can't stand the fact that average Kenyans don't support hunting. They consider it a cruel sport pursued by people from the developed world, an activity that has no real benefit for them." Isiche observes that the ban hasn't always excluded all consumptive wildlife use. As the Mpala director Margaret Kinnaird notes, cropping—the annual killing of a specific number of certain animals for meat and by-products—was allowed for some private lands in the 1990s. Though Kinnaird feels the program was generally successful, Isiche considers it a failure.

"It was heavily abused," he says. "On many of the lands, the number of animals killed was far greater than the quotas. More than that, it created a negative image of Kenya; it diminished our brand, if you will. Look, Kenya has few natural resources. Really, when you analyze it, wildlife and the name we've made in valuing wildlife—that's what we have. And the cropping program damaged that. The idea that many in the West promulgated, that it put food on the table for hungry people, was erroneous. Little of that meat actually got to hungry people on the *manyattas*, the people who needed it. Instead, it was sold to the highest bidder, for the benefit of the landowners. From that perspective, the meat that came from cropping actually had very low value; it would've been worth much more if it had stayed on the animal, where it would've maintained a higher value as an ecotourism resource."

Isiche feels the whole argument of consumptive versus nonconsumptive wildlife use misses the point. The real issue is land use, not wildlife use. If the land is to be put to its best and highest use, wildlife preservation will be a natural adjunct. In this, he shares some common ground with Anthony King, Mike Norton-Griffiths, and other opponents: "The important thing is to maximize the arid and semiarid lands for wildlife use," he says. "That will mean better zoning. Most critically, we have to stop encouraging intensive agriculture in areas where it's completely unsuitable. Right now, the government is buying up land in Isolio and settling farmers on small parcels. It's utterly unworkable, because it's simply too dry there. People will never be able to farm reliably; all that will happen is the wildlife will be killed, the habitat destroyed, the soils eroded. A few years from now, people will be starving, we'll be sending food, and we'll have lost the area for wildlife forever. On the other hand, if we manage it as pastoral reserve—a place where we could establish stocking limits and encourage joint use of the land as grazing range and wildlife habitat—we'll be feeding people and maintaining wildlife habitat simultaneously. We'll have a sustainable system."

That, of course, is the nub of the conflict: not so much the definition of "a sustainable system," but the ancillary activities that are appropriate within such a system. If Norton-Griffiths and Isiche were to sit down over a couple of cold Tusker beers, they would agree that Kenya's semiarid private lands are the last best hope for reviving and preserving the nation's wildlife patrimony; that settlement and development at the margins of parks and reserves should be actively discouraged, and instead these areas should be managed as buffer zones where both wildlife and pastoral activities could coexist; that simultaneous use of private lands for the support of both game and pastoral people is essential; that regulated stocking levels for cattle, goats, and camels are necessary; and that any pecuniary yield from the wildlife must be returned to the people who live on the land.

Where they differ is on the appropriate use of wildlife, and this difference, so to speak, makes all the difference. For Norton-Griffiths, King, Thouless, et alia, wildlife must be viewed dispassionately to save it, at least in Kenya. Wildlife is, as Isiche himself says, one of Kenya's few resources. Thus, it must be legally and rationally exploited to provide for the people; otherwise, the people themselves will exploit it as they see fit until it disappears. The emphasis, then, is on maintaining and improving habitat and the management of game numbers. Game that can be taken without affecting base populations *should* be taken, with the proceeds—trophy fees, proceeds from culling operations, meat—going to local people.

But for Isiche, this ignores two essential points. First, as a growing number of people throughout the world believe, wild animals are not simply meat on the hoof. They manifest intelligence and emotional complexity. Several species—most relevantly where Kenya is concerned, elephants—approach the human degree of awareness. This isn't a matter of religion or philosophy, insists Isiche; rather, it is a position supported by hard science. Our advances in ethology and animal neuroscience thus impose a burden: the protection of individual animals as well as the habitat that supports them. Second, as Isiche points out, wildlife is by no means prospering in all the countries that do allow hunting. More to the point, he says, even the hunting success stories must be taken with a grain of salt.

Hunting proponents point to South Africa as a nation that has greatly expanded its wildlife numbers through a program that allows stocking, culling, and hunting on private land. Further, South Africa has done more than merely jack up the numbers of animals it markets to hunters. Wildlife typically is behind fences in South Africa; even Kruger National Park, which covers twenty thousand square kilometers, is mostly behind wire; this prevents wildlife from raising havoc on adjacent pastoral and agricultural land and helps keep poachers out. Still, as can be seen in Kenya, fencing has a downside; if it protects critical lands and wildlife, it also truncates ecosystems and blocks migration routes. In the best of all possible African wildlife habitats, fencing would be eliminated or at least minimized. And to a degree, that's what's happening in South Africa today; in many areas, the fencing is coming out as private landowners are expanding their profitable wildlife operations or working in conjunction with the government to provide auxiliary habitat at the margins of parks and reserves. Kruger and adjoining reserve lands in Mozambique are also coordinating management strategies.

Isiche, however, counters that hunting abuses in South Africa have been well documented. "They're notorious for canned hunts—stocking very small fenced enclosures with the animals of choice, including lions, so the hunters can shoot them easily, and the animals have no possibility of escape. It's really appalling, and it's a widespread practice." Indeed, canned hunts have long been an embarrassment to the international hunting community and, if considered as the primary metaphor for hunting in general, could certainly provide credence to Isiche's claim that the Kenyan model is the only reasonable alternative for wildlife management.

Most big game hunters ascribe to the concept of "fair chase"—hunting wild animals on a range of sufficient scope to provide the beasts a good chance for escape. But significant numbers of well-heeled hunters remain wholly comfortable with the idea of shooting pen-raised animals in fenced enclosures of a few acres. While such canned hunts are considered utterly repugnant by ethical hunters, the practice, as Isiche states, has long been a staple of the South African hunting industry, and the preferred quarry is lion. In excess of three hundred lions are killed in South Africa each year, virtually all of them domestically raised, then released for "sport." Each lion represents about forty thousand dollars in foreign exchange for fees, licenses, safari costs, and taxidermy and trophy shipping expenses. Indeed, the breeding of lions for such hunts is a major business in its own right; at its peak in early 2009, the South African Predators Breeders Association employed five thousand people.

Canned hunts first got widespread exposure in the late 1990s, when the BBC broadcast a documentary that included footage of a lioness being shot in a small enclosure while her cubs looked on. The program induced revulsion in the British viewing public—and ultimately throughout the developed world. IFAW and other animal rights groups took up the standard and have been hammering on canned hunts ever since, and in 2009, they accomplished a definitive breakthrough. On June 12, a South African High Court upheld legislation that stipulates lions and other feline predators must be allowed to range freely on private lands for two years before being hunted. Prior to the ruling, the lions were shot a few days after being released onto hunting "reserves."

As covered by Mike Cohen in the Bloomberg Report, the court's decision, while hailed as a victory by animal rights groups, raised havoc in the South African game and agricultural sectors. Carel van Meerden, the head of the Predators Breeders Association, declared the decision a disaster and predicted that the entire lion hunting industry would be closed. Other authorities acknowledged that the number of lions shot in South Africa may well be reduced, but there is general consensus that lion hunting will continue under the new rules. Meanwhile, South African authorities are considering what to do with the "excess" domestically raised lions that likely will result from the ruling. At the time of the decision, almost three thousand lions were being raised in captivity throughout the country. Now that many of them will not be able to be shot as part of a canned hunt, they are of little or no value to their owners. South Africa's Department of Environmental Affairs declared it could not predict the fate of the supernumerary lions; euthanasia, however, is considered likely.

IFAW can thus point to major triumphs, most particularly when dealing with black-and-white images that broad segments of civilized society find repugnant. But it doesn't fare so well when addressing gray or ambiguous areas—issues that integrate culture, habitat, land use, and politics and may have no simple solution. Recently, the organization ran into public relations difficulties while implementing a much-heralded program to move approximately sixty elephants from Malawi's Phirilongwe region to Majete Park in the south of the country.

The elephants were depredating crops in Phirilongwe, and farmers were retaliating; the conflict had resulted in casualties to both villagers and elephants. The transfer was going along fairly well until word got out that the elephants wouldn't necessarily receive better protection at Majete, which is run by the African Parks Foundation, a mainline conservation NGO. African Parks, it turned out, was happy to take the elephants, but it didn't share IFAW's view that no wild animal should ever be deliberately killed; indeed, African Parks considers all reasonable options in the management of its reserves, including subsistence and trophy hunting. Peter Fearnhead, the CEO of African Parks, noted his organization was neither pro-hunting nor anti-hunting but was committed to the long-term sustainability of its reserves. And while the group had no current plans to introduce hunting at Majete, Fearnhead continued, it would certainly allow it if the alternative was degradation of the park's habitat.

IFAW, deeply embarrassed by Fearnhead's observations, quickly secured a commitment from Malawi's Department of National Parks and Wildlife that elephant hunting would not be allowed in Majete, and the translocation project resumed. Given the poor quality of governance in Malawi, however, it is likely the only people who took the Parks and Wildlife commitment seriously were IFAW's many credulous donors. Certainly, no resident Malawian believed it.

Moreover, the move was opposed by many people in the Phirilongwe District, who saw it as a usurpation of their rights and a seizure of potentially valuable assets. Indeed, the elephant relocation was pilloried for undercutting nascent efforts to establish a wildlife sanctuary in the district, one that could have drawn tourists and money in its own right. Further, said IFAW opponents, removing the elephants would hasten the destruction of Phirilongwe's remaining wildlife habitat, since the absence of the menacing beasts would allow people to invade their former redoubts, cut down the forests, and cultivate the land, ultimately leading to soil erosion and siltation into nearby Lake Malawi.

It would've been far better to have fenced the elephants out of neighboring farmlands, claimed an ad hoc local group called Friends of Phirilongwe: the elephants would then be secure behind the wire, croplands and people would be safe, and an opportunity would be created for a Phirilongwe wildlife reserve, likely resulting in increased revenues for the impoverished area. Implicit in such a scenario, of course, was the possible utilization of the elephants for meat, trophy fees, or both; left alone in a fenced reserve, the elephants would have overpopulated their range in relatively short order. IFAW is almost as influential in Malawi as Kenya, however, and the complaints of dissident Phirilongwe locals came to naught. Indeed, a statement released by the Friends of Phirilongwe noted that not only was a 2005 document signed by the region's chiefs requesting a fence instead of elephant removal ignored, but also the tribal leaders were pointedly told by government authorities to keep quiet and do nothing to disrupt the move.

IFAW continued moving elephants, ultimately declared the project a success, and promoted it heavily on its Web site, the unhappiness of Phirilongwe locals opposed to the project notwithstanding. Nor was the long-term carrying capacity of Majete addressed. Because elephants are elephants—extremely large, relatively fecund, indomitably migratory beasts that raze all vegetation when confined behind wire—a day of reckoning is inevitable for Majete. Sooner or later, the elephant population will expand beyond the carrying capacity of the park. Large numbers will either have to be moved elsewhere—or killed. IFAW has not solved the problem; it has merely postponed the problem's resolution.

Norton-Griffiths, of course, would have built the fence in Phirilongwe, created a nature reserve, established a cull quota for the elephants, and returned the benefits—in meat and money—to local villagers. In other words, it's unlikely he will be getting together with Isiche anytime soon for those convivial beers.

CHAPTER 9

An Inalienable Right

The Arusha express bus from Nairobi takes about an hour to crawl past the sprawling, dust-colored suburbs and frayed satellite towns south of the Kenyan capital. Then the land opens up, though it hardly presents a cheery prospect: great vistas of red dirt swales and hills scattered lightly with thorn trees. The land is "cow burnt," as Edward Abbey would have described it: grazed down to mineral earth, with hardly a blade of grass standing. My companions on this trip represent a rich diversity of cultures. Stolid Maasai elders commingle uneasily with pallid German backpackers, who laze in their seats, eyes closed, listening to tunes on their iPods. Somali matrons, faces partly obscured by black *hijabs,* hands meticulously painted with henna arabesques, share a meal of chicken, rice, and *muufo,* a type of pocket bread. Overhead, the sky is the color of curdled milk, dominated by a high, hot sun. The bus travels through miles and miles of southern Kenya, and the only wildlife in all that parched expanse is a small flock of helmeted guinea fowl, jittering chickenlike as they forage across the raw, red dirt.

As the bus draws near the Tanzanian border, the topography assumes greater relief: small stony mountains separated by wide, pleasant valleys. Some of the land is cultivated here, and the uplands are heavily vegetated by trees and scrub. These hills support game, I'm told, including some of the rarer antelopes—lesser kudu, gerenuk, and duikers. Past the border, the land becomes even more welcoming. It is greener, for one thing; more rain has fallen here than in Kenya during the weeks preceding my trip. There is grass in the fields, the cattle are fatter, and the crops of maize and beans are lush. Arusha, our destination, is a pleasant city of moderate size, with broad streets shaded by mature trees. It lies at the foot of Mount Meru, a volcanic cone that is a double of Mount Kilimanjaro, albeit in reduced dimensions. Meru's wooded parkland and montane forest still support significant populations of big game, including Cape buffalo and elephants. Arusha was the jumping-off point for most safaris during the golden age of African trophy hunting, back when Hemingway and Robert Ruark hunted, and Tanzania was still a British colony known as Tanganyika. Arusha, in fact, remains Tanzania's primary tourist center, and safaris for both hunters and wildlife viewers typically are arranged here.

Perhaps the most salient things striking the visitor coming overland from Kenya are that Tanzania has fewer people, also that they seem better nourished. Further, they appear more relaxed; there isn't that sense of tension, of incipient violence, present in many Kenyan towns. Much of the credit for Tanzania's mellower vibe must be given to the country's founder. Julius Nyerere not only imposed a socialist economic model on his country; he also did everything in his power to quash tribalism and infuse the populace with a sense of national identity. As a result, the country's citizens tend to think of themselves as Tanzanian first and Sukumba, Kimbu, or Chagga second.

Of course, people aren't sitting around campfires singing Kumbaya. There is still plenty of crime in Tanzania. Most incidents involve simple theft: Tanzania is an impoverished country, even poorer than Kenya; per capita income in 2008 was the equivalent of thirteen hundred U.S. dollars in Tanzania and sixteen hundred in Kenya. Still, some of the crimes seem unique to this part of the world. In Arusha during a recent visit of mine, the local press was aflame with stories about the trade in albino human body parts. Albinism is a relatively common condition in northern Tanzania, southern Kenya, and Burundi, and the skin, hair, and bones of albinos are considered potent good luck talismans. As a consequence, Tanzania's two hundred thousand albinos live in constant fear of being killed for their constituent parts. At least forty albinos were murdered in the country during 2008 and 2009, and the government responded forcefully, sentencing several of the killers to death. Still, even these grisly homicides are driven at least as much by poverty as by superstition; the trade in albino talismans is lucrative.

Given the poor economy, it would be logical to assume Tanzania's wildlife is as straitened as Kenya's. But the game is relatively abundant.

This is partly due to Tanzania's unique location, encompassing as it does some of the richest wildlife habitat in the world, including the Serengeti Plain and the Selous Game Reserve. But it's also because human population density is lower in Tanzania than in Kenya. At 945,000 square kilometers, Tanzania encompasses almost twice as much land as Kenya, but its population is only slightly larger. There is more room for people, livestock, and wildlife.

Also, many people think the relative abundance of game in Tanzania is due to the emphasis Nyerere and subsequent leaders have put on its resource value. Tourism has always been a bulwark of Tanzania's fragile economy: in good times and bad (or in Tanzania's unique case, bad times and worse), visitors flock to the Serengeti to see the great wildebeest migration and the stunning concentrations of plains game in general. But unlike Kenya, Tanzania also allows—indeed, encourages—hunting. And not just for wealthy foreigners. Certainly, trophy hunting is a major industry in Tanzania: vast portions of the country are divided into hunting blocks, which are leased to professional safari companies for large sums of money. But subsistence hunting also is allowed in Tanzania; it is, in fact, considered an inalienable right. For a nominal fee, any villager can obtain a permit that will allow him to take plains game for the pot. Wildlife thus has palpable value for poor rural Tanzanians, say hunting advocates. Knowing they will be able to derive benefit from wild animals, farmers and herders don't have to be convinced to keep them around; the conservation of game becomes a matter of proprietary interest.

This sense that wildlife is a resource held in common, that it exists to benefit people, is ingrained in national culture, says James Kahurananga, the African Wildlife Foundation's program director for the Maasai Steppe Heartland. Kahurananga's office is in a low building off a shaded lane in downtown Arusha. He is a small man, highly animated, brimming with an ebullience that seems irrepressible. Tomes and periodicals are crammed into shelves lining the walls, and his desk is piled with papers, journals, and reports. "It's natural to us," says Kahurananga. "I myself come from a tribe with strong hunting traditions. I used to do some hunting with my father and grandfather, using bows and arrows."

Kahurananga says consumptive and nonconsumptive wildlife uses are compatible and can properly be viewed as a matter of zoning. Parks, such as the Serengeti, can be rigorously managed as no-hunt zones. In other areas, he says, hunting can be allowed, as long as reasonable take quotas are maintained. "They might be areas that are used exclusively for hunting," he says, "say, areas that have difficult access, little or nothing in the way of infrastructure or accommodations, and minimal scenic value. Other areas can be managed for both hunting and nonconsumptive wildlife uses. It requires some competent management, but it can be done."

Kahurananga acknowledges there are hunting abuses in Tanzania—corrupt dealings in the lease of hunting blocks, excessive quotas, outright poaching. But that, he continues, is nothing new for Africa; those kinds of problems come with the territory. In the end, he insists, legal hunting still provides an incentive for poor rural people to conserve the wildlife that lives around them. "I've been all over Kenya," he says, "and I can say flatly that their system is not working. I would advise the authorities there: please allow hunting and consumptive use. Otherwise, you will end up with nothing."

Kahurananga notes there is no "unused land" in Kenya, Tanzania, or virtually anywhere in Africa south of the Sahara. All of it is employed for something by human beings—generally, grazing or intensive agriculture. Even the parks, he observes, adhere to the doctrine of beneficial use: they bring in tourist dollars. The idea that land can be set aside solely for the benefit of wildlife, he says, is pure delusion. "If you are going to save wildlife, first you have to save the land," he says. "By that I mean the uses of the land that are conducive to coexistence with wildlife."

In the best of all possible situations, that could be limited to wildlife viewing, Kahurananga allows. "If you have a large property with a well-known and luxurious lodge that attracts plenty of tourists, fine—good for you," he says. "But how many properties in Tanzania or Kenya are like that? Very few. More likely, you're talking about a private ranch or a group ranch—say, fifty thousand acres or so. You have cattle, but you also have some wildlife. But you have no lodge, you have no capital to build a lodge or market it, and even if you did, your property is almost inaccessible. It's hard to get to from the usual tourist routes. And it probably doesn't have the concentrations of wildlife that draw the crowds. Your wildlife acts like real game. It doesn't congregate all together in one place where it can be easily photographed. It runs from people, it hides in the brush, it's hard to see. So what do you do with a place like that? If you can't derive any legitimate use from the game, you're going to eliminate it. Because it'll compete with your livestock for forage, or if it doesn't do that, it'll eat your livestock directly."

For such a property, he continues, authorities can either write it off as potential habitat or allow people to derive profit from the wildlife. "Establish quotas, certainly, but really allow them to manage their animals—to sell permits, to kill it for food or other products. Only then will people become protective of wild animals. IFAW and other groups think you can somehow convince people to *care* about wildlife because of their beauty or their intelligence. There isn't that tradition here, and for a very good reason—simple human survival is difficult enough."

The possible benefits of its hunting policy notwithstanding, Tanzania has major difficulties in managing its wildlife resources. Poaching and institutionalized corruption top the list. In 2009, the Berlin-based group Transparency International ranked Tanzania 126 out of 180 countries surveyed for corruption; that represented a drop of 24 places from 2008, hardly an encouraging trend. Still, Tanzania fared better than its northern neighbors: Kenya was ranked 146 in 2009, and Uganda ranked 130. Corruption, then, is not unique to Tanzania; it is endemic to the continent and can be mitigated only through societal changes that force good governance and discipline in law enforcement rank and file.

A 2003 white paper by the Lawyers' Environmental Action Team, a Tanzanian public policy group, focused in particular on the latitude accorded officials who oversee the hunting sector: "[An] examination of the provisions of the wildlife law governing the hunting industry reveals that authorities charged with the control of the industry have been invested with tremendous unchecked powers. It has been noted that courts of law have decried this and recommendations to trim down these powers in order to avoid arbitrary abuse and misuse of the power for self-interests have been suggested." Unfortunately, nothing substantive has been done to change the situation. But Kahurananga feels relatively minor policy adjustments can be made to ameliorate the malign consequences of corruption to some degree, effecting real change for the benefit of wildlife.

"A great problem in Tanzania—well, Africa in general, but Tanzania is my primary concern—is the lack of training facilities for wildlife managers," Kahurananga says. "I was fortunate enough to obtain my higher education in the United States, but we obviously can't train our entire force of wildlife managers in the developed world. We need to be able to do that here, in Tanzania." Such schools wouldn't have to be heavily endowed institutions with lavish facilities, Kahurananga emphasizes. Competent instructors would be the most important thing: people versed in modern wildlife management practices, who could, in turn, train a large cadre of biologists, rangers, scouts, and wardens. Or alternatively, Kahurananga says, recruits could serve apprenticeships in the field with senior researchers and rangers.

"We have a great many people in this country who already have the bushcraft skills," Kahurananga says. "What they lack is the technical training. One way we could fund this might be through foreign partnerships—with governments, corporations, or NGOs. For that matter, East Africa's wildlife would be much better off if IFAW and other groups put some or all of the money they're spending on sensationalistic advertising campaigns and public relations and 'education' into *real* education for wildlife managers."

While addressing Tanzania's larger problem of poor governance is beyond the scope of any individual or single organization, Kahurananga emphasizes that pressure must be maintained in specific regard to corruption in the hunting sector. In this one area, he says, world opinion counts—Tanzania depends too much on its wildlife to ignore international outrage. Echoing the determination of the Lawyers' Environmental Action Team, he focuses on hunting block dispensation. "The way they're granted—by whim, as a favor, or more generally for money— must be addressed," he says. "Everyone knows it's a very basic and serious problem, and we need increased pressure inside and outside the government to change things."

Hunting blocks in Tanzania are supposed to be founded on solid conservation principles, including firm quotas, and in theory, at least, they are granted only to concessionaires who have demonstrated a commitment to ethical hunting. In practice, things are different. Typically, says Kahurananga, the best blocks go to politicians in power who either exploit them themselves with no regard to quotas or any other regulation, or they sublease them to cronies or fly-by-night safari company owners who pay substantial kickbacks. "True, some of the blocks are operated by reputable companies and are run well and ethically," Kahurananga says. "But the poorly run concessions provide animal rights groups with a lot of ammunition. We could make a much better case for the benefits of regulated hunting if we could clean up this sector."

Jonathan Howells, the managing director for Robin Hurt Safaris in Tanzania, has similar feelings about the country's hunting sector. Robin Hurt is one of the larger safari companies in Tanzania and generally is considered among the best. The firm operates its concessions along strict conservation-based guidelines, emphasizing ethical hunting and fair chase to its clients. I interviewed Howells at his company's Arusha headquarters shortly before the beginning of the annual hunting season.

The compound was a frenzy of activity, with employees taking inventory and loading equipment onto trucks for the long drives to the hunting blocks.

"Frankly, the past few years haven't been particularly good for the hunting business," says Howells, a fortyish ex–British Royal Marine commando who looks like he could still undertake a combat mission with aplomb. "It has become highly politicized; it's just very unstable. In 2006, for example, the government decided to ban lion hunting halfway through the season—this was while we had clients in the field who had shot lions, and we had other guys with lion hunts booked. Then two weeks later, they rescinded the ban. It caused terrible difficulties. And in 2007, about two weeks into the season, the government tripled trophy fees; for lions, for example, it went from $2,500 to $7,000. We felt honor-bound to keep to the original price list we had quoted our clients, so we ate the additional fees. It cost us about $200,000."

Such erratic policies are not good for either the Tanzanian economy or effective wildlife management, says Howells. Ultimately, it will push hunting companies to countries with more stable policies—South Africa, Namibia, and Botswana. "Hunting isn't just part of the culture in this country," Howells says. "We're also a big part of the economy. Our basic rate [in 2008] for a twenty-one-day safari is $46,000. On top of that, add $16,400 for government fees, about $30,000 to $40,000 for the permits for the game animals that are taken, plus another $15,000 or $16,000 for the trophy processing and shipping."

In addition, says Howells, some companies charge additional client fees to support local communities. Robin Hurt, for example, adds a 20 percent levy to the game permit fees strictly for the benefit of communities within their hunting blocks. "In one block, we have thirteen villages, and each one of them got $2,500 last year [2007]," Howells says. "In another block that had fewer villages, each got $5,500. That's real money in rural East Africa; it went to *boma* [corral] construction to protect livestock from predators, apiary projects, maize mills, supplementary rations. That money is making a real difference."

Robin Hurt also pays compensation to villages who suffer livestock depredation from lions. The benefits of this policy are mutual: the villagers obtain generous cash payments for their livestock, and Robin Hurt is able to maintain a healthy lion population on its concessions for its clients. "I know there have been some problems with livestock compensation programs, but it has worked very well for us," says Howells. "We haven't lost a lion on our blocks to poisoning in seven years."

But payments from safari companies to local communities can only go so far, Howells emphasizes. Without good governance, he says, any wildlife policy, whether it incorporates hunting or not, will not measure up. "It is very frustrating," he says. "Ideally, a significant part of the money we pay to the government should be earmarked for the Wildlife Department for more anti-poaching patrols, better equipment for the scouts and rangers, and habitat improvement. But it all goes into the general fund. And from there, it can go to any number of places—or people—but very little if any of it gets devoted to wildlife conservation."

Howells acknowledges there are heavy abuses by some hunting companies; he seemed deeply embarrassed, even angry by this fact. "I know Craig Packer [a University of Minnesota wildlife biologist and authority on lions] has been making a lot of noise about this, and unfortunately it's true," he said. "We have a standing policy in our company that no lion can be shot that is younger than five years old. You have these fly-by-night companies that shoot lions over their quota and that shoot young lions. Lions move around a lot, and they by no means stay in any one hunting block, so we've had shady companies operating next to our concessions who have shot specific lions that we had been taking great pains to conserve."

Still, Howells insists that wildlife should flourish in Tanzania as long as ethical hunting companies are integrated into the system. "We have one hunting block that is five thousand square kilometers," he says. "When we went there in 1992, there was very little game; I can recall only one small herd of buffalo. No lions, very few leopards. We started a rigorous anti-poaching program. For those first years, we were removing ten thousand snares annually. Now we're only taking out a hundred snares a year. We have three thousand resident buffalo, and we typically see twenty-five leopards a hunt. The lion population is healthy. So when you combine a good hunting company with community involvement, you end up with a wonderful situation. But poor governance results in corrupt hunting policies and unethical hunting companies. That's our biggest problem here."

Like Kahurananga, Howells thinks Kenya would benefit by a repeal of its hunting ban. He also doesn't think that will ever happen. "The anti-hunting NGOs are calling the shots up there," he says. "That won't change. They have the resources, and they're willing to pay whatever it takes to not only maintain the status quo but expand their operations. They'd like to see a similar policy in Tanzania. I doubt they'll be successful, but one never knows. They have the funds, the vision, and they're exceedingly patient."

But animal rights advocates aren't the only people who have doubts about Tanzania's hunting policies. On the other side of town is a former coffee estate, now a plush resort favored by hunters and ecotourists going off or coming back from safari. This is a satellite enterprise of Burka Coffee, a venerable Arusha firm owned by the Rechsteiner family. Though many of the long-established coffee groves are disappearing around Arusha, Burka still cultivates about fifteen hundred acres of trees, producing about a thousand tons of high-grade Arabica coffee annually.

Alex Rechsteiner, who runs much of the day-to-day business of his company, has invited me to dinner. As the sun sets in a welter of gold, salmon, and magenta, we have a couple of drinks. The grounds are beautifully landscaped, and even here on the outskirts of the city, wildlife intrudes: fruit bats swarm over the ripe clusters of dates depending from tall palms, and bush babies squall from the jacaranda trees. Rechsteiner is a lean, dark-haired, handsome man in his midthirties; he is deeply serious. One gets the sense that he has carried the weight of responsibility, family and corporate, for a long time. It is hard to imagine him as a frivolous or even lighthearted child. A second-generation Tanzanian of Swiss-German antecedents, he is deeply involved in his country's conservation issues. He is a principal of the conservation group Friends of the Serengeti and spends much of his free time out on the plains, working on various projects or simply enjoying propinquity with the game.

As we are poured an excellent white wine from South Africa and served entrées of Nile perch, Rechsteiner expands on his views of wildlife management, hunting, ecotourism, the international animal rights advocacy movement—and, most pointedly, the future of megafauna in East Africa. His perspectives are deeply informed and highly textured, but they can be summed up succinctly: he is not optimistic. "I just can't see a happy end to the problems we face here," he says, picking abstemiously at his food. "When you look at the alternatives, it's difficult to see how you can arrive at a workable solution—there is so much against it."

Rechsteiner is particularly dubious about hunting as a means of investing wildlife with value to local communities. At one time, sport hunting in Tanzania made sense, he says. The human population in the country was relatively small, the animals were abundant, and hunting amounted to a sustainable enterprise, one that added value to wild lands and provided handsome returns to the safari companies, reliable employment for tribal communities, and funds for habitat management. "It was also a useful tool for stabilizing certain species in specific areas," Rechsteiner says. "But the goal posts have shifted. Tanzania isn't the same place it was when it was Tanganyika, and the world isn't the same world."

Tanzania is facing many of the same problems as Kenya when it comes to preserving wildlife, says Rechsteiner, including a rapidly increasing human population and the relentless conversion of open range to intensively cultivated croplands. But hunting must also be considered a significant threat, he says. "Compared to other countries, Tanzania still has relatively large populations of game," he continues. "But compared to the past, we've seen tremendous losses in wildlife; we're in an ever tightening spiral of declines. And hunting is a significant part of the problem."

Both trophy hunting and subsistence hunting are contributing to the declines, says Rechsteiner. If all the professional hunting companies operating in the country acted like Robin Hurt, he says, sport hunting wouldn't be an issue; indeed, professional hunters would be invaluable allies in the conservation of Tanzania's wildlife. Although Robin Hurt isn't necessarily a lone exception in a corrupt sector, the firm still stands out in an industry that is less than pristine. Many companies are overly liberal in interpreting the quotas on their concessions, Rechsteiner says, or if the owner of the concession is a powerful and influential Tanzanian, he will often feel free to chop it up into several blocks, each block with the same quota of the original concession. Thus, a concession that had an annual quota of say, three lions, now becomes four concessions, each with a three lion quota; twelve lions are then taken annually off a tract that could at best sustain a kill of one-fourth that number.

"And it's not just a matter of difficulties with individual companies," Rechsteiner says. "There also has been a huge spike in the number of hunting outfits operating in Tanzania. Twenty years ago, there were maybe ten professional hunting companies working here; now there must be close to two hundred. That increased pressure is having tremendous impacts."

Community hunting is also depleting game, emphasizes Rechsteiner. The national "right to hunt" is popular in Tanzania, a pledge made and kept by Nyerere to share one of the country's few abundant natural resources. But such a "right," Rechsteiner says, is no longer practical in today's Tanzania, a country that has more than doubled in population since its independence in 1961. "Resident hunting has been a prime mover in wildlife declines," says Rechsteiner. "To a very real degree, the declines in game in many areas have tracked the increase in human population. Sport hunting, at least, can be a tool. If everything works as it should, trophy hunting adds value to wildlife, and that value can be transferred to the communities. But with resident hunting, the only value of the game is as bushmeat. In a protein-poor country like Tanzania, that's real value—but it's still very, very low compared to the values associated with sport hunting."

Plus, observes Rechsteiner, resident hunters kill a large number of animals compared to the number killed by sport hunters: the meat, after all, is everything. Resident hunters are often extremely competent, and it doesn't take them long to utterly expunge big game from vast portions of the landscape. "Though some protected blocks are doing okay, game has decreased massively in the northern part of the country," says Rechsteiner. "The habitat is pretty good to excellent. So you have to conclude the issue is hunting—excessive sport hunting to a degree. But resident hunting probably is the biggest reason, along, of course, with poaching; that never goes away. Poaching, snaring, predator poisoning—it's always with us, and it isn't properly taken into account when hunting policies are established."

Though the hunting ethic is culturally enshrined in Tanzania, there are some signs that the animal rights agenda is making a bit of headway in the country. It is not the purist doctrine championed by IFAW, but it is nevertheless recognition that animals have standing as sentient beings. Still, this shift is not due to a changing social ethos: it's wholly grounded in pragmatism.

In the Kilimanjaro District, observes Alex Songorwa, the head of the Department of Wildlife Management at Tanzania's Sokoine University of Agriculture, local villagers vigorously support hunting restrictions on their common lands. "They live in an area that is heavily visited by tourists, and they realize they can make more money from photo safaris than from hunters," says Songorwa. "But to attract nonhunting tourists, they need a lot of game on their land—wildlife that is comfortable around people, which means wildlife that isn't hunted. So they're working with safari outfitters and some of the NGOs to stop the hunting."

The local languages don't have a phrase that accurately conveys the concept of "animal rights," continues Songorwa, so the villagers refer to the concept of "animal human rights." The oxymoronic phrase is now in wide usage in the Kilimanjaro region—not just by hunting foes, but

by hunting advocates—and accurately (if awkwardly) sums up the difficulty of accommodating rural African mores to an ethic developed in the
cities of Europe and North America. Songorwa continues, "Supporters
of hunting will say, 'Yes, animals have animal human rights, but I also
have human rights to food, and my human rights account for more than
an animal's human rights.'"

In any event, Kilimanjaro residents are having difficulty enforcing Kenyan-style hunting proscriptions. "The locals support a hunting ban for the region, but the central government doesn't recognize
their authority," Songorwa says. "Hunting policy is determined at the
national level, not by local chiefs and elders. So the central government
is maintaining its hunting quotas for Kilimanjaro, and that is causing a
lot of conflict."

It is dangerous to speak in generalities, but Tanzanians seem more
invested in their wildlife than Kenyans. Perhaps it's because Tanzania
simply has more wild animals and a lower human population density
than Kenya or that Tanzania's population is not as urbanized. Maybe
it's because average citizens can still hunt; the taste, the ceremonies, and
the traditions of bushmeat still resonate throughout the general population. In any event, the benefits and downsides of hunting notwithstanding, the colloquy on wildlife policy seems both more sophisticated and
less doctrinaire than it does in Kenya. Still, the basic problem is the same
in both countries: declining wildlife populations. Tanzania may contain
more animals than Kenya, but it is basically in the same boat. The graph
line is heading down at a steep, unrelenting angle.

"The thing is that southern Kenya and northern Tanzania—where
the great concentrations of game are located, in the Serengeti and the
Maasai Mara—are one ecosystem with shared wildlife and shared
migration routes," observes Enock Chengullah, the wildlife program
director for the Tanzania Natural Resources Forum. I interviewed
Chengullah, a man with a winning if somewhat melancholy smile, late
one afternoon at his office on a quiet Arusha back street.

Ideally, says Chengullah, the Mara-Serengeti system would be managed under a single authority vigorously supported by both Kenya and
Tanzania. But each country enforces its own laws on its portion of
the system—and poorly at that. The consequence is that Africa's great
showcase for wildlife is being pillaged relentlessly of its wildlife. "You
can buy bushmeat very easily in Nairobi," says Chengullah. "You'll be
told it's from legal cropping, but it's from the Mara or eastern Serengeti.
The poachers come from far away, and they're hosted by local villagers,

who share in the meat and profits. It's organized, it's efficient and the governments of both countries have done nothing to stop it. They promote the wildlife through their tourism bureaus, but even as they urge the tourists to come, the game disappears. There is no will to change things."

Certainly, as Chengullah says, there is no official impetus for change and no sufficient source of funding to enforce such change. But change—and beneficial change at that—is manifest in the Serengeti system. It is not, however, coming from the public sector.

CHAPTER 10

Buy (or Lease) It and They Will Come

From Arusha to the Serengeti is a leisurely all-day drive. First you transit through pleasant pastoral lands, punctuated occasionally by small, neat villages. The cattle are sleek, the people tall, erect, and punctilious in address. Around noon you come to the Rift Valley escarpment, which you ascend in a series of thrilling switchbacks. At a pullover, you look south to a far alkaline lake surrounded by parkland and patches of dense forest. This is Lake Manyara National Park. It is here that Iain Douglas-Hamilton conducted his groundbreaking work on the social structure of African elephants, research that is now holy writ for the animal liberation movement. Indeed, elephants—and buffalo—can be discerned plodding along the shore, and far to the southwest the surface of the lake seems obscured by a pink mist: flamingoes.

You drive on across a plateau that is heavily cultivated, then take a jog over to Ngorongoro Crater. The agricultural activity—and commerce, for souvenir shops are common along the roadway—continue almost up to the border of the Ngorongoro Conservation Area. But at the gate, where tourists pay a substantial entrance fee, triple-canopy forest commences. It is like entering a time warp, an evulsion from the Africa of the twenty-first century, followed by an abrupt thrust into the primeval past. The air is cooler and tastes faintly of nectar and herbage; birds throng the trees. You come to the lip of the crater with little warning, and it lies before you—an eerily perfect caldera twelve miles in diameter and two thousand feet deep. There are more than twenty thousand large wild animals in Ngorongoro, and you can spot many of them easily from the overlooks—the zebras, wildebeest, and buffalo, the rhinos, the huge bull elephants carrying eighty-pound tusks. You can also see the numerous vans crammed with tourists doodling across the crater floor, converging on lion kills and other elements of interest. Ngorongoro is, generally speaking, a functioning ecosystem, but it is by no means wild.

As you approach the Serengeti Plain, however, things are different. Virtually all traces of human habitation disappear, save for the road itself. The Maasai call this place the Serengit, the Land That Goes Forever, and when you venture out upon it, you feel like a voyager, not a tourist. The grass goes to the horizon, and the horizon always recedes.

My hosts on this trip are Rian and Lorna Labuschagne. Though they are now residents of Tanzania, in the truest sense they are habitués of the entire continent, spending their free time shuttling from Kenya and Tanzania to Botswana and South Africa, then over to Mali and Burkina Faso, visiting friends, game reserves, music festivals, and bazaars. Tall, fiftyish, mesomorphic, easygoing but sardonic in humor, Rian fought insurgents of the South West Africa People's Organization and Cuban advisers in Angola as a young South African conscript. Though he no longer serves as a director of the Ngorongoro Conservation Area, he and Lorna are still working in conservation, but in an entirely different capacity—they're now in the private sector.

Prior to entering the Serengeti National Park proper, we stop near Olduvai Gorge for lunch. Wildebeest skulls dot the ground, and Thomson's and Grant's gazelles stand less than a hundred yards away, twitching their tails as they graze. It is at the end of the dry season, and the grass is sparse and sere. The big concentrations of game are to the west, Rian says between bites of his cold quiche. "They're getting some rain there, and things are greening up. I don't know if we'll be able to intersect the wildebeest migration, but we'll give it a try."

The wildebeest, of course, are the main tourist draw for northern Tanzania and southern Kenya. Each year, between 800,000 and 1.2 million Serengeti wildebeest and tens of thousands of Burchell's zebras complete a great seasonal round; from the southern Serengeti in January, they move north and west to arrive at the Maasai Mara in October, then head south again, constantly following the rains and the grass.

I'm tremendously excited at the prospect of witnessing the migration and can literally feel my heartbeat quicken as we enter the park. But as we motor across the plain, there is no evidence of the great masses of moving game; in fact, animals are rather scarce. We see quite a few Maasai giraffes, ostriches, some topi, and, of course, the ubiquitous gazelles. We come across a dead Nile monitor lizard by the side of the road and the bloated corpse of a hippo, complete with scavenging crocodiles, in a small stream. Farther along, in a copse of fever trees by the same stagnant creek, we are blocked by a traffic jam of Land Rovers. All their passengers are leaning out the windows and the sunroofs with their cameras. Off in the grass, a leopard slinks along; I'm as guilty of anthropomorphizing as anyone, and to me the cat seems deeply irritated by the interruption of his hunt. I'm endeavoring to be the perfect guest, cheerful and uncomplaining at all times, but Lorna—an exceptionally perceptive person—senses I'm somehow disappointed that the Serengeti isn't exploding at the seams with wildlife.

"Don't worry," she says. "You're going to see a *lot* of game at Sasakwa."

As we head west toward Lake Victoria, the air thickens with moisture. The grass is heavier and higher, and it is greening up; the plain has given way to a more rumpled topography, a rolling parkland with abundant trees. We pass through Robanda, a small but relatively prosperous town, and Rian mutters unhappily. This particular settlement, an inholding of private land surrounded by the Serengeti National Park and adjacent game reserves, is an issue of great contention among conservationists. Serving as a node for poachers who come from far and wide to depredate the Serengeti ecosystem, it nevertheless has considerable support among its political representatives in the Tanzanian government. Rian acknowledges he has no idea what can be done about the situation.

"Frankly," he observes, "I don't like talking about it."

Just past the village, the road cuts south. We are nearing our destination: Sasakwa Lodge at Singita Grumeti Reserves. The preserve area covers approximately 350,000 acres of fee-title and leased land in the Grumeti Corridor, a great swath of terrain that stretches along the Grumeti River and serves as a conduit for the game migrations between the Maasai Mara and the Serengeti. As such, it is one of the most important game reserves in Africa, but that isn't the only thing that makes it remarkable; it also is privately owned. The Grumeti Reserves are the project of multibillionaire Paul Tudor Jones, a hedge fund manager renowned for predicting—and profiting from—the 1987 stock market crash. Along with an uncanny talent for making great amounts of money, Jones is an ardent conservationist and Africanophile. In 2002, he started the Grumeti endeavor, ultimately taking on Singita, a South

African ecotourism group, as a managing partner. Today, the Grumeti Reserves is a top-end tourist destination, supporting two hyperluxurious tent camps and a main lodge within its borders. The Labuschagnes are Jones's point people in his real estate and conservation ventures in East Africa, and they supervised the construction of the project's facilities.

As we pass the unmarked border into the Grumeti Reserve holdings, Rian reminisces about the challenges of hauling everything required—from native stone and wood to antique furniture and venerable, first-edition books—to the hilltop site that supports Sasakwa, the main lodge. "It wasn't that you were just worried about getting everything done on schedule," he laughs. "Sometimes, you weren't really sure you were going to get it done at all."

As Rian talks, I notice something: animals. We see some small groups of topi—big, fawn-colored antelope with blue-gray haunches and forequarters. There are some Burchell's zebras, and off in the distance, their heads towering above the thorn trees, a couple of Maasai giraffes. The farther we drive into Grumeti Reserves, the more abundant the wildlife: over there, a large herd of Cape buffalo; there, a family of hyenas loping through the grass. More zebras, more topi, more gazelles, a string of impalas bounding across the road. Game is everywhere. Finally, we debouch onto a large plain fronting a sizable hill. Atop the promontory is Sasakwa Lodge—from a distance, a glitter of glass and flashes of pale stone. On the plain is a vista right out of the late Pleistocene—the kind of sight I expected to see when we crossed the Serengeti. There are great herds of topi and zebras interspersed with a smaller number of wildebeest—perhaps ten thousand animals in total, all intently grazing the emergent green grass. Far away amid the trees, great dark bulks are slowly moving: elephants. Rian stops the Land Rover, and we get out. Not far from us is a dark stain on the earth, clotted with vultures and jackals: a lion kill. The tsetse flies descend on us joyously, and we swat at them as we watch the game. Except for the distant grunting and nickering of the beasts, all is utterly quiet. By some instinct, we talk softly, almost in whispers, though the animals are by no means alarmed by our presence.

"Some biologists came out here recently and looked at this and told us this is the largest concentration of topi confirmed in the Serengeti ecosystem in forty years," Rian recalls. "I wish you could see it when the wildebeest migration is moving through. This plain is *black* with them."

This extravagant number of animals is altogether appropriate. Not

FIGURE 6. Like the plains game and predators, elephants have made a spectacular recovery at Singita Grumeti. They are easily observed from Sasakwa, the main lodge, as they browse the adjacent acacia forests. (Courtesy Singita Game Reserves)

only does the Grumeti Corridor serve as a conduit between the Maasai Mara in Kenya and the Serengeti Plain; also, it is tremendously rich habitat in its own right. But when the Labuschagnes were first laying the foundations for Sasakwa less than a decade earlier, the surrounding countryside was eerily empty of wildlife. It wasn't a matter of slack time between migrations; the game was starkly, permanently absent. The only large mammals active in the landscape, recalls Rian, were bipedal: poachers, in other words. Any quadruped that wandered into the area was promptly shot. "We'd sit up on the hill at night and just watch the jacklights," says Lorna, referring to the powerful spotlights illegal hunters use to locate quarry after dark. "There was this background staccato of gunfire. It was very—distressing."

Nor were the poachers poor locals out to obtain a bit of meat for the pot, says Rian. Sasakwa is difficult to reach, well beyond the range of most regional villagers who must travel by shank's mare. To hunt the area, motor vehicles are required, and only wealthy Tanzanians can afford cars or pickups. Rian recalls one poachers' camp that had been brazenly erected right below the hill where construction of the lodge had begun. "There were four guys—none local, all from the coast," he says. "When we got there, they had sixty antelope heads strewn around

FIGURE 7. Eland at Singita Grumeti Reserves. The game has made a stunning recovery since the reserves were established, a result of rigorous patrols by highly competent game scouts and rangers, many of them ex-poachers. (Courtesy Singita Game Reserves)

the camp and a ton of drying meat. They were highly indignant when we kicked them out."

Although Jones had legal title to the land, often that is not enough in Africa. Ownership must be enforced on the ground, because deeds mean nothing to men who are used to wandering where they please and shooting whatever they want. While overseeing construction of the lodge and satellite facilities, the Labuschagnes also recruited an anti-poaching unit for the Grumeti Reserves—basically, a private cadre of 120 game scouts. Rian's military training and combat experience came in particularly handy here. He outfitted the men, all locals deeply steeped in the intricacies of bushcraft—and many of them ex-poachers—in uniforms of his own design, trained them in modern law enforcement techniques, infused them with an esprit de corps, and paid them salaries that were excellent by Tanzanian standards. They patrolled incessantly, removing snares, chivying poachers. Within a year, the illegal killing mostly had ceased. The game started to return, and ultimately it burgeoned. "That's the thing about this part of Africa," observes Rian. "The habitat is generally in very good shape. All what's really needed is game protection; if the animals aren't killed or harassed, they'll do just fine."

The road skirts the plain, then wends between a few small hillocks angling toward the higher hill that is capped by Sasakwa. Large groups of impalas and some eland lounge under the trees, watching the Land Rover pass. An *askari* (guard) in a starched khaki uniform salutes smartly as the vehicle passes through the gate at the foot of the hill leading to the lodge. The road vectors sharply skyward, and then suddenly we are at the summit, confronting a building that seems a kind of hyperelegant palazzo, one subtly infused with the architectural precepts seen in the old colonial homes of Laikipia. I'm somehow reminded of La Cuesta Encantata, the mountain near the central California coast hamlet of San Simeon that supports Hearst Castle, William Randolph Hearst's Lucullan residence. Sasakwa, mercifully, avoids the rococo flourishes, the nothing-succeeds-like-excess impulses that characterize the castle and its grounds. But the end result is the same—a melding of an incomparable landscape with a remarkable edifice. During the day, the lodge is largely an open-air structure, the great doors of its major rooms swung wide into long passageways. Native stone constitutes the walls and the paving. Vast, slightly rolling sward and flower gardens, thick with butterflies, end in a wall at the brink of the steep slope running down to the plain. The views are beyond the purplest of adjectives: they seem to grab you in long claws by the forebrain, drag you over to one of the lounge chairs, and push you down. Fine telescopes allow you to zoom in on the individual animals on the savanna. You are served cold drinks and snacks. At night, you dine on haute cuisine; beyond the windows, a billion stars burn down from the darkened welkin. Ultimately, you are escorted to one of the eight private "cottages" to sleep—beautiful stone two-room bungalows, each with a private plunge pool. The staffers who work at Sasakwa are omnipresent but never intrusive, always on hand to provide something to eat or drink or to arrange a game drive, a horseback ride, a balloon flight, or appointments with the on-call masseuse or manicurist.

The luxury, in fact, is stifling to anyone not to the manor born. You can't peep past the door of your bungalow without an *askari* snapping to attention and asking if he can escort you somewhere. This is partly because of Sasakwa's peerless standard of service, but it also is a matter of safety, of minimizing liability. Sasakwa is an island surrounded by an African wilderness teeming with dangerous animals. A guest who decides to take a stroll down the hill on his own—even walk back to his cottage after several postprandial ports—could run into a Cape buffalo, elephant, lion, or puff adder, with predictably unpleasant results. Yet

FIGURE 8. Lions spar at Singita Grumeti Reserves. The reserves have one of the largest populations of charismatic predators in Tanzania. (Courtesy Singita Game Reserves)

this is precisely the lodge's greatest attraction: it is a snug capsule of civilized amenities anchored in one of the world's last truly untamed places.

Of course, this kind of experience is expensive—thirty-two hundred dollars or more per couple daily. This steep price is deliberate on Jones's part, for a variety of reasons. First, apparently Jones's natural inclination is to do things to the most exquisite and refined degree possible. Second, Grumeti supports a variety of ancillary endeavors to benefit locals, including primary and secondary schools, a scholarship fund, and sustainable agricultural projects. Once operating costs are covered at Grumeti, all revenues go to a fund supporting the surrounding communities. Third, if the lodge were within the price range of most people, more people would come. Jones wants the minimal number of guests paying the highest possible price; he wants to see his plains thronged with wildlife, not wildlife-besotted tourists. Finally, Jones is a businessman, and the Grumeti Reserves, in the end, is a business venture. By best estimates, Jones has invested more than seventy million dollars of his own money into the project; he doesn't expect a profit, says Rian, but neither does he want to throw money into the property indefinitely. Grumeti ultimately must pay its own way; that's why Singita was brought in as a managing partner. Despite the larger good it is serving,

FIGURE 9. Community residents on a tour of Singita Grumeti Reserves. Singita has initiated a number of programs for locals, including scholarships, game scout training, and commercial and agricultural loans. The hope is to provide the communities with a palpable stake in the reserves' success. (Courtesy Singita Game Reserves)

Grumeti is first and foremost a business and secondarily an exercise in environmental and social equity.

And integral to the Grumeti Reserves' business plan is hunting, Rian observes—not much, but some. Grumeti Reserves essentially consists of three old hunting blocks, and Jones continues to pay the full complement of trophy concessions for each, though very little game is taken. The maintenance of the hunting tradition at Grumeti is partly due to Jones's belief that ethical hunting is a noble and salutary endeavor. Jones is an avid bowhunter and has bagged a Cape buffalo—one of the most dangerous animals to hunt with a large-bore rifle, let alone a bow. But he allows hunting in some areas of Grumeti also because it helps the reserve pay its own way; considered client by client, hunting safaris typically generate far more income than photography and game-viewing safaris. Hunting therefore is an option Jones is determined to keep open.

The private enterprise approach to African conservation is unusual but not unique. In Mozambique, Greg Carr, an American, lapsed Mormon, Internet multimillionaire, and philanthropist, is basically funding the rehabilitation of the fifteen-hundred-square-mile Gorongosa National Park out of his own pocket. Gorongosa was once one of Africa's richest wildlife reserves, but its game was wiped out during the twenty-year civil war that engulfed Mozambique beginning in 1977. As noted earlier in this book, ranchers on the Laikipia Plateau in Kenya are also attempting ecotourism projects on their own properties that collectively encompass most of the regional ecosystem. But these ventures and Carr's are not proving easy to implement. In Gorongosa, Carr has managed to reestablish much of the wildlife, and tourists are once again returning. But he has encountered considerable resistance from local people, who resent his attempts to restrict their avid clear-cutting and slash-and-burn agriculture on nearby Mount Gorongosa, the source of half the water that enters the park. And in Laikipia, the challenges facing conservation are multiple—drought, war among the different pastoral tribes, latent antagonism between the central government and the region's remaining white ranchers, general population pressures, and, of course, the dispute between ascendant animal rights groups such as IFAW and old school habitat conservationists.

Jones also has significant long-term problems in Grumeti, and, again, most boil down to human numbers. While he has largely succeeded in protecting a great chunk of the Grumeti Corridor, and thus assuring the continuance of the annual wildebeest migration from the Maasai Mara to the Serengeti, he has his back to the wall. Just west of Grumeti is a crescent of heavily settled agricultural land; it is pressed against the eastern shore of Lake Victoria on one side and the reserves on the other. The human population of this region is swelling. The herds of cattle and goats are expanding as well, and the land is under increasing cultivation. It seems unlikely that Grumeti Reserves can remain isolated from the exigent needs of its western neighbors. At the very least, poaching will increase as the human population presses eastward; the invasion of livestock is probable as well. It is by no means clear whether Grumeti Reserves will prove viable in the long run. That points to a larger issue facing private conservation ventures in Africa. The best of intentions, the most effective management techniques, and the deepest of pockets ultimately may mean little if conservation initiatives are not driven by local communities.

In North America, projects similar to Grumeti and Gorongosa are under way—most notably, the efforts of erstwhile media mogul Ted Turner to transform a big chunk of the American Midwest into a kind of "buffalo commons." He has purchased more than two million acres on the high plains and is planting them with native grasses and stocking them with native fauna. If the vision he shares with a growing number of allies holds, wolves will once again harry buffalo calves through the tall grass, black-footed ferrets will hunt in sprawling prairie dog towns, and grizzlies will amble down from the Rocky Mountain front to dig for tubers and gophers on the plain. And because the rule of law and relatively sound governance characterize society in the United States, there is little doubt that Turner's plan is sustainable. The high plains conservancies that are now developing have been organized for the most part under long-term trusts, with the weight of the courts and the oversight of legions of well-paid attorneys supporting them. They will endure. But in Africa—Tanzania included—central governments are weak, and laws are subject to all the vagaries that money can buy. And even the laws that are maintained on the books are poorly enforced. Fiats from on high do not work; they simply have no force. For something to function, it has to be implemented and wholeheartedly accepted at the village level.

Alex Songorwa thinks Jones has made good progress on several fronts. "First, he has secured the integrity of the Grumeti ecosystem," Songorwa says. "He has beefed up anti-poaching patrols tremendously. He has bought up all the hunting quotas in the region but hardly uses them. And you see the results—the game has rebounded to a very impressive degree. He also is winning over the communities. He funds local enterprises and really supports education, right up to providing scholarships at the university level. I'm aware of at least one student at my own university who is supported completely by Jones. He has changed the way local people think about conservation; I believe he has created something that can endure."

Not everyone agrees with Songorwa. "Jones has accomplished remarkable things in Grumeti," says Tom McShane of Advancing Conservation in a Social Context. "But I'm not sure how long his project can be maintained. During his lifetime? Probably. But what happens after that? We need long-term protection for the Serengeti ecosystem, and that's extremely difficult for any outsider, no matter how well-intentioned and well-funded, to address."

Part of the problem, of course, is the deep-rooted distrust many Africans feel for the *muzungu*: the white man. The scars of colonialism have by no means faded in East Africa, and any endeavor that imposes strictures on the land tends to stimulate opposition. In an article on the Gorongosa project that ran in a 2009 issue of the *New Yorker*, Philip Gourevitch reports that a villager, dubious of Greg Carr's intentions and opposed to any policy that would restrict access to the region's forests, relates a local parable of the Monkey and the Fish. It goes like this: A monkey taking a stroll by a river looks into the water and sees a fish.

Thinking the fish is drowning, the monkey grabs it and hauls it out of the water. The fish flops around, and the monkey thinks the fish is expressing its gratitude at being saved. Of course, the fish dies, and the monkey thinks: too bad—if I had come along sooner, I could've saved him.

Many people living near Gorongosa, implies Gourevitch, feel they are the fish, and Carr, the quintessential do-gooding *muzungu*, is the monkey. The same could be said of Jones and villagers just beyond the Grumeti orbit or any other African conservation project involving large amounts of capital and foreigners with ambitious plans. No matter how progressive the undertaking, no matter how equitable its implementation, there will be some degree of regional resistance because the decisions are not being made by local people. And if the resistance lasts longer than the funding, or the simple will of the founding visionary, or the dedication of subsequent managers, the project is not sustainable.

But local management usually means business as usual. In the case of Gorongosa that translates as the continued diminution of the forest through fuel gathering and traditional agriculture; with Grumeti, it is chronic poaching and invasion by livestock. The villages within the Grumeti sphere of influence may support Jones and his vision, but the pastoralists and farmers encroaching from the margins have no reason to champion the reserve—quite the opposite.

Still, there is no arguing with results. Grumeti Reserves may or may not prove a long-term solution, but it must be acknowledged that the project is succeeding here and now, and succeeding spectacularly. At the very least, it is providing a respite—a speed bump on the road that is leading inexorably to the Serengeti's demise. And that in itself is valuable; anything that can delay catastrophe raises hopes that catastrophe may somehow, in the end, be avoided.

On my last afternoon at Grumeti, I get in an open-sided Land Rover with Rian and Lorna. We drive out on the plain fronting Sasakwa and watch the huge herd of topi and zebras. Then we drift into the woodlands, past a large fenced enclosure where some black rhinos browse, part of a project to restock the Grumeti Corridor with this signature and beleaguered species. We stop near a pride of lions, bloated from a recent kill, lolling in the rich, honey-colored light of the westering sun. We proceed past a large aggregate of Cape buffalo, switching their tails against the tsetse flies gnawing at their black hides, fixing us with contemptuous gazes, then on through the trees, where we abruptly find ourselves in a herd of elephants. Rian stops the Land Rover. The elephants are upset by our sudden appearance. The dominant matriarch of the herd is particularly irate: she bellows fiercely, flares her ears, and charges forward for a few yards. I once again feel that looseness in my limbs and the vaguely ill sensation that seem to characterize my encounters with testy megafauna. Rian refuses to move the vehicle.

"You don't want to spoil them," he explains. "If you let them push you around, they get used to it, get bolder. It makes them more dangerous." The matriarch trumpets again, arching her trunk, her anger palpable. She lunges again and looks—to me, at least—like she's preparing to launch into an unrestrained charge. Then she abruptly turns and lumbers back to a calf that was lingering in some bushes. She wraps her trunk around the young animal in a way that seems doting, hyperprotective, and the two of them sidle away, finally joining the main group; the older elephant never stops glaring and roaring at us.

The obvious anger of the matriarch, the bond she evinces with her young, the—for want of a better term—deep intelligence guiding her actions: it haunts me, makes me think of George Adamson's contention that shooting elephants should be a capital crime. But if it weren't for Jones's vision and the reality of the Grumeti Reserves, these animals wouldn't even be here; they'd be long dead, their ivory gone to the illegal but thriving workshops in Vietnam and China. If part of the price for maintaining Grumeti is some occasional trophy hunting—the shooting, say, of an ivory-laden old bull elephant, one infirm, bereft of clan and position—then isn't it worth it?

IFAW staffers, of course, would say no; the idea would strike them as deeply repugnant, immoral even. But that elderly bull would be dead within months in any event, feeding scavengers and contributing his ivory to any enterprising local who comes across his remains, and ultimately his tusks would end up in the black market. If taken by a wealthy hunter, however, that old bull would generate close to a hundred thousand dollars toward the preservation of the Grumeti Corridor. He would assure continued life for the fierce-eyed matriarch and her calf.

Rian starts up the Land Rover and we slowly drive away. I find that trying to cipher the moral mathematics of hunting such magnificent beasts as the elephants we've just encountered—or buffalo or lions—leaves my head throbbing. But one fact is unassailable: I am happy to be at the Grumeti Reserves. I'm happy to have seen it, happy to know that—for now, at least—it exists.

CHAPTER 11

Even the Cows Must Pay

The town of Nanyuki is expanding, moving out slowly from its modest urban center into the surrounding scrublands. Still, it takes perhaps fifteen minutes to transit temporally from the twenty-first-century Kenya of Internet cafés, minimalls, and coffee shops selling lattes to young backpackers and NGO staffers to the Kenya of the past ten thousand years, the Kenya of the immutable herder with his stick and his emaciated cows nuzzling for a surviving blade of grass among the dust and rocks. Because that's how it is as you head north from Nanyuki: you're driving along rutted streets flanked on each side by buildings in various states of decay, past hotels and bus depots and iron mongers' shops. Impromptu open-air markets mark the crossroads, with hawkers selling everything from wilted vegetables to pirated CDs and flip-flops; almost everything manufactured originates from China. Then the buildings dwindle and abruptly cease. You're in a kind of transition zone of beaten earth and destitute *manyattas,* with trash driven across the landscape by a parched wind. A bit farther are some eucalyptus plantings, the thin, evenly spaced trees·destined for the charcoal kiln.

Then it's all moth-eaten bush receding to far hills. Go-away-birds perch on some of the acacia trees, and the occasional spotted eagle cuts the sky. And of course, there are the ubiquitous herders and their cows and goats. Not a great many of either: the forage is scant, a drought is gripping the country, and already the livestock have begun to perish. But they remain, these animals and their tenders, the masters of this land, tenuous as their hold may be.

My driver, Matthew, has a good general fix on our destination—the ranch of the Honorable (Francis) Ole Kaparo, a former speaker of the Kenyan parliament, a Laikipia Maasai leader, and without doubt the biggest of the "big men" in and around Nanyuki. The trouble is—as usual in rural Kenya—there are no address placards, no mailboxes along the road. Occasionally, a graded track meanders off into the bush. Matthew knows one of these tracks leads to Kaparo's compound; it just takes us a while to find it. He stops by a herdboy of eight or nine who is slowly driving some cows among road. The lad is thin as a heron and dressed in what looks like a soiled flour sack pulled over his head. The two chat amiably, and the boy abruptly points down the road, toward the way we have come; he makes a waggling motion with his hand. Matthew wheels the car around: "We passed it."

A mile down the road we stop by a narrow drive blocked with a cable strung between two metal posts. I notice good fencing separates the property from the road, and the trees and brush on the opposite side of the wire are relatively lush; unlike most of the surrounding country, this land hasn't been overgrazed. Matthew unhooks the cable, and we drive through. Birds are suddenly everywhere: weaver finches of various types, spur fowl, superb starlings, wagtails, the big go-away-birds, myriad species I can't place. Matthew, an avid birder, identifies them all for me as we progress. It once again occurs to me how rich this highland country can be, given some precipitation and a respite from the relentless gnawing of the livestock.

We drive perhaps a mile and come to a kind of high stockade constructed from planks: Kaparo's compound. A couple of *askaris* stand by the gate and greet us politely. Nearby a herd of spotted cattle—sleek and fat compared to their counterparts on the other side of the road—stand in the shade of some thorn trees, chewing their cud. I remark on the animals, noting their admirable condition. Matthew nods. "He must keep cattle," he says, speaking of Kaparo. "He is Maasai." I've been in the country long enough to pick up on the deeper implications of Matthew's remark. Cattle are a traditional store of wealth in East Africa, considered more as cash-on-the-hoof than mere livestock. Cows are used freely as a true medium of exchange, to pay for everything from a dowry to land or a car. They are employed to settle debts or to satisfy civil judgments.

But to the Maasai, cattle transcend even this evaluation. No matter his place in society (politician, chief, or simple herdsman), no matter where he lives (in a Nairobi high-rise or a mud-and-wattle hut on the Serengeti), every Maasai male is, in his heart, a cattleman. The urge to own cattle is as natural, as urgent to him, as eating or breathing. The Maasai cow is loved. It is washed, petted, serenaded, curried. A favorite cow that has been devoured by a lion or expired from rinderpest is mourned deeply, sometimes with the fervor approaching the loss of a family member. Kaparo, one of the most powerful people in Kenya and a wealthy man by any account, has no pecuniary reason to keep cattle. Nor does he keep a great many of them, as demonstrated by the excellent condition of his rangeland. But as Matthew observed, he *must* keep cattle: he is Maasai.

One of the *askaris* unlatches the gate to the high fence and disappears inside. He returns in a few minutes, opens the gate wide, and motions us in. Something is pulling at my brain as I walk into the compound, which is composed of a large, low house surrounded by expansive lawns and gardens, the whole circuited by the tall palings. Then it hits me: lovely as it is, this residence nevertheless is built along the lines of a standard Maasai *manyatta:* a central residence surrounded by a well-fenced corral. His position notwithstanding, Kaparo continues to maintain the cultural precepts that shaped him as a boy. I remember what Laurence Frank once told me: "The Maasai are a deeply conservative people." Not conservative in any kind of flag-waving, jingoistic American sense of the word, of course: rather, conservative in that change generally is anathema to them. They already know the ideal existence—life on the Serengit, the land that goes forever, surrounded by one's cattle, one's family, one's clan members. Any deviation from this state can only be for the worse.

Kaparo greets me on the veranda of his home and graciously ushers me in. Typical for a Maasai man, he is tall. He carries some extra pounds, a testament to his position in society: men of wealth and influence are expected to eat well in this part of the world. His demeanor is calm and reflective, his voice soft. The interior of his home smells deliciously of skillful cooking; his wife and some of his grown sons, sitting around a long table, are finishing off a late and lavish breakfast. Kaparo sits me down with his family, introduces me to his spouse and children, and gives me a cup of hot, milky tea. As we talk, his family slowly continues their meal, generally ignoring our conversation.

Though he holds no public office at the time of our interview, Kaparo continues to exert his influence over government policy through political allies in both Nairobi and the countryside. He is particularly concerned about the Draft Wildlife Bill, the pending legislation that, depending on its final version, could either end Kenya's hunting ban or continue it. He speaks candidly of both his allies and his foes—in itself a marker of his power, given the diffidence I have noted among lesser East African politicians and functionaries when addressing policy issues and personalities. He directs his most pointed broadsides against the International Fund for Animal Welfare.

"IFAW is trouble," he says, sipping his tea. "It is as simple as that. These foreign animal rights groups—they have become the biggest hindrance in establishing any meaningful and effective wildlife policy. They have immense resources, and they use them to subvert the wholly legitimate rights of communities and landowners to use wildlife." Kaparo disparages IFAW members as clueless urbanites who have no grasp of the fundamentals of Kenyan rural society and wildlife conservation and the sustainable limits of land and water.

"They live in Nairobi, and they are only knowledgeable about law and legislative policy," he said. "Don't get me wrong—that, along with their money, is what makes them so effective. They are extremely well-organized, and the moral and financial support they receive from their partisans in Europe and North America have made them dominant. We—pastoral people—are poorly organized and poorly funded. But they have no grounding in *real life*. They don't understand how things work, out here where the animals and the communities must coexist. Moreover, the policies they force don't directly affect them; they live in the cities, after all. But their policies certainly affect us—the people who actually share the land with the wildlife. We don't tell them how to live, but they tell us how we *must* live."

Kaparo abruptly changes the topic to livestock, and we briefly discuss the challenges of raising cattle in the semiarid pastoral lands of northern Kenya: the lack of reliable precipitation, the scant forage, the abundant diseases and parasites, the constant threats from predators and rustlers. Cattle stealing is an endemic problem for all the pastoral tribes; raids and counterraids between clans and communities constitute a tradition reaching back millennia and continuing to the present time. This is due partly to cultural underpinnings; young *moran* traditionally have demonstrated courage and martial prowess, virtues highly esteemed in pastoral communities, by killing lions and participating in cattle raids. But cattle rustling also occurs because cattle are currency; they represent immense value to pastoral people, and items of value are scarce in the rangelands. It is true, says Kaparo, that the Maasai and other pastoral tribes esteem their cattle for emotional, even spiritual, reasons. On the other hand: "This is Kenya," he says, signaling for more tea from a maid who is hovering nearby with a fresh pot. "More to the point, this is Laikipia. It is not Nairobi. In all the rural areas of this nation, we understand reality very well. We have that grounding in real life that I mentioned. And what we understand is that nothing, and nobody, eats for free." He stirs his tea slowly. "Our cattle are very important to us, but they are not pets. Like everything else, they have a debt. Here, even the cows must pay."

Given this inflexible accounting, then, the idea that wild animals are somehow sacrosanct, that they are exempt from paying their life debt, is absurd. Most of Kenya's wildlife lives on private lands outside the parks and reserves, but the stability of the situation is by no means assured if laws proscribing the legal use of wild animals are maintained, Kaparo says. Kenya's swelling population demands that the land is put to productive uses; there can be no alternative. The efforts to turn private lands into game reserves supported by ecotourism have been successful only to a point: "It can be part of the solution but not the whole solution. 'Green' tourism is sensitive to any number of factors—the quality of the lodges, the concentrations of game, civil unrest. We have plenty of evidence that it isn't enough to support the community lands."

Moreover, observes Kaparo, ecotourism is a capital-intensive endeavor, and capital is a resource that most tribal homelands lack. The funds required to construct lodges agreeable to foreign tourists and provide the necessary guides and security are beyond the reach of virtually all the pastoral communities. Nor is the only feasible alternative—partnership with a company or individual willing to invest in such projects—particularly attractive. Experience has taught the communities that significant investments from an outside developer can benefit the developer but not necessarily community members—the people who live in *manyattas* and herd goats and cattle. In the end, the tourists may come, and profits may well flow to the investor. Some ancillary benefits to the tribe in the form of a clinic, a school, a new well, may accrue. But somehow, the people who live in the *manyattas* and herd livestock still live in *manyattas* and herd livestock, except now they may find greater restrictions on their rights to graze their cattle, collect firewood, farm, kill depredating wildlife, or take an antelope for the pot. Thus, their traditional way of life, pastoralism, has been compromised significantly and for relatively little in the way of recompense. Further, tradition must not be considered lightly in such a context, Kaparo warns: experience has taught the pastoral tribes that the cultural verities that have guided them over thousands of years are their greatest asset, a patrimony not to be spurned for a handful of Kenyan shillings and promises of rich cargo.

"So it shouldn't be any surprise that the communities generally view wildlife as a problem," Kaparo says. "The people are prevented from benefiting from it in any way. They can't hunt it. They can have trouble getting compensation when a lion kills their cattle. And the way things are set up, ecotourism ventures can make things even worse—they end up with more restrictions and little or no direct payoff."

The wildlife legislation that IFAW is pushing only exacerbates an already untenable situation, says Kaparo. "It not only confirms the [big game hunting] ban but extends it to fishing, bird hunting; it could be construed to include insects, even microorganisms. It would be a complete catastrophe. Sport hunting for spur fowl and guinea fowl produces quite a bit of income for some of the community lands, especially those held by the Samburu. This bill would eliminate that and provide nothing in return. It could also make many standard agricultural practices technically illegal."

What's needed at this juncture is neither more legislation that further restricts pastoralist rights, nor convoluted ecotourism schemes, Kaparo continues; instead, a little common sense is in order. "One thing animal rights advocates overlook when they praise Kenya's wildlife policy is the simple fact that there is no law compelling people to keep wildlife on their land," Kaparo says. "The law simply disallows legal hunting. But poaching, snaring—the illegal killing of game—is impossible to control. And animals killed this way are impossible to market legally, so their only value is as bushmeat and contraband products. For the initial purveyor, the return is low. So the simple solution for the pastoralist is to eliminate wildlife completely. No wild animals, no problem; they aren't killing your cows, they aren't eating your grass, they're not spreading livestock diseases. If we want game on private land twenty or thirty years from now, we have to provide incentives, not additional impediments."

Josep Oriol and Alayne Cotterill rent a small, snug home on a ranch not far from Kaparo's compound. Both are deeply involved in the nuts-and-bolts of wildlife conservation: Cotterill is the lead field researcher for the Laikipia Predator Project, and Oriol is a partner in Conservation Capital, a group that plans and funds private wildlife conservation ventures in East Africa. They are an extremely attractive couple. Cotterill is in her thirties, tall, blond, slim, with large blue eyes and finely wrought features. Oriol is about the same age, trim and muscular, dark where Cotterill is fair. They somehow would look more appropriate attired in couture clothes, lazing at a sidewalk café on a Paris boulevard, than hanging out on the back verandah of their Laikipia home, dressed in T-shirts and khaki shorts, knocking back a couple of cold Tuskers. They are, however, the real deal: able habitat conservationists who spend months of each year living rough in the bush.

Cotterill's expertise is lions and hyenas; in the course of her work, she has snared and tranquilized scores of them, fitting them with telemetry collars so their movements can be tracked. Part of her research focuses on the ways these predators behave and interact with each other and their environment. But the bigger goal is their conservation. Working in concert with local ranchers, Cotterill keeps track of potentially trouble-some predators, advises pastoralists on their presence, helps construct *bomas* to protect livestock, and generally promotes the idea that big meat-eating animals can live in relative peace with cattle, goats, and camels. This is, of course, a challenging vocation even in Laikipia, where wildlife on private lands generally is accorded better treatment than in other parts of Kenya.

Like Kaparo, Cotterill feels hampered by Kenyan wildlife policy. It sounds like a paradox, she says, but there would be more lions in Laikipia if authorities and habitat conservationists had a freer hand in control-ling them. "Right now, there are maybe 200 or 250 lions in Laikipia," she said. "But with policy change, the region could easily accommodate twice that, with no real drop in plains game populations or significant increase in cattle predation. But that's not going to happen under the cur-rent situation."

Cotterill explains that Kenyan agencies, specifically the Kenyan Wild-life Service, have become so infused with an animal rights perspective that problem wildlife have become impossible to address effectively. Not long ago, an injured lion near the Maasai Mara had been identified as a livestock killer. In such situations, the effective response is to kill the lion. Once a lion suffers a chronic injury and begins killing livestock, it becomes virtually impossible to rehabilitate; full recovery from a seri-ous wound or broken bones is unlikely under any but the most seren-dipitous circumstance, and a lion that begins killing cows will keep kill-ing them. But instead of dispatching the lion, the Kenya Wildlife Service trapped it, moved it to another area, and released it—a move that was hailed by Kenyan animal rights advocates as progressive and humane but one that was roundly condemned by habitat conservationists, since it merely shifted the burden from one group of pastoralists and ranchers to another. Too, lions released into new territories likely will encounter lions that already live there, who will either inflict new wounds or kill it outright.

"Nobody sees that when it happens, of course, so everyone pushing the translocation option keeps their halos," says Cotterill. "Really, it's maddening. The biggest conservation problem we're facing is the lack of good control for problem animals. One lion can kill hundreds of domestic animals. They not only impose tremendous burdens on local people, but they create a great deal of ill will for wildlife in general."

Kenyans are not passive people and tend to deal with problems directly. The only sympathy rogue lions will engender in this country is among the relatively few animal rights advocates headquartered in Nairobi. Virtually everyone else fully supports the swift termination of any animal, especially a predator, that threatens human life or property. Most if not all of the time, says Cotterill, pastoralists or farmers will take their complaints to the authorities, but they will act with dispatch if official response is sluggish. At that point, the problem will be eliminated through poison, snare, or spear.

"What makes it especially frustrating [with regard to lions] is that very often the problem animals are the ones trophy hunters prize," Cotterill continues. "Typically, they're the old males. They've been supplanted by younger males in the pride and are on their own. Their teeth hurt, because they're worn and broken. They're getting slow. Without a pride, it's difficult or impossible for them to catch wild game. Basically, they're entering the last months of their lives. So they turn to cattle—or people—and start pissing everybody off. Under current law, that animal can't be legally killed by the locals or a professional or trophy hunter. But the situation is intolerable; you can't have a dangerous animal wandering around killing cows or people. So the locals are going to poison the lion and leave it to rot. And along with the lion, everything else that eats meat in the vicinity dies—vultures, bat-eared foxes, jackals." But if you could sell the rights to kill that lion, says Cotterill, it'd generate tens of thousands of dollars, and local pastoralists could be well-compensated: "Then you'd suddenly switch to a situation to where a liability becomes a source of profit. Lions would be valued, not despised."

The lion problem points to a larger issue, observes Oriol: the costs of maintaining wildlife on the land are high. Echoing Kaparo's epigrammatic observation that even cows must pay for the grass they eat,

Oriol maintains that successful wildlife conservation plans are those that incorporate as many layers of income as possible. "You really need to maximize the opportunities," Oriol says. "Donors are certainly important—wealthy foreigners with a passion for African wildlife who want to fund large-scale conservation endeavors, NGOs, whatever. But those investments by themselves can have little or nothing in the way of return, and ultimately an investment that doesn't pay back is looking at failure, especially in Africa. In the end, you have a situation where the wildlife on your land is going to be poached, cropped, or subjected to trophy hunting. The first alternative costs you; it reduces your assets. The second two pay. Cropping is less remunerative than hunting, but it's more appropriate for some holdings—say, a place that has lots of Burchell's zebra."

And in any conservancy endeavor, Cotterill interjects, flexibility is paramount. Doctrinaire positions—an obvious aside to IFAW—are, she says, tantamount to failure. "For it to succeed, it's a process, like zeroing in a rifle," she said. "You always have to be tweaking it. Adaptive management is the only management that works around here."

Oriol is currently involved in putting together a one-hundred-million-dollar conservancy deal in the Niassa region of Mozambique, a project that excites him immensely. The management plan he is helping develop for the Niassa Reserve will emphasize, in stark contrast to Kenya's policies, both the preservation and regulated use of wildland resources.

Niassa, explains Oriol, is a chunk of pristine forest, savannah, and wetland the size of Switzerland in the northeastern portion of the country, on the Tanzanian border. Most of Niassa was declared a reserve in 1954 but has never been properly managed as a wildlife refuge. For most of the fifty-five years following its founding, Niassa was a mere paper reserve—or worse, a hunting ground for political elites and poachers. It is only lately that progressive policies have begun to be implemented on the ground, including the designation of a core zone where all hunting is completely banned.

From the late 1970s to the early 1990s, Mozambique was swallowed in civil war, turning into a conservation black box; nobody knew what was happening to the country's wildlife, though the worst was suspected. Indeed, after the shooting stopped in 1992, it was obvious that much of the wildlife had been depleted. But significant pockets of game remained while the human population was relatively low as a result of war casualties and the flight of refugees. Moreover, the habitat was largely intact, particularly in Niassa. The persistence of land mines and the abundance of tsetse make Niassa unsuitable for ambitious livestock operations, so the wildlife quickly expanded with the cessation of open warfare.

Niassa today is brimming with game, not only Cape buffalo and elephants, but also other charismatic species, including sable antelope: the legendary black antelope of the bushveldt that can weigh in excess of five hundred pounds and sports massive, backward curving horns. "There are almost twenty thousand sable in Niassa now, making it the largest population in Africa," says Oriol. "It's a tremendous opportunity down there; we just need to get it right."

More specifically, getting it right means making sure Niassa residents share in the resource, continues Oriol. While Africa wildlife enthusiasts may look at Niassa and see a World Heritage Site ripe for heavy regulation, the locals see the woodlands, the water, and the wildlife as assets. That latter view can't be given short shrift, Oriol warns. Indeed, care must be taken to make sure the wildlife is identified as something that can benefit local communities; otherwise, the animals of Niassa will succumb wholesale to snaring, spearing, and poisoning, just as in Kenya. That's why simply declaring Niassa a government protectorate and assuming tourism will provide sufficient revenue is a specious strategy, says Oriol: "Whenever you remove an asset from an equation and assign it to the government, you have created a tax," he says. "You turn it from something that can provide goods and services to something that must bear costs."

In ten or twenty years, says Oriol, Niassa will have developed enough infrastructure so that ecotourism might provide sufficient incentives to preserve the wildlife. "But how much wildlife would be left then if you didn't have other means of providing income during the interim? Not much. So instead, we're looking at preserving core zones—say, areas that support species of concern or particularly large concentrations of game. All uses will be nonconsumptive here; these will be the areas reserved for ecotourism. But around these we'll have buffer zones where regulated hunting and other compatible consumptive uses are allowed."

Oriol acknowledges that criticism of both trophy and subsistence hunting in Africa is legitimate. "Yes, there are problems—real problems. But those problems are being used as an argument to eliminate hunting rather than reforming it. That's no good either. Hunting can be a very useful tool in conservation strategy, and we have to use every tool available to us."

Ultimately, the issue comes down to social equity, says Cotterill, "and that's something of an irony. Because social justice is a major talking point with NGOs like IFAW. They claim that preserving wildlife for 'the nation' is a major social justice issue. That's why they pay their staffers salaries that are commensurate with salaries in developed countries—they want to emphasize their 'fairness.' And that means IFAW staffers are truly rich by Kenyan standards. But is it social justice for a pastoralist to lose two or three of his twenty cows because of existing wildlife policy? Basically, you have a group that maintains a highly recompensed staff in Nairobi—literally, a privileged class. Meanwhile, the policies that those staffers promote result in tragic consequences for rural Kenyans. It is the impoverished pastoralist who must pay—and pay and pay—for these policies. Where's the social justice in that?"

CHAPTER 12

Elephant Man

Max Graham could easily engender envy in any but the most well-favored and accomplished man. Well over six feet and exceedingly fit, he is also almost ridiculously handsome, with carved features, white regular teeth, a mane of glossy chestnut hair, and a three-day beard that artfully keeps him from being too pretty. Spend a little time with him, and you can't help but notice that women of all ages and stations—fellow field researchers, NGO staffers, shopkeepers, vegetable vendors—palpitate slightly when he engages them. Professional achievement complements his fortunate genetics: he is one of the most respected wildlife biologists in Kenya. Only a superbly sunny, self-deprecating, and companionable disposition makes his obvious alpha maleness bearable; he is so genuinely sweet-natured that you can't help but wish the best for him.

And that's a good thing, because Graham is embarked on perhaps the most difficult mission in East African wildlife conservation: maintaining and ultimately expanding the region's elephant population. Actually, that's not quite it. Graham is the director of a University of Cambridge program on human and wildlife conflicts, with elephants as the primary subject of research. He has implemented a pilot program in Laikipia that, he hopes, will prove sufficiently effective to warrant expansion to the rest of Kenya and beyond. Given the controversies that wild elephants stimulate in the regions where they live, Graham needs every scintilla of goodwill that his academic credentials, amiable personality, natural talent for public relations, and good looks can generate.

Graham notes there's some good news on Laikipia's elephants, or at least it seems that way when you look at the population statistics. Their numbers expanded from fifty-two hundred in 2002 to seventy-four hundred in 2008. But these figures, says Graham, belie inherent difficulties in continuing the expansion, or even the long-term maintenance, of the region's herds. The uptick in Laikipia's elephants, he observes, was largely due to the general era of peace and stability that the species enjoyed from the early 1990s through 2005.

"During this period poaching declined dramatically," says Graham, "and there was significant investment by the government, NGOs, and private landowners for wildlife-friendly development projects. That's not to say that Laikipia's elephants didn't face any stresses—they did. But everything considered, this was a pretty good time for them."

But Laikipia is not an inviolate preserve patrolled by regiments of well-armed, well-funded rangers. With the exception of a few national reserves, it is under private ownership. Livestock culture of one form or another—modern ranching on tracts owned by foreign investors or white Kenyans, quasi-nomadic pastoralism on the tribal holdings—dominates the economy. That means elephants often show up in places where they are not welcome and often end up engaging in activities that are deeply displeasing to landowners—stomping cattle, charging livestock herders, laying waste to croplands and flower gardens.

Such forays are not lightly tolerated by ranchers and pastoralists; indeed, they are met with emphatic resistance. An emblematic construction in Laikipia is an elephant repellent device consisting of a series of large electrified cables dangling from a lintel over a ranch compound driveway. The cables are long enough to touch the backs of any inquisitive elephant, delivering powerful, dissuading shocks. Just as often, elephants are harried away from areas where they are not welcomed. They may be chased by angry herders, roused by flash-bangs (nonlethal grenadelike charges), or peppered with bird-shot. Those exhibiting habitually dangerous behavior may be killed, though this is relatively rare. These regular and unpleasant encounters with human beings have made Laikipia's elephants unpredictable in their behavior; they are known as some of the testiest elephants in Kenya, far less tractable than those found in Tsavo or Amboseli (though the elephants found in those parks, or anywhere else in Africa, can hardly be considered cuddly and friendly).

Such tensions notwithstanding, Laikipia's elephants flourished from 1990 to 2005. Not only were their numbers up, Graham observes, but also their social fabric had mended. Family groups exhibited stable inter-actions. Migratory behavior had begun to emerge, with elephants feel-ing comfortable enough to reestablish some of their old routes through Laikipia to contiguous portions of the Northern Frontier District. The Lewa Wildlife Conservancy, a community-based organization, has helped protect millions of acres in northern Kenya, establishing land for both traditional pastoralism and wildlife. Elephants have benefited tre-mendously from this one initiative alone, says Graham.

But those encouraging trends are being countered by some ominous developments; one in particular is having devastating effects. "Since the late 1990s, there has been a huge influx of armed Somalis into [northern Kenya]," Graham says. "The response of the government was to arm the local communities so they could protect themselves and their property. That was understandable, but it's had some unfortunate consequences."

Specifically, the government's decision to create an informal home guard sidestepped the issue of existing conflicts among Kenya's resi-dent communities. The Pokot, Turkana, Marakwet, and Samburu tribes all feel deep enmity toward Somalis, but they also are at odds with one another over grazing land and water sources. Cattle raiding among the four tribes is a tradition that extends back thousands of years, and the practice invariably is accompanied by combat and bloodshed. While it is a matter of debate whether the Somalis have been checked in their dep-redations by providing northern Kenya's tribes with automatic weap-ons, it is clear that the policy has intensified the internecine carnage among the country's pastoral communities. Before, they had spears, *run-gus,* and the occasional single-shot shotgun or old Enfield rifle; now they have AK-47s.

When I was in Kenya not long ago, the newspapers were filled with accounts of the Pokot-Samburu "war" along the Great Rift Valley: vir-tual tribal armies were engaged in pitched battles, and the body count was high. In the hotel bars of Nanyuki, old-timers told stories of ranch-ers who had witnessed firefights from their living-room windows. "A friend of mine and his wife had to sit there and just watch these peo-ple shoot each other up," a man with a massive frame, magisterial paunch, sun-ravaged face, and satchel-sized hands told me over a cou-ple of Tuskers. "Some Samburu came up to their house with a terribly wounded friend and asked them for help, but they couldn't do it. If they had, the Pokot would've found out and taken the fight to them. It's a bloody mess."

Of course, when people are fighting one another over the basic means of subsistence, wildlife is apt to get short shrift. "It is pretty much a given that the game can't flourish where the locals own a lot of automatic weapons," Graham drily observes. "The wild animals, including elephants, have been wiped out or driven out in most of the areas where the fighting is going on. We're going to have to deal with this decision to put guns into the northern territories for a long time to come."

Obviously, tribal conflict is no anomaly in this part of Africa: Rwanda, where close to one million Tutsis died at the hands of Hutu militants in 1994, is less than three hundred miles from the southern border of Kenya. Kenya's central government is weak. But sooner or later, it will, in all likelihood, be able to exert sufficient pressure—through either armed troops or financial incentives—to stifle the pastoralist conflict to the point that it's at least at an angry simmer rather than a full boil. And while wandering groups of herders armed with assault rifles are devastating for wildlife, the long-term impact is less than an ambitious development project would be—say, a big hydropower plant or a new asphalt road. If the habitat remains intact, the animals will return once the relentless killing stops. "Wildlife populations around here can be directly correlated to available space," observes Graham. "That's especially so for elephants. If we can maintain large expanses of reasonably good habitat, we can have elephants. In Kenya, most of the habitat that meets those conditions is in the north—Laikipia and the Northern Frontier."

These districts constitute about half of Kenya. They're the best candidates for enhancing the country's megafauna, not because they're rich and lush, but rather, the opposite is true. They're valuable for what they lack. They do not have deep, well-watered soils. On the contrary, they are arid or semiarid with poor, thin soils. They are suitable only for grazing, and limited grazing at that. Because the land is so poor, it has never been heavily populated by humans. Wildlife, however, can and does thrive here, as long as poaching is controlled. Beyond this common necessity for basic law, however, the strategies for megafauna preservation—more to the point, elephant preservation—differ.

At this writing, the Northern Frontier is a no-man's-land, roamed freely by *shifta* and Somali irregulars. The foremost strategy for securing this vast region as habitat, then, is precisely that: *securing* it. There must be an armed presence of sufficient size and competence to stifle the brigands and allow the presence of scientists and game managers. The problem is a large one, but it is by no means insurmountable. The Northern Frontier is lawless, but it isn't held by an organized army. Given the harshness of the country, even the bandits are scarce. As Ian Parker and his compatriots demonstrated fifty years ago when they patrolled the Northern Frontier, the district can be reasonably secured with relatively few men, as long as they are dedicated, well-supported, and ably led.

Things aren't quite the same in Laikipia. For the newcomer, Laikipia looks similar to the Northern Frontier District: vast expanses of scrubland conforming to a rugged topography of peaks, bluffs, deep gorges, and rolling plateaus. But there are significant differences that may not be immediately apparent. First, Laikipia is semiarid, while the Northern Frontier is truly arid: Laikipia may receive up to six hundred millimeters of rain annually, but the Northern Frontier District gets half that or less. This difference in precipitation means Laikipia's land is correspondingly valued more highly than land in the Northern Frontier. Laikipia may be sparsely settled, but it supports far more people than the Northern Frontier—too many, in fact, to allow the free movement of elephants. "Laikipia," says Graham, "is a human landscape." Elephant preservation in the region, he says, therefore depends on good fencing, not to keep the elephants enclosed in specific areas, but to exclude them.

"It's already well along," says Graham, speaking of the fencing of Laikipia. "There's a 163-kilometer fence running from east to west that separates potential cropland from some large ranches where elephants are tolerated, and there's a project to the north that protects approximately 45 square kilometers of elephant habitat."

A word about elephant fencing: it is not at all comparable to the fencing used in North America either to keep wildlife out or to contain livestock. In the United States, an eight-foot-tall mesh fence on hefty metal stakes is considered adequate to exclude everything up to and including elk. Bison fencing is far more robust, often consisting of welded metal pipe. But no self-respecting African elephant would be deterred by such barriers. An effective elephant fence is by its very definition an electric fence: high-tensile electrified wires run through industrial insulators that are fixed to massive metal or hardwood posts sunk into concrete. Sometimes trenches are dug along the wire as well. Elephant fences are expensive and require a great amount of labor to erect and maintain. And it can all be for nothing.

"There's no such thing as an elephant-proof fence," says Graham, smiling pensively as he recollects some instances of elephants that were undeterred by one impediment or another. "Usually it only takes about three months for some of them to figure out a barrier. Sometimes they'll stack branches on the wire to short it out. Or the dominant ones will push smaller elephants through to the same effect. Maintenance and repair is a given; you can't just put up a fence and walk away, expecting that everything will be fine."

Indeed, one of Graham's greatest problems in devising strategies for human and pachyderm coexistence is dealing with the elephant that is too smart for everybody's good, including its own—the elephant that cannot be contained by any fence, regardless of design or construction. IFAW and other groups invariably oppose killing such highly intelligent and contrary animals, favoring translocation instead. But tracking, darting, and transporting such a wily, wild, and immensely large beast typically involves a great deal of planning, money, and human hours—all of which are in short supply for Graham and other field scientists involved in the nuts and bolts of elephant conservation. "On top of that, your chances of successfully relocating the animals are pretty low," he observes. "If you're going to put them into an area that doesn't have any elephants, it's probably unsecured, and they'll be poached or immediately run into trouble with local communities. If there are elephants in the area, the new elephant may not make a successful transition to a new group. There's no guarantee it will be accepted and survive." All of which can make translocation of Laikipia's fence-busting elephants impractical. "I'm not saying it's never an option," Graham continues. "Sometimes it makes sense, and when it does we'll do it. There are also other things we could look into, such as cutting the tusks [of elephants that use them to short out wires], but we're not geared up to pursue that at this point."

Sooner or later, then, the question must be raised for Laikipia: How many elephants? Fenced holdings, no matter how expansive, ultimately won't be large enough for a burgeoning elephant population. A fenced preserve containing elephants is a preserve that must address excessive elephants or face utter habitat destruction; no animal, save *Homo sapiens,* is as adept at destroying woodlands as elephants. In his meetings and seminars with locals, Graham covers a wide range of nonlethal alternatives for elephant control, including fencing and aversive therapy techniques employing nonlethal devices such as flash-bangs. But he can't avoid the Malthusian dialectic implicit in elephant conservation in modern African: restoring an elephant population can quickly lead to too many elephants, devastated habitat, and then, once again, no elephants.

"It's clear to me that we may have to consider culling at some point for some properties," Graham muses. If and when that point is reached, however, implementation of a culling program will be problematic. First and foremost, Graham says, the craft of elephant shooting is almost extinct in Kenya. Efficient and humane elephant culling depends on the ability to kill entire family groups with brain shots in a few seconds—the kind of skills possessed by only a few people in Kenya today, specifically, retired and aging rangers and wardens such as Ian Parker.

In fact, elephants are already being killed today in Laikipia, as a matter of practical and ad hoc necessity. On one of my trips to Kenya a few years ago, residents of a small aggregate of *manyattas* near Mpala had just polished off the last scraps of meat from a rogue elephant that had been charging around the countryside for some time, stomping cattle. The beast had been messily—and by all accounts, inhumanely—dispatched by Kenya Wildlife Service rangers, who had peppered it with automatic weapons fire. "It was a goddamn mess," said one researcher who was working out of Mpala at the time. "I mean, it was precisely the opposite of a clean brain shot from a large-bore gun fired by an experienced hunter. The KWS rangers are poorly trained, and they certainly don't have the weapons or expertise for dealing with elephants."

Such a demise, unfortunately, is probably as good as it gets for Laikipia's outlier elephants. "A lot of them are speared," Graham says. "I wouldn't have said this five years ago, but it's clear to me we may have to establish an elephant-shooting school at some point. We need to start training people now, because in a few years this entire skill set will be lost in Kenya."

And that brings Graham up against his second, and larger, problem in establishing a coherent culling program: government policy. Under the current wildlife laws, the killing of each animal must be approved by the Kenya Wildlife Service and, in most cases, carried out by KWS staff. This makes efficient culling impossible; as noted, the KWS is incapable of fielding sufficient numbers of properly armed and trained staffers to deal with rampaging megafauna. The recent attempts to change the Wildlife Conservation and Management Act to accommodate some killing of game would have allowed elephant culling, but for now the requirements for establishing a legal cull are too ponderous even to consider such a strategy.

"Of course, elephant killing is ongoing," Graham says. "We're just leaving it to the poachers on one hand and the farmers and pastoralists who are threatened by elephants on the other. Laws that expressly forbid the killing of wildlife in any and all circumstances do nothing to save wildlife in Africa and actually work to the opposite effect by creating tremendous resentment among community members. Without the legal authority to kill elephants as necessary, we're decreasing our ability to conserve them."

Given the limitations of space in Laikipia and the exigent biological requirements of elephants, the "utilization" question becomes crucial, Graham continues. As noted elsewhere in this book, an elephant that must be removed for bad behavior still represents a tremendous resource for local people: literally tons of meat and, in the case of old bulls bearing heavy ivory, hefty trophy fees from sport hunters. The line between dispassionately identifying, shooting, and consuming problem animals and unregulated killing can be a fine one, but it must be walked in Laikipia if a sizable and stable elephant population is the goal. The alternatives are not acceptable, says Graham. If elephants are rigorously protected but their populations are not controlled, they will ultimately destroy Laikipia's rangeland, then crash in numbers. If active protection is abandoned, the herds will be wiped out by poachers or farmers protecting their holdings. Ultimately, the only model that can work is protection of both the elephants and the range, with a program that allows locals to derive benefits from excess animals.

Legal hunting is even more crucial for the Northern Frontier District, says Graham. "To a significant degree, that's the real hope for Kenya's elephants," he says. "Assuming we can establish adequate security, it represents a tremendous chunk of habitat. But its economic potential will always be limited. It's hot as hell, it's incredibly desolate, and security will always remain an issue, even if it's improved to the point that wildlife can rebound. In other words, it has virtually nil ecotourism potential. No tourist would want to go there. But hunters *will* go. They aren't put off by remote places, poor or nonexistent infrastructure, even danger. They actually like it—it's part of the experience they're seeking. If the Northern Frontier District is going to realize its full wildlife potential, it needs an economic driver, and trophy hunting is one of the options that could actually work. During Kenya's colonial period, the Northern Frontier was considered a prime safari district, world renowned among trophy hunters—it could be again."

But if Graham supports policies that allow regulated utilization of Kenyan elephants, he is quick to qualify his position. Any authorized consumption must exclude the ivory trade. Trophy hunting is one thing: legal ownership of constituent parts would be assigned to the hunters who shoot the animals, and no commerce in ivory would be allowed; the tusks would be relatively easy to register and track. Indeed, there is virtually no incentive for a wealthy hunter to chop up and sell his ivory. A man who can pay fifty thousand dollars or more for a successful elephant hunt isn't going to sell the primary memento from the experience. Allowing communities to trade in the ivory they obtain from elephant culling, however, would be a catastrophe. The growing middle class in China has created a concomitant demand for ivory products, and the Chinese government has shown no inclination to stem the illicit trade.

"Right now, ivory is selling for fifteen hundred to two thousand dollars a kilo on the black market—the only market that exists for it," says Graham. "Even a small elephant will carry ten kilos or so of ivory, so the profit potential is enormous. If we allowed even a 'regulated' trade in ivory, every poacher from here to Somalia would pile in and wipe out all of Laikipia's elephants in nothing flat. Equatorial Africa—the Congo and Cameroon—used to have huge herds just ten years ago, and the illegal ivory trade has almost eliminated them. Any kind of legal market would just accelerate the process."

Still, benefits derived from conservation must devolve to the communities if elephants—indeed, large game animals in general—are to survive in Laikipia. And a successful model for this already exists, says Graham: the Northern Rangelands Trust (NRT), a subsidiary project of the Lewa Wildlife Conservancy. Lewa has its origins in the five-thousand-acre Ngare Sergoi Rhino Sanctuary, established in 1983 by Laikipia ranchers David and Delia Craig. The sanctuary has since undergone a name change and a dramatic expansion: it now stands at forty thousand acres and supports 440 species of birds and 70 mammal species. The Craigs were also cofounders of the nearby Ol Pejeta Conservancy, which operates under similar policies and contains the largest population of black rhinos in Kenya.

In 2004, Lewa engaged with the Kenyan government and other regional conservancies to form the NRT, an umbrella organization that promotes the creation of wildlife corridors, the sustainable use of resources, and the improvement of local communities on three million acres of land. "Lewa did an incredible job setting up that trust," said Graham. "They did a tremendous amount of outreach with the communities, made them full partners in every sense. They were patient, and they were driven by pragmatism, not doctrine. Some very astute and sophisticated trade-offs were involved. Conservation goals were balanced with land rights, agricultural needs, and tribal community support. But in the end, they effectively protected millions of acres of habitat. I think the Northern Rangelands Trust has a very good chance of succeeding, and that's because it was put together from the bottom up, not the top down."

More broadly, Lewa and its subsidiary trust represent the best hope for Kenya's wildlife, says Graham. The parks have largely failed, as has the no-killing-under-any-circumstances rationale that has driven the country's wildlife policy for the past thirty years. "Not all of the private conservancies are working well," Graham concedes. "But those that are have some common qualities. They serve the local communities well, and the local communities therefore support them. They have good security. Outside these conservancies the game is just getting hammered, so we should look to them as a good template. But we also have to allow them to thrive; ultimately, they need to do more than ecotourism, some cattle grazing, and a little bird hunting."

And that means giving them autonomy over the wildlife on their land. The centralization of wildlife policy has been disastrous for Kenya's game, observes Graham: it enforces responsibility on the communities but allows them no authority and provides them no benefits. Wildlife management must thus "devolve to the local level. There must be opportunity for enterprise and innovation. As it stands, the centralized policy serves the Kenya Wildlife Service and national government, and that's about it. If you want to do anything, you have to go through paper chases and bureaucratic engagements at the national, regional, and district levels. At every tier, you have to pay 'facilitation' fees, and those are often beyond the means of the community leaders. In other words, current policy makes wildlife a burden, a prohibitive cost for the communities rather than an opportunity. Until we turn that around, I'm not sure elephants have a long-term future in Kenya."

CHAPTER 13

The Sage Reconsiders

If you fly over parts of Tsavo today—and I challenge anyone
to do so, if you have the eyes for it—you can see lines of
snares set out in funnel traps that extend four or five miles.
Tens of thousands of animals are being killed annually for
the meat business. Carnivores are being decimated in the
same snares and discarded. I am not a propagandist on
this issue, but when my friends say we are very concerned
that hunting will be reintroduced in Kenya, let me put it
to you: hunting has never been stopped in Kenya, and there
is more hunting in Kenya today than at any time since
independence. [Thousands] of animals are being killed
annually with no control. Snaring, poisoning, and shooting
are common things. So when you have a fear of the debate
about hunting, please don't think there is no hunting. Think
of a policy to regulate it, so that we can make it sustainable.
That is surely the issue, because an illegal crop, an illegal
market is unsustainable in the long term, whatever it is.
And the market in wildlife meat is unsustainable as
currently practiced, and something needs to be done.

—Richard Leakey, in an address to the
  Strathmore Business School, Nairobi

Situated near the western shore of Long Island, Stony Brook University
is separated from Kenya in ways other than distance. The northeastern American hardwood forests that surround and intrude on the campus bear little resemblance to the acacia scrublands of Laikipia and
the Northern Frontier District and are ecologically disparate from the
plains of the Maasai Mara. Forty miles up the road are the Hamptons,
among the most exclusive of America's bosky exurbs and a remove from

the slums of Nairobi that can be measured in light years. At this season in New York State, very early spring, the crocuses are pushing up from the humus, but the temperature is brisk to the point that a warm coat is requisite for comfort. In Kenya, meanwhile, the Long Rains have arrived in force after an extended drought, but the rich crop of grass sprouting in their wake is quickly being grazed to the nubbin by the millions of cattle and goats that inhabit the country.

So it seems a little odd that Stony Brook—as un-African a venue as one is likely to find—is the home of the Turkana Basin Institute, an organization devoted to the ongoing study of the crèche where those of the genus *Homo* took their first faltering steps before matriculating to the larger world. In the most basic terms, we are all East Africans: the fossils of the Great Rift Valley and its surrounding environs prove that. These trace remains of our earliest ancestors were Richard Leakey's initial passion; they are now, it seems, his last.

Leakey was born and raised in Kenya and first gained renown as an understudy—and occasional antagonist—to his father, Louis Leakey, the paterfamilias of modern paleoanthropology. Richard and his crews made several celebrated finds, including "Turkana Boy," a skeleton of a twelve-year-old *Homo erectus* who died about 1.6 million years ago, and crania and skulls from other hominids, including one from a new species, *Australopithecus aethiopicus*. He currently continues this work, dividing his time between Kenya and the institute offices in Stony Brook.

Still, Leakey isn't best known as a paleobiologist. His middle years were not devoted, as his time is now, to the painstaking excavation of hominid fossils from the sandy matrices of the Rift Valley. They were, instead, a time of adventure and violence. As the most famous and most effective director of the Kenya Wildlife Service, Leakey was given carte blanche by then president Daniel arap Moi to stanch the destruction of Kenya's wildlife generally and win the Ivory Wars in particular. And he did it. Leakey was as tough as rhinoceros hide, fearless, and by most accounts utterly incorruptible. He was hard-nosed in the prosecution of his mandates, and poachers were often pursued under shoot-to-kill orders.

Leakey served with the Kenya Wildlife Service from 1989 to 1994. The game came back under his leadership—and, it must be noted, under the hunting ban. Many people who have only a passing knowledge of Leakey's role in wildlife conservation, however, assume his support of the hunting proscriptions was a matter of deep philosophical commitment. But this wasn't the case. Things were more complicated than that.

The Turkana Basin Institute consists of a suite of offices on one of the upper floors of a social science building on the Stony Brook campus. It is here that I interview Leakey, who has only recently returned from Kenya. All the offices in the institute complex are utilitarian; luxury appointments are obviously not a consideration here. But Leakey's office, while relatively large and affording a pleasant view of the campus, is positively Spartan. The desk and accompanying furniture are the kind you'd see in the office of any midlevel government bureaucrat. Personal mementos are scant. Yet the overall impression isn't one of shabbiness or professorial absent-mindedness. Quite the contrary, in fact: Leakey's office is neat, organized; it somehow conveys the sense of a well-planned camp. It is as though he has taken the disciplines necessary for a tolerable life in the Kenyan bush and applied them to the genteel environs of Stony Brook. I almost expect to see a pair of boots perched on a trunk or chair, elevated so scorpions won't crawl into them at night while he sleeps.

Now in his midsixties, Leakey looks much older than his years. At the time of my interview, he is dressed in a rumpled, donnish sweater. His hair is white. His face is seamed, and his skin has that blotched, abraded appearance typical among many Africans of English descent who have spent their lives exposed to the fierce equatorial sun. His movements seemed labored, which is not surprising: he lost both legs in a private plane crash in 1993. Rumors have abounded ever since that it was due to sabotage by elements of the Moi administration displeased by his rigorous oversight of the Kenya Wildlife Service, which minimized opportunities for graft. Leakey, self-effacing and stoic by nature, will not speculate.

Leakey resigned from the KWS in 1994, after his opponents accused him of racism and agency mismanagement. Some of his adversaries claimed corruption in the KWS flourished under Leakey. His responses to these charges have ranged from irritation and disgust to simple silence; the impression he leaves is that a formal defense is beneath his dignity. Accusations aside, one fact is clear: under Leakey, the KWS was able to stem poaching.

There is a question foremost in my mind as I sit down with Leakey, and this is it: Why was the KWS effective only during his tenure? Its antecedent organization, the Wildlife Conservation and Management Department, was feckless. And since Leakey left, the KWS has become notorious for inefficiency, incompetence, and arrant—rather than merely rumored—corruption.

Leakey sighs at the question, looks out the window, and essays a faint smile. "When I agreed to take that job," he says, "it was under the condition that I would not be answerable or available to any government minister or director. I would only be answerable to the [KWS] board [and Moi]." That made all the difference, he said, because that condition immediately put the service beyond the influence of any given politician. Typically in Kenya—throughout much of Africa—any high-ranking government official who wants a favor or a payoff only has to summon the head of a given ministry to his or her office for a private chat. The demands are made clear: the staffer has no option but to acquiesce. "[In Kenya], nobody in a subordinate position can stand up to bullying from a government minister," Leakey said. "That, essentially, remains the source of corruption and dysfunction—that any influential politician can disrupt any law or policy. By putting myself beyond that influence, I was actually able to get something done. My staff saw I was beyond political pressure, and that created a tremendous esprit and dedication to our work."

Leakey also drafted a seven-volume policy document for KWS staff that spelled out goals and duties—the so-called Zebra Book. Among other points, the Zebra Book (which remained official policy from 1991 to 1996) emphasized wildlife monitoring, tourism impact assessments, and partnerships with communities living adjacent to parks and reserves. "It provided clear guidelines and left no doubt as to our mission," he says.

Acknowledgment of the wisdom of the hunting ban was implicit in the KWS's mission. But, Leakey emphasizes, his support of the ban was specific to the time and place: Kenya in the 1980s and 1990s. Any idea that he was philosophically opposed to the taking of game under any and all circumstances was simple misunderstanding or wishful thinking. "The line I took then on legal hunting, including elephant hunting, was based on political reality," Leakey says. "Kenya couldn't run an effective civil police force that could combat corruption and control its porous borders, so how could you legalize hunting and not expect it to get out of control? Say you did a count in an area and determined that you could establish a sustainable annual quota of three hundred elephants— well and good. But the quota would've meant nothing; once the shooting started, three hundred dead elephants would've quickly turned into three thousand."

That was then. And now? Again Leakey flashes that brief, almost wan smile. "Oh, now the situation is much, much worse," he continues.

"I am in no way opposed to the idea of hunting, but we couldn't simply introduce legal hunting now; in most places, there's not much to hunt. We'd first have to create a system that invests value in game, then work up to options—whatever they are—that allow people to realize that value. I also don't think hunting should be perceived strictly as a pursuit for white, foreign elites. That generates tremendous resentment—both for the activity and, indirectly, for the wildlife. One thing is clear, however: the hunting ban in and of itself means nothing at this point. The current system has been an utter failure, and wildlife throughout Kenya is being relentlessly eliminated. We need an entirely different way of thinking."

Leakey favors a flexible, multifaceted approach to preserving Kenya's wildlife, but any option, he emphasizes, has to accommodate private enterprise. It is not that he is a reflexive capitalist: rather, his opinion relates to the Kenyan zeitgeist. Kenyan society, generally speaking, does not subscribe to the socialist ideals of Julius Nyerere, ideals that still hold considerable sway in Tanzania. For better or worse, Leakey observes, Kenya is entrepreneurial. This is especially so in matters of land. The old impulses for community—that is to say, tribal—holdings are falling away. Years ago, he notes, most of Kenya's people lived on tribal lands that were held in common. These lands were the basis for pastoral culture, and there was no formal title to them. Now all is changed: "Today, every Kenyan aspires to own a title deed to some land. Whether it is the right thing or the wrong thing is another issue. But land is being adjudicated, and private ownership is taking place."

And when land is held by individuals, Leakey notes, wildlife goes from being a public trust to either an asset or a liability. This fact must now be acknowledged and incorporated into Kenyan wildlife policy, he insists. As it stands now, most of the land is held privately, but the government "owns" the wildlife; people are expected to support game on their land but derive no benefit from it. To ensure the presence of wildlife on private land, says Leakey, there must be some benefit returned to the land's owners.

"I have sheep, I have cattle, and wildlife doesn't mix well with sheep, cattle, and goats," Leakey observed at Strathmore. "I grow grapes [in my vineyard]. Wildlife does not go well with that either. The baboons destroy my crop every second year. I don't do it for money, I do it for fun—but wildlife is a damn nuisance if you are a landowner trying to make your living on agriculture. I would be prepared . . . to consider letting the wildlife in my area use my land, but shouldn't I be able to make some money from it? And this should override the issue of consumption hunting [and] nonconsumption tourism. This is a principle of life. You cannot have national policy enshrined in a national constitution that gives private ownership and democratic rights . . . and then, on the other hand, takes away your right to use your asset to enrich yourself. We can control what you do with your land, but it [must] be within the context that it is fair and that gives market value to that land."

There is not necessarily any need to cast about for radically new models that conjoin private enterprise with conservation goals, Leakey emphasizes. Such templates already exist; for decades, they have been refined and applied in the developed world. The approaches typically taken by the Nature Conservancy, he avers, are especially worth noting. In North America, the Nature Conservancy has protected large ecologically important properties by either buying them at fair market value or establishing long-term conservation easements on them. In the latter cases, the owners retain title to their lands, but the allowable economic activities are rigorously defined. Cattle ranching may still be sanctioned, for example, but stocking levels are tightly controlled. Other strictures typically are enforced: fencing livestock out of riparian zones is a common practice. Habitat restoration programs—reforestation, expansion of wetlands, reestablishing native grasslands—also are usually part of the deals. The landowners, in effect, lease their land for the long term in exchange for a large cash payment and the right to pursue activities that don't impinge on major ecological values.

Still, says Leakey, flexibility is essential. "One size doesn't fit all. Public lands require different approaches than private lands, obviously. As a nation, we [Kenyans] take great pride in our inventory of public lands. But the nomenclature doesn't mean much these days. Is a 'park' really a park when thousands of cattle are illegally grazed on it and all the game is snared and poached to oblivion? So at this point, private management of the parks looks like a pretty good alternative. National governments typically don't run airlines or railways well. The same can be said, at least in Kenya, of national parks. Why not give ten- to fifteen-year concessions on the parks, with yearly inspections to make sure the terms are being honored? If the conditions aren't being met, the concession can be yanked. This could even be done by local authorities, the people who live near the parks and are most affected by their management. They could negotiate the management for specific protected areas—demand a high degree of resource protection and a fair share of the revenues. With this kind of arrangement, there is no real incentive

FIGURE 10. Richard Leakey, the first director of the Kenya Wildlife Service and the world's most celebrated paleoanthropologist. Leakey took a hard line on poaching during his years with the KWS and is widely credited with stopping the elephant slaughter of the late 1980s and early 1990s. He is not, however, opposed to regulated hunting, culling, and game cropping. (Courtesy Royce Carlton, Inc.)

to cheat. As it stands now, all the incentives *support* cheating. Or perhaps we can actually let the people own the parks—buy shares in them. Again, the incentives would be on preserving and enhancing what we have, not depleting [it]."

In any event, says Leakey, "KWS is a complete failure. It is clear we can't manage our wildlife through the civil government, which is utterly dysfunctional. We need to try new things. The lust for land is destroying wildlife. And that's a dynamic we won't be able to change; we can't put the desire for land back in a box. It's part of our society now, so we have to direct it, use it to promote conservation goals. It's our only real chance."

Leakey parts with some in the conservation community who claim that nonconsumptive wildlife policies compound the tragedy of diminishing game by threatening pastoral societies. Anthony King of the Wildlife Laikipia Forum, for example, feels that trophy hunting and subsistence hunting allow pastoral communities to augment their income and diets while pursuing traditional lifestyles.

But "weakening" pastoral culture is not the same thing as threatening the tribes that currently practice pastoralism, Leakey emphasizes. Indeed, a switch from cattle herding to alternative livelihoods may be in the best economic and social interests of any given pastoral community. Further, he notes, pastoralism is part and parcel of the threat to the game. It's one thing when a few thousand Maasai, Samburu, and Turkana are herding their cattle across the rangelands; it's another when millions of them are doing it, and their cattle likewise number in the millions. Cattle husbandry doesn't necessarily result in the utter extirpation of wildlife and wildlife habitat from the landscape, as intensive agriculture does, but its effects are negative nevertheless—profoundly negative, when the numbers of cattle and cattle keepers are as high as they are in Kenya. Not only does the livestock compete with the game for forage and water, but also the pastoralist impulse to overstock the range invariably leads to erosion, which in turn permanently degrades the land's carrying capacity for both wild and domestic animals. Predators, of course, typically are destroyed by pastoralists if they even sniff in the direction of a goat.

Tourists may swoon at the sight of a Maasai *moran* in traditional dress guarding his cattle, says Leakey, but that in itself is insufficient reason to "preserve" Maasai pastoralism. "There is no reason why people living adjacent to the Maasai Mara Reserve should be expected to continue to herd cattle wearing *shukas* and [carrying] spears when they want to send their children to Strathmore or Harvard," Leakey observed to his Strathmore audience. "They have got to get some return on their money. And if they can't get it through wildlife, then they must be allowed to get it another way. If they get it another way, then the Maasai Mara collapses. It is not a question of them suffering; it is a question of collective action to make sure they benefit and we all benefit as Kenyans."

Leakey continues this line of thought in our interview. "Practically speaking, pastoralism *must* pass away," he says. "What are you going to do? Demand that [pastoralists] say no to cell phones, to antibiotics, to modern products and services in general? These technologies change societies. People all over the world want them, and they will have them."

I mention the ubiquity of cell phones I had noticed among Maasai of the Serengeti during a recent trip. The *moran* kept them in beaded pouches around their necks, using them to text relatives and, as mentioned earlier, to check cattle prices in Nairobi, Mombasa, and Dar es Salaam. Wherever I stopped, several Maasai would amble up to the Land Rover and ask to use the cigarette lighter to recharge their phones.

"Well, there you have it," Leakey says. "Pastoralism is not immutable, nor should it be. In fact, change of the culture is the only real hope conservation has in Kenya. You can only be a good conservationist when you have a decent house and enough food on your table to think beyond immediate survival needs. You can only esteem the lion when you aren't worried about him eating through your main store of wealth. Probably the single greatest problem in the pastoral lands is high population growth—too many people putting too many demands on the land. Why is that? Pastoralists need large families. They need children to herd the stock, *moran* to protect the villages. A man wants a lot of children so he will be cared for when he gets old. But with material progress, the need for many children isn't imperative; the opposite, in fact, holds true. Education of the children becomes paramount, because education results in more income, more goods, better prospects in general. But educating children costs money, so families will have fewer children in order to educate the ones they have."

Leakey maintains he understands the impulses of the International Fund for Animal Welfare, Born Free, the Humane Societies in the United States and the United Kingdom, and other animal welfare groups. He even, he says, shares some of their goals. "I believe, for example, that wildlife shouldn't be snared, that birds should be caged and fed prop-

erly, that zoos should have exhibits that allow their animals a sem-
blance of their natural habitats," he says. "But it is difficult to make a
jump from that to saying animals shouldn't be hunted with rifles out
of 'principle.' I don't understand that principle. Life and death are the
most basic of realities, especially where wildlife and the environments
that support them are concerned. That's what natural systems are all
about, and to say otherwise is to confuse the essential message about
conservation."

The animal rights groups active in Africa mean well, Leakey continues, "but for conservation to succeed in Africa, you can't shove human
rights aside for animal rights. Unfortunately, that's the impression [ani-
mal rights] groups are leaving—that an elephant or lion is worth more
than a human being, that if a lion eats your cow, well, that's how things
are sometimes. You can't shoot the elephant raiding your crops or the
lion killing your livestock, you can't hunt for meat; you just have to take
it, you have to 'support' wildlife because it's the right thing to do." And
ultimately, says Leakey, that philosophy will fail in Kenya and all across
Africa. Or more likely, it will fail and simultaneously be championed
and "officially" supported: it will remain the law of the land, people will
take all the money the animal rights groups offer—and the game will
still be poached, poisoned, and snared to extinction.

"As I said, I sympathize with the animal rights groups to a certain
degree," Leakey says. "But I would like to see them refine their goals, to
address issues where they can have a real impact. By that I mean they
should stick to domestic animals and their problems. The abuses here
are horrendous: check out any abattoir, look how cattle and donkeys
and goats are treated on farms and ranches. Focus on industrial poultry
production, where hens are kept crammed in batteries where they never
see the sun and can barely move. These are real abuses, and they cry out
for real action. But they're not getting anything like the attention paid
to elephants, a species that can't be logically addressed simply by defining its 'rights.'"

And why is that? Leakey ventures one of his tentative smiles again.
"Well, there isn't as much money to be raised from the plight of a don-
key as from the plight of an elephant, is there? And as far as that goes,
I have to add that IFAW and other groups aren't as powerful in Kenya
as they were a year or two ago, and money—I mean the lack of it—is
the cause. IFAW gets most of its money from public donations, and its
marketing materials featuring big-eyed African animals threatened by
hunters and poachers were always very effective in raising funds. But

the global recession took a big bite out of [IFAW's]) income—for now, anyway. When the times get better, people will donate again."

A sizable segment of the conservation community does not share Leakey's opinion that IFAW's influence has waned, of course. In any event, Leakey feels the fight between animal rights and traditional conservation is a sideshow. In the longer view—the only view the paleobiologist considers reasonable—this fight will be subsumed by larger issues. "We need to look at past periods of climate shift to understand the changes that are coming down on us, changes that will completely alter everything, including conservation," Leakey says. "The warming climate, marine acidification, the inexorable growth of human population—these will put stresses on wildlife and wildlife habitat that are beyond anything we are now addressing."

At a certain point, Leakey continues, these threats may well require a triage approach to conservation—or beyond that, a kind of ark strategy: a gene bank for wildlife, artificial habitats where animal diversity can be maintained until conditions improve. And ultimately, they *will* improve, he emphasizes: there is no stasis in nature. The world's human population may well hit twelve billion, but it cannot sustain that figure. One way or another, human numbers will fall. That could allow the restocking of the game lands with "ark" specimens.

"That's providing the habitat hasn't been utterly degraded, the topsoil destroyed, in the process," he says. "And here, I'm somewhat optimistic. As I said, I believe the passing of pastoralism is inevitable, no matter what is happening or not happening with conservation. Forty or fifty years from now, it will largely be an historic phenomenon, due to the universal determination people have for improving the fortunes of their children. In a way, I'll deeply regret it: inevitably, cultural richness will be lost. But it will also present opportunities. As pastoral peoples exercise the greater options available to them, stocking levels on the rangelands inevitably will decrease. They could well recover their habitat potential, allowing restocking with wildlife. So the important thing now is to prepare, to expect major, even cataclysmic changes, and take the longest possible perspective. Conservation is not necessarily a 'failure' if it doesn't accomplish its goals in ten years—or even one hundred years."

Leakey and I chat a bit longer before his sidelong glances out the window convince me my interview with him is nearing an end. It is lunchtime. After exiting the campus, I drive to the adjacent hamlet of Stony Brook. It supports a few businesses, including a Thai restaurant.

I eat pad thai; it is skillfully prepared though bland, apparently skewed for Yankee palates. After dining, I walk back to my car. I'm working up a few notes when I see Leakey and a colleague heading to the restaurant. He is limping but is stable on his artificial legs, and though he looks weathered, even a bit frail, he also appears completely serene and peaceful. I think of those hominid fossils that have constituted much of his life's work and given him the gift of a deep, geologic sense of time. From his point of view, the decline of the game, even the collapse of civilization or the extinction of our own species, must be considered part of a great adventure—the unfolding of life on earth. It is a matter of flux, not beginnings and endings. I find myself striving to share his optimism, but I am not altogether successful.

CHAPTER 14

Commodifying Conservation

My colleague and I sit down at a table in a small restaurant by the banks of the Zambezi River. It is dusk, and clouds of *Anopheles* mosquitoes are rising from adjacent wetlands. The insects are hungry and resolutely questing in our direction. Malaria is rife here in Caprivi, a panhandle-like province of Namibia wedged along the borders of Angola, Zambia, and Botswana. It is a disease I've contracted once before, and I don't care to renew my acquaintance. The waitress, as though divining my unease, places a burning insecticidal punk under our table and hands us menus. I anticipate the list of fare, for I've been traveling through Namibia with my companion, Greenwell Matongo, for over a week, and I'm familiar with the national cuisine: meat. And more meat.

Namibia isn't really a felicitous destination for vegans. Vegetables, in fact, are generally disdained here. Go into a supermarket, and the meat counters are vast, stocked with everything from beef, pork, and mutton to game, dazzling arrays of sausages, windrows of hams and other cured meats, and huge selections of biltong, the dried meat that is consumed as both a staple and a snack throughout sub-Saharan Africa. But the vegetable section usually isn't a section at all. It's typically a small counter or even just a shelf or two with some wizened apples, a pile of spuds, some onions, perhaps a few withered carrots and wilted cabbages.

I certainly have nothing against animal protein, but I pine for green vegetables and fruit if I can't have them daily. Greenwell, the former chief game warden for the Namibian Ministry of Environment and

FIGURE 11. A sign in front of a Windhoek hotel restaurant notes the available game entrées. Meat from harvested wild animals is available throughout Namibia, and regulated cropping and hunting are cornerstones of the nation's conservation policy. (Glen Martin)

Tourism and currently the World Wildlife Fund's community outreach liaison for the country, scoffs at my persnickety ways. "When it comes to meat, we say, 'bring it on,'" he laughs. He orders a heaping platter of oxtails. By now I've steeled myself to his derision and even understand it: as a traveler, I've always believed in accommodating myself to local mores and food, and whining about the absence of salads is poor form. Besides, Namibian meat is lean and delicious. The animals are fed on the local pasturage and browse and never finished in a feedlot. Namibian beef would be considered organic, grass-fed, boutique meat in the States, retailing for up to twenty dollars a pound. Here, it is the norm.

But I eschew the beef. I instead order the oryx steak, a fillet taken from one of the elk-sized, wickedly horned antelope that are emblematic of Namibia. Literally: they are on the country's seal. Other game is also on the menu—springbok, zebra, and kudu. In almost any other country on the continent, except perhaps for South Africa, such offerings surely would be "bushmeat," a product of the illegal wildlife trade. Here, though, the meat is sanctioned, certified, the yield of a government program that sustains local communities, private landowners, and wildlife habitat. By eating this oryx steak, I am, paradoxically, contributing to the preservation of oryx and other game. I consume it with an untroubled conscience. Greenwell checks out my clean plate while I sit back with a toothpick.

"Congratulations," he says. "Now you're eating like a Namibian."

I'm not in Namibia, however, as a game-besotted foodie. I'm here to compare—to look at the Namibian model of conservation and contrast it with the Kenyan model. They are utterly disparate: in Kenya, of course, hunting is completely proscribed, while in Namibia it is not only allowed but celebrated. Which model, I want to know, is working better?

Certainly, there is a sense of anticipation, of hope in Namibia that is palpably absent from other countries in the region. Perhaps that can be attributed to the superfluity of high-quality protein, but I suspect it has more to do with the abundant land (319,000 square miles compared to Kenya's 224,000 square miles), low human population (two million compared to forty million), relatively rich natural resources (e.g., fisheries, wildlife, uranium, and diamonds), and a stable, democratically elected government. Corruption is not unknown in Namibia, but it is generally restrained. In 2008, the country ranked sixth on the Ibrahim Index of African Governance, an annual survey that evaluates the ability of forty-eight sub-Saharan nations to deliver essential goods and services to their citizens. Generally speaking, the roads are better in Namibia than in California. Windhoek, the capital, is a sparkling city of three hundred thousand set in gently undulating acacia savannah. The other towns—they can hardly be called cities—are uniformly neat and prosperous; litter is almost nonexistent. The vast countryside is either wild and uninhabited or well-maintained rangeland.

Founded only two decades ago, Namibia is a young nation, another element in the energetic, relatively upbeat outlook of its populace. But the history of the land is incarnadine. Inhabited by a number of pastoral and hunting tribes up through the nineteenth century, the region was declared a colony by Germany in 1884, a result of Wilhelmine concerns over growing British influence throughout Africa. This engendered great resentment among many of the tribal inhabitants, particularly the Herero and Nama, who rebelled in 1904. The German response was brutal—more than that, it was genocidal. Lieutenant General Lothar von Trotha was called in to quell the uprising; he issued an order of extermination (*Vernichtungsbefehl*) to his troops: "Within the German boundaries, every Herero, whether found with or without a rifle, with or without cattle, shall be shot. Signed: The Great General of the Mighty Kaiser, von Trotha."

About sixty-five thousand Herero were slaughtered, reducing the population by 80 percent. The Nama suffered roughly ten thousand casualties, amounting to half of their population. Following the violence, the surviving native inhabitants were stripped of their land and subjected to Apartheid-like social and economic strictures.

Following World War I, British-held South Africa administered Namibia as a territory under a League of Nations mandate. This situation remained in force when South Africa's white minority declared its independence from Britain in 1934. When the league was superseded by the United Nations in 1946, South Africa refused a revised trusteeship agreement, because it would've entailed more rigorous oversight. Namibia was then administered as a kind of unofficial province of South Africa, though it wasn't formally incorporated into the country. Nevertheless, the standards of Apartheid applied throughout the territory, and tribal resentment grew.

In 1966, the Southwest Africa People's Organization (SWAPO) initiated military action against the South African occupiers. The guerrilla war that ensued was long and hard fought, raging through both Namibia and Angola. Finally, in 1988, South Africa agreed to a United Nations peace plan. Namibia declared independence for all its territory in 1990, with the exception of Walvis Bay, a coastal town that remained a South African enclave until 1994.

Though he is only in his midthirties, Greenwell retains vivid memories of the war. His father was a member of SWAPO's inner circle and currently serves as a government adviser. His uncle was a renowned fighter who was killed in combat and is considered a national hero, a martyr in the fight for independence. Except for a few years in India, when his father served as a diplomat-in-exile for SWAPO, Greenwell grew up in refugee camps in Angola and the Congo. He recalls several air raids on the Angolan camps by the South African Air Force that resulted in heavy civilian casualties. And he remembers long years of hunger, when there was little to eat except pap, the ubiquitous, stiff, cornmeal porridge that is a staple across the sub-Saharan region and is known as *ugali* in Kenya. "As kids, we basically raised ourselves in the camps," Greenwell recalls. "The adults were off fighting or dealing with diplomatic matters."

SWAPO was socialist in its political underpinnings and was supported by the communist bloc during the years of heaviest fighting. Indeed, Cuba committed thousands of soldiers to fight alongside SWAPO troops, and Fidel Castro is highly esteemed throughout Namibia today. But on attaining Namibia's independence, Sam Nujoma, the head of SWAPO, veered from a rigid, vertically integrated centrist model for the new state, instead investing much of the economic and political power at the local level. This generally sat well with Namibian citizens, most of whom are highly entrepreneurial. Nujoma remains a revered figure throughout the country, primarily for his success in establishing a stable society and his rejection of the African "Strong Man" model: he stepped down from the presidency in 2004 and returned to his native village of Etunda for extended rustication. In casual conversation, Namibians refer to him as "the founding father" without irony. His international reviews are more mixed, primarily because of his close ties with Zimbabwe's iron-fisted dictator, Robert Mugabe, and his insensate rants against homosexuality.

From the beginning, the SWAPO government recognized the importance of wildlife resources and addressed the issue in Article 95 of the national constitution: "The State shall actively promote and maintain the welfare of the people by adopting international policies aimed at the following: maintenance of ecosystems, essential ecological processes, and biological diversity of Namibia, and utilization of living natural resources on a sustainable basis for the benefit of all Namibians, both present and future."

The constitution, notes Greenwell, establishes conservation as a primary national goal, but it is not "conservation" in a general sense. Instead, it is conservation that is to be pursued along a specific path toward a definite end: conservation promoted for "the welfare of the people," conservation geared toward "the utilization of natural resources on a sustainable basis," conservation conceived "for the benefit of all Namibians."

In other words, says Greenwell, as we address ourselves once again to a bountiful meal of succulent, range-fed Namibian meat—kudu for me, this time—the ultimate goal of Namibian conservation isn't the preservation of wildlife. It is, instead, the improvement of prospects for the average Namibian. By conserving and enhancing wild ecosystems, wildlife will thrive, affording abundant economic opportunities: ecotourism, trophy hunting, subsistence hunting, game cropping, trade in wild botanicals. "We are completely committed to conservation," Greenwell says. "But that doesn't mean we're committed to saving individual wild animals. Our conservation programs require us to *utilize* wild animals. In Namibia, people always come first."

Conservation in Namibia is multitiered. National parks cover approximately 17 percent of the land, including the entire coastline. Freehold conservancies—basically, farms that provide ecotourism and hunting opportunities—account for an additional 4 percent of the land, and tourist concessions and community forests account for another 1.5 percent. Finally, community conservancies currently cover 17.5 percent of the land. As of this writing, sixty-four such conservancies are in place, with about twenty more under formation. Ultimately, the country should support eighty community conservancies, according to Chris Weaver, the World Wildlife Fund's point man in Namibia. As with the freehold conservancies, trophy hunting and other sustainable uses are encouraged, subject to quotas approved by the national Ministry of Environment and Tourism.

At the WWF offices in Windhoek, I talk with Weaver, a spare, erect man with a thick shock of gray hair, angular features, and a raptorlike way of taking in things, before Greenwell and I head out to visit some of the conservancies. Prior to the late 1960s and early 1970s, Weaver observes, conservation policy in the territory could hardly be considered enlightened. More to the point, cattle production was the sole concern of both the tribal pastoralists and white landowners. Wildlife, officially, was "vermin" for all the predictable reasons: predators ate the livestock, while native ungulates ate the same grass that the cattle ate, and grass is seldom an abundant resource in Namibia, especially during the dry season. Even more significant was disease. In Namibia, wild antelopes, buffalo, and other herbivores transmit a variety of viral, bacterial, and protozoan maladies to livestock, including hoof-and-mouth, anthrax, tuberculosis, bovine pleuropneumonia, bovine malignant catarrhal fever, trypanosomiasis, and African swine fever. "Having wildlife-free land made it easier to sell [or lease] your farm," says Weaver. "It was a good marketing point. There was no incentive to maintain wildlife and every incentive to wiping it out."

For the most part, Namibia's game laws in the 1960s and early 1970s were minimal and generally ignored. Then in 1975, spurred by wildlife's profit potential, the territory adopted the Nature Conservation Ordinance. This, Weaver says, became "the Bible" for Namibian conservation policy, though prior to independence it sometimes was honored more in the breach than in observance. The ordinance was a result of two things: the efforts of local conservationists who felt wildlife could best be preserved by endowing it with real value and the growing realization of landowners that they could turn a buck from the wild animals on their land. The demand for African trophy hunting opportunities has remained more or less stable over the past fifty years, despite the simultaneous rise in animal rights activism. When Namibia's white landowners realized they could sell the rights to shoot a kudu for two thousand dollars or so, they became nominal conservationists, underscoring their regional reputations for stolid pragmatism.

The ordinance established four categories of game: vermin, which included baboons and some predators; huntable wildlife, covering common species such as springbok, kudu, zebras, oryx, buffalo, and warthogs; protected game, mainly rarer antelopes such as roan and sable, which may be hunted under tightly controlled quotas and circumstances; and specially protected game, which included CITES species of international concern, such as elephants, black rhinos, white rhinos, and cheetahs.

The ordinance was a good law, but enforcement was spotty when Namibia was under the thumb of Apartheid-era South Africa, and the war for independence made it irrelevant in any event. During the years of fighting, much of the game disappeared, wiped out for bushmeat by the contesting armies. And in the first years following independence, wildlife wasn't much of a priority as SWAPO scrambled to establish basic institutions of governance. "By 1993, the game in the communal areas was at historic lows," Weaver recalls. "The habitat was there, but not the animals. People were concerned with feeding themselves, and wildlife still had the status of vermin. Nobody wanted lions eating their cattle or elephants chowing down on their crops."

Soon after independence, the government was stable enough to once again consider wildlife policy. And officials quickly recognized, Weaver said, that the game could be brought back and that it could benefit citizens if it was managed as a resource and profit center. Community lands were thus granted the same rights over resident wildlife that white landowners had long enjoyed. Additionally, special loans were made available to disadvantaged Namibians to purchase land from willing white sellers. From this genesis, the first community conservancies evolved. As with the remaining freehold farms, the government reviewed and approved wildlife consumption policies and quotas. But the animals, along with the products and profits realized from their use, accrued to the communities.

"The first four conservancies were created in 1998," says Weaver.

"[WWF] helped [the conservancies] establish the tenders for each species to be utilized—basically, the price that would be charged the professional hunter arranging the hunts. When communities saw what they could get—twenty thousand dollars for an elephant, ten thousand dollars for a lion, for example—all of a sudden the entire dialogue changed. Poaching just *stopped,* because now, there was tremendous social pressure against it. Before, when you killed an animal, you weren't adversely affecting anyone. More likely, you were contributing to the common good—killing a predator that was eating everybody's goats, maybe bringing in a tasty buffalo or antelope to the village. But now if you killed a lion or elephant, you were depriving everybody of the ten thousand to twenty thousand dollars that the lion or elephant represented— big money and a big loss for the community. You went from hero to pariah."

I saw this dynamic manifest at the Salambala Conservancy in Caprivi. A holding of the Subia people, Salambala is relatively small for a Namibian conservancy—about 230,000 acres. Still, Caprivi is lush compared to the rest of Namibia, watered by the Zambezi and Okavango; wetlands and fertile savannas are abundant, and so is the game. A lot of animals live in Salambala, and each one is valued by conservancy members for the money and meat it represents. Like all Namibia's conservancies, Salambala works off an annual quota approved by the Ministry of Environment and Tourism.

I am impressed with the detail of the 2010 quota; nineteen species are listed. The year's take for elephants is eight, with six going to trophy hunters, one culled for community uses, and one dedicated to "traditional authorities," for example, the chief and conservancy committee members. Many traditional game species are on the quota, including impalas (with a take of fifty), buffalo (seven), zebras (fifty), kudu (four), and waterbuck (four). But hippos are also listed (four), as well as crocodiles (three), baboons (six), and black-backed jackals (two). These last species typically are not greatly sought after by trophy hunters, but some people are willing to pay to shoot them on safari, and Salambala is happy to oblige, as long as the take is sustainable. The quota even extends to the holding's game bird population. The 2010 take for white-faced ducks was 100, the same for spur-winged geese, while 150 turtle doves, 50 guinea fowl, and 70 red-billed francolins could be shot.

At the time of my conversation with Greenwell, the quota for wildebeest is eight, and that accounts for the general unhappiness Greenwell and I encounter outside the plastered cinderblock building that houses

FIGURE 12. Conservancy warden Elvis Mwilima examines the remains of a blue wildebeest that was illegally killed at the Salambala Conservancy in Caprivi. Conservancy officials had identified the poacher—a community member—and were actively seeking him. (Glen Martin)

the conservancy's administrative offices. Committee members are gathered around a table piled with animal parts: severed hoofs, fragments of hide, and piles of dark, twisted viscera, all redolent of decay. These are the remains of a blue wildebeest, explains conservancy chairman Robert Simjambo, the conservancy committee chairman. Simjambo is tall, thin, and magisterially erect; his face is lined from privation, yet there is no hardness to it. When he speaks, it is always with an easy smile and a soft, mellifluous voice, which can be misleading, because he is very upset by the scraps of this wildebeest, especially because he has learned it was poached by a community member

"We know who did it, he knows that we know, and he is now hiding from us," Simjambo says, gazing neutrally at the black reeking remains. "But we'll find him. And he will pay." Later, I ask Greenwell just what "paying" entails. It will certainly result in jail time, he says cheerfully, and perhaps a good drubbing as well. (Spontaneous beatings, I have observed, are considered appropriate and salutary ancillary punishment for crimes in sub-Saharan Africa.) That wildebeest, he continues, represented more than 12 percent of the conservancy's annual quota: it was a major theft of tribal resources, and theft is not taken lightly anywhere in Africa. "The success of the conservancies is linked directly to the change in status of the game," Greenwell continues. "Before, it was vermin, competition, a threat. Now it is property, with real value. You don't take property here, no matter if it belongs to a person or a community. There are consequences."

Salambala is trying to diversify its income base. Livestock has always been part of the Subia culture and economy and remains important. At the time of my visit, work was well under way on a modest guesthouse to accommodate tourists. Plans are also on the boards for a fairly ambitious aquaculture project, and many of the residents produce carvings and other items to sell at a gift shop located on Caprivi's main highway. Timber is sustainably harvested and marketed through a national certification program. Hunting, however, brings in most of the revenues.

Yet revenues owed and revenues collected are two different things. On all the conservancies, community leaders contract with licensed professional hunters, who then bring clients out to community lands to hunt for substantial fees. Professional hunter fees to Salambala range from about N$500,000 to $1 million annually, says Simjambo, or about US$70,000 to $140,000. The problem for Salambala is that their contracted "PH" is N$538,000 in arrears. The community members have filed a civil case to collect and have revoked the hunter's contract, but it is unclear when they'll see any of the money owed them.

"Professional hunters reneging on their contracts is one of the biggest problems facing the conservancies," says Greenwell. "In [Salambala's] case, I think it's more a matter of the hunter being a terrible businessman than a crook. But either way, it makes things very hard for the conservancies. The ministry knows it's a problem, and it's trying to weed out the good operators from the bad. They're also thinking about changing payment systems, requiring more money up front at the beginning of the hunting season."

Enforcement of the game laws is strict throughout the country, and most officials, both federal and local, take their missions seriously. Because part of their job is ameliorating conflicts between humans and wildlife, the work often becomes serious beyond the doctrinal or legal senses: it is overtly dangerous. When Greenwell was the chief warden for the Ministry of Environment and Tourism, much of his time was spent tracking and destroying rogue animals. He has many stories from this period, and a disconcerting number end with ". . . and then we were all yelling, 'Shoot! Shoot!'"

FIGURE 13. Elephant crossing sign on the Caprivi Strip, Namibia. Growing in number, Namibia's elephants are causing conflicts with locals and inflicting significant damage to habitat. Most wildlife managers favor culling as a means of keeping the population within bounds. (Glen Martin)

One yarn involves a lion that had been wounded by a poacher and had charged Greenwell and his cadre of game scouts. The lion gravely mauled two of the men before it was brought down in a blaze of rifle fire. Another involved a herd of elephants that had been terrorizing a farming hamlet, intimidating the residents, and laying waste to their pumpkin patches. After unsuccessfully trying to rout the animals with nonlethal means, Greenwell and his men determined that shooting one of the dominant adults was the best way to drive the group off. After a midnight stalk through a pumpkin patch, Greenwell shot one of the animals but didn't kill it outright. He and his trackers trailed the elephant through heavy cover the next morning, finally cornering and killing it. "Shooting an elephant is the last resort in a case like that; plus it's really scary following a wounded one through the bush," Greenwell recalls. "But the plan worked—the herd completely left the area. They understand what it means when one of them is shot."

One story, however, doesn't end with demands for gunfire; that's because Greenwell and his men got there too late. "I got a call from a village elder about a leopard that had been killing their goats,"

Greenwell recalls as we drive west from Caprivi through vast expanses of bushveldt. "He told us that he was setting out with a couple of guys to track it. I told him, no, don't do that; wait until we get there. We left immediately."

But distances are long in Namibia, and it was hours before Greenwell and his crew got to the village. By then, the elder and two young men of the settlement already had left. The group was easy to track, and before long the scouts found them. "They were all sprawled out on the ground, covered in blood," Greenwell says. "The elder was dead, and next to him was the leopard, also dead. Their bodies were still very warm, and their wounds were still fresh. Whatever happened had happened just minutes before we got there. The other two men were terribly mauled but alive." Greenwell and his scouts quickly ministered to the two survivors and got the story. "They had tracked the leopard to some termite mounds, and one of the mounds had a big warthog burrow dug out at the bottom," Greenwell says. "So the elder goes over and looks down the hole, which is a big mistake: you never, ever just stick your head into holes or caves when you're tracking a leopard." The leopard, of course, was in the burrow, and it boiled up and killed the elder. Then, true to the continental reputation of the species, it attacked the other two men instead of running away.

"They were able to kill it with spears, but not before they were almost killed themselves," Greenwell says. "It was really a terrible incident." On the other hand, he notes, it reinforced the fact that tracking dangerous game and similar jobs are best left to the wardens and scouts. "The ministry really takes [animal] conflicts seriously, and they try to respond right away. And that's essential for conservation in this country. If you lose the trust of the locals, if they think you don't take their problems seriously, they'll deal with animal issues themselves, and that's bad for both them and the wildlife."

Salambala represents a certain kind of conservancy: diversified in economic strategy, moderate in size, with a relatively large human population. Nyae Nyae is another kind. At 2.5 million acres, it is extremely large. Although it, too, is located in northeastern Namibia, it is remote from human population centers and sparsely populated itself; only around two thousand members of the Ju'hoansi San inhabit the holding. (The San were known as "Bushmen" until relatively recently, but the term is now generally considered pejorative.) Nyae Nyae means "a place without mountains, but rocky" in the San language. The land is covered with broad-leaf hardwood and acacia bushveldt, and several great pans fill with water after the rainy season, sustaining large concentrations of game and birds. The conservancy is situated next to Khaudum Game Reserve, a big chunk of utterly wild habitat that expands the general wildlife carrying capacity for the region. True migratory behavior is manifest by several species, including elephants, at Nyae Nyae and Khaudum.

Along with the Damara and Nama tongues, the San language employs a variety of lingual clicks and pops that are impossible for most outsiders to master. Greenwell, who speaks five tribal languages, English, and Afrikaans fluently and German with a high degree of competence, understands most San conversation but doesn't attempt to speak it. "It would be too easy to say something offensive or insulting without knowing it," he explains. "The clicks sound the same to most people, but there are very subtle differences in them that mean a great deal."

The only settlement at Nyae Nyae is at Tsumkwe, where a rustic lodge, a gift shop, and the conservancy offices are located. I meet several members of the conservancy committee at the small building that serves as the administrative hub. Like many people who first encounter the San, I am struck by their appearance. They are small and gracile, with light tawny complexions and a singular peppercorn hair pattern; their eyes are likewise distinctive—wide-spaced, almond-shaped, often with epicanthic folds. The San have always been nomadic hunters, and their tracking skills are so refined that they seem superhuman. Greenwell has worked with San trackers, and he has many stories of them unerringly following wildlife across rocky barrens where he could see nothing that would indicate an animal had passed: "And I'm not all that bad of a tracker myself," he says.

The three men I meet—Dan Jackson, Gcao Clemens, and Cwi Cnassie—are punctilious but almost languid; they seem distinctly unenthusiastic, if mildly amused, by my presence. Our conversation is carried out through an interpreter. English is the official language of Namibia, but few of the San speak it; most, however, are fluent in Afrikaans, and that is the language we employ. They explain the quotas for the conservancy's various species and the community's annual harvesting of devil's claw, a large tuber that is dug, dried, and shipped to Europe, where it's esteemed by New Age herbalists for its reputed medicinal properties. Trophy hunting and devil's claw harvesting, I learn, are pretty much the sole sources of income for the conservancy. A scheme to incorporate the operations of the lodge with a small fly-in camp for well-heeled ecotourists is on the books, but that's about the extent of future economic plans.

I ask the three men what they want from the conservancy, and they are quick to answer: developed water and the continued freedom to pursue the traditional San way of life. Depending on the season, Cnassie explains, water is scarce or nonexistent over much of the conservancy. Most of the San live outside Tsumkwe in small camps. Developed water (boreholes with hand pumps, small reservoirs) makes extended living in the bush possible—indeed, by San standards, exceedingly comfortable. Other than that, San ambitions for goods and services are modest.

What *is* critical to the San, aside from water, is game access. The San are the only people in Namibia who are allowed to hunt year-round, with virtually no restrictions, save that they must use traditional techniques and weapons, for example, handmade bows and spears and poisoned arrows. Much has been made of the fact that very few San pursue a completely traditional life these days. Most now wear Western clothes and come into settlements at least occasionally for staples such as salt and tea. Alcohol abuse is also a problem for the San. But that does not mean they do not remain true to the essential verities that define them as a people: most particularly, to be San means to hunt.

I ask the conservancy committee members about the importance of hunting to the San, from both the individual and the community perspectives. It is the first time I see them animated. They have been lounging in their chairs, responding to my questions politely but in an enervated fashion. Now they sit upright and smile broadly. "It's everything to us," says Jackson. "I need to hunt—we all need to hunt. After I'm doing conservancy business for a while, after I spend much time in Tsumkwe, I have to get out and hunt. I need to be in the bush with my friends, hunting game. It is not just a matter of meat. We need the meat, but we also need to hunt. We have always been hunters." I am reminded of Sitting Bull's pronouncement on the ethos of hunting: "When the buffalo are gone, we will hunt mice; for we are hunters, and we want our freedom." Unlike the Hunkpapa Sioux, the San are not a martial people, but they would understand this sentiment very well.

After concluding the interview, the San all stand, and we shake hands: they use an elaborate and modified version of the U.S. grab-and-clasp soul shake of the 1970s, and they laugh when I muff it. Greenwell and I then drive to the office of Andries Alberts, a young Boer who is the chief warden at Nyae Nyae for the Ministry of Environment and Tourism and a part-time professional hunter. Alberts is tall and fit, with a friendly, open face and three-day beard. He is dressed in dusty, field-stained khakis. On an urbanite of similar age, his emergent whiskers would be a fashion statement. For Alberts, they simply mean he has been too engaged with duties in the bush to shave. Alberts's office has a big desk piled high with papers and surrounded by a few battered chairs. A number of dogs of indiscriminate breeding lie sprawled on the cool concrete floor. They grin and slap their tails when Greenwell and I walk in but otherwise refuse to move.

We talk about the challenges of maintaining a conservancy of Nyae Nyae's size. When it was first established in the late 1990s, Alberts says, there was relatively little game on the holding; it had all been wiped out because of war and intensive persecution by neighboring farmers. "We brought in three thousand head of different species," Alberts reminisces. "Hartebeest, oryx, blue wildebeest, kudu, springbok." Alberts has a large scar below one eye from a springbok that horned him when he was taking it off the truck; he also has numerous interesting cicatrices from a leopard mauling. "That didn't have anything to do with restocking, of course," he grins. "The leopards have always been here and are doing very well."

Today, Nyae Nyae is replete with game, not just the stocked varieties, but a wide suite of species that, like the leopards, have rebounded in numbers or migrated from outlying areas. Nyae Nyae has some of Africa's highest concentrations of rare predators, such as African wild dogs, and the avian life is positively extravagant. Poaching, observes Alberts, is almost nonexistent, not just because of his constant patrolling, but also because every San is a de facto game scout of the highest competence. Because the San live in the bush and hunt constantly, virtually nothing escapes them: any poacher who shows up is quickly reported and apprehended. Each tribal member receives an annual distribution from the hunting and devil's claw collection receipts, though most money is directed to the community's critical infrastructure projects, particularly water systems. "All in all, this is a successful enterprise," Alberts says. "Income for the conservancy and its members averages about N$1,400,000 annually."

I note the potential for increasing the value of the conservancy's "product": a luxury lodge that could accommodate many ecotourists, for example. Alberts shakes his head. San culture, he notes, puts no premium on wealth; indeed, the concept of accruing individual wealth is considered somewhat odious. San life is communal life; meat and goods are meant to be shared. "The San are not entrepreneurial," he says. "Maximizing profits is not a concern for them. They remain a deeply traditional people—they know who they are, they know what they want. And they have Nyae Nyae more or less where they want it."

Nyae Nyae has its problems, of course. Its vast size helps insulate its wildlife and essential ecosystems, but it does not exist in a vacuum. Incursions from the pastoral Herero and their cattle are a major concern. Also an issue is the wildlife itself—elephants, specifically. The Nyae Nyae–Khaudum system has an abundance of elephants—too many of them, says Alberts. Conflicts with farmers and pastoralists have increased dramatically over the past few years, and the elephant numbers are such that the vegetation is starting to show a clear impact. "People who've never seen it don't understand the damage elephants can inflict on the range," he says. "When they could migrate continentally, it was never an issue, of course. But now that their migration options are reduced or nonexistent, it's a huge concern. In semiarid areas like this, they can do damage that takes the land years or decades to remedy."

The only practical solution, Alberts says, is the quick and efficient elimination of a large number of elephants. Trophy hunting isn't an effective mechanism; family groups in problem areas must be identified and quickly shot. Even in Namibia, however, such a strategy is difficult to implement because of the international charisma of the African elephant. At the time of my conversation with Alberts, the government was intent on capturing sixty of Nyae Nyae's elephants and moving them to other regions—an extremely expensive, difficult, dangerous, time-consuming, and laborious project of little benefit to the San, for no meat will be distributed. Nor would such a program make much sense for elephant conservation, Alberts adds: most areas that can support elephants in Namibia already have elephants.

Still, such problems must be considered minor when compared to the conservation challenges facing Kenya. By any reasonable metric, Nyae Nyae is a consummate success. This is brought home to me as Greenwell and I drive the 150 miles on dirt track through rolling bushveldt back to the main road. Though game is abundant, it is not as concentrated and immediately visible as it is in a national park; the land is too vast, and the bush is too thick to allow for easy viewing. Also, many of these wild animals are hunted at least occasionally; they are, in fact, wild. The propinquity of human beings disturbs them. As we drive along, I find myself drifting in and out of a hypnagogic state, until suddenly I'm brought to full awareness by an animal slinking across the road. It is obviously a predator of some kind, and Greenwell stops the truck. The creature is standing broadside to us, not ten yards away: a feline that looks like a hypertrophied tabby cat. I realize I'm looking at an African wild cat, one of the most cryptic of the continent's predators. I'm thrilled; anyone can see a lion in a national park, but to encounter one of these lesser known, far more secretive carnivores is a rare experience. To me, it seems to say: Nyae Nyae works.

From Nyae Nyae, Greenwell and I drive west, toward the coast. The land becomes increasingly arid, the vegetation sparser. Occasionally I see springbok ghosting across the landscape, but the game doesn't seem particularly abundant. But when we pull the truck over and stretch our legs, the ground is trampled with tracks and festooned with droppings from a wide array of beasts. As with any desert environment, much of the wildlife is nocturnal or crepuscular, and not easily spotted.

We spend the night in a small town bordering Etosha National Park. Like many of the parks in Kenya, Etosha—at fourteen thousand square miles, one of the largest reserves in Africa—is almost wholly fenced. This allays concerns about wildlife diseases spreading to cattle but also effectively limits animal migrations and imposes ineluctable limits on conservation. In time, says Greenwell, it's hoped that the wire can be removed from portions of the park, particularly on the southern borders; Etosha will then have contiguity with a number of communal conservancies and freehold farms, greatly increasing the region's ecological resilience. "We may be able to control livestock diseases through a multidiscipline approach that doesn't rely strictly on fencing," says Greenwell. "Improved monitoring and treatment are obvious options. And as tourism and wildlife utilization become increasingly integrated into the economy, you'll see less resistance to the idea of removing fences. If people see economic opportunity in a changing policy, they'll be less inclined to fight it."

The next morning, we drive south. The landscape exhibits a basin-and-range topography, and the reds and ochers of the raw rock and earth are concentrated by the white light and pellucid air. We pass men and women of the Himba tribe herding cattle along the road. They are among the most rigorously traditional people in southwestern Africa, plaiting their hair with ocher, dressing in animal skins and beaded decorations, including anklets designed to prevent snakebites. We go through Okombahe, a small settlement that serves nearby mines, where tin and precious stones of various kinds are extracted. We then turn southeast along a track and proceed for several additional miles through rolling terrain dotted with thorn trees. Finally, we come to a group of people sitting on folding chairs under a spare copse of acacia. A few other trucks

FIGURE 14. Members of the Tsiseb Conservancy meet with Namibian government officials to discuss compensation for wildlife damage and other issues. The meeting was sometimes heated, but afterward everyone shared a hearty repast of springbok. (Glen Martin)

have recently pulled up—officials from the Ministry of Environment and Tourism. This is a meeting of the Tsiseb Conservancy, a holding of more than five thousand square miles inhabited by Damara pastoralists.

Though it looks utterly vacant, Tsiseb supports plenty of game: along with the ubiquitous springbok (approximately seventeen thousand), there are elephants, steenbok, klipspringer, kudu, oryx, and ostriches. Predators are likewise abundant. There are no lions on Tsiseb, but there are plenty of cheetahs, in part because lions are absent; lions kill cheetahs as a matter of course. Leopards, hyenas, and jackals are common. The conservancy makes money through a trophy hunting concession, the sale of live game, and also through ecotourism: community members serve as guides to nearby Brandberg Mountain, a massive granite plug that is Namibia's highest peak and the site of thousands of Neolithic rock paintings and carvings.

It quickly becomes clear that this meeting—an annual overview of the conservancy's business—is no love fest. Several members of the ministry are present, and while the community members accord them the respect anyone in uniform reflexively receives in Africa, no one is shy about expressing his or her dissatisfaction with the way things are going in Tsiseb—or with the central government. Several people make snide comments about the "fancy new trucks" driven by the ministry officials, who laugh uneasily. Leading the meeting are the conservancy's committee members, and there is open hostility between some of their number and several people in the larger audience. An observer can't help but note that the committee members seem sleek, well-fed, and stylishly dressed in comparison to the conservancy residents, virtually all of whom are thin and poorly clothed.

Opening the meeting, committee chairmen Nickey L. !!Gaseb (exclamation points denote lingual clicks in the Damara and San languages) prefatorily notes, "This is a general meeting, not an elephant meeting," meaning a variety of issues will be discussed, not simply those associated with damage to crops and infrastructure by rampaging elephants. "Ask whatever you want, but please—don't make yourself a nuisance. We can fight, but we must fight positively, so we can improve the conservancy." !!Gaseb then launches into a long disquisition about the need to shake up the conservancy leaders and staff. "That includes the committee," he says, running his eyes over his fellow committee members, who return his gaze blandly. "Some of them are lazy; they're not doing the work. And that also goes for the mountain guides and game guards; many, many of them just aren't doing their jobs. We can't have that."

The crowd's reaction to this is mixed, and it quickly becomes apparent that incompetent staffers and committee members aren't the foremost issue of concern. A middle-aged woman stands up and addresses the committee: "A hyena bit three of my goats," she says. "And that was just last week. All of us are losing goats to hyenas and cheetahs. When are the government and the committee going to do something about that? What about controlling these animals? Last year, we heard there was going to be a government program to pay us for our livestock. What about that? Nobody is getting paid anything!"

A man stands up and, despite !!Gaseb's earlier warning, complains about elephant damage. "As everybody here knows, they tear up the water pipes and destroy our pumpkin plantings," he says. "We need government help to teach us how to live peacefully with these animals."

Cletius Maketo, a warden for the Ministry of Environment and Tourism, explains that the compensation program for animal damage is nearing the implementation stage and urges patience. "We are in the process of printing the forms now," says Maketo. "But remember, the payments will be limited, and some things won't be covered—elephants destroying infrastructure, for example. The program is mainly for the compensation of livestock losses from predators."

The complaints keep coming. One man declares that some donkeys that were purchased and killed for bait by a trophy hunter have given local leopards a taste for livestock. Another man stands and demands a solution to the conservancy's perennial water problem. "Where I live, we have a single bore hole to serve us, and it is contaminated by animals," he says. "The elephants come down and dirty it, and we have to drink it. This isn't the first time we have asked for help; this problem has been with us for fourteen years. People are sick from this filthy water. We need action now, but the committee members are not responsive." The crowd breaks into applause, and the man smiles shyly and sits down.

It seems to me that Tsiseb's residents are openly disdainful of the committee—indeed, that they are disenchanted with the conservancy in general. But when I buttonhole a few meeting attendees during a break, they seem nonplussed by my questions. Yes, they acknowledge, they are unhappy with some of the committee's members and their decisions. But there are always problems between committee officials and rank-and-file residents: that is the nature of community politics. And as for the conservancy itself—should it be abandoned? Unanimously, they say no: people have very real gripes about the administration of Tsiseb but not about the basic tenets that sustain the conservancy. "It's a hard life here," says one man. "But if we were all out on our own, it would be harder; both the people and the land would suffer. We have to make Tsiseb better, but no one wants to abandon it."

On a light breeze, I pick up an aroma of cooking meat wafting from a huddle of small brushwood shelters about a quarter-mile away. I mention that something smells delicious. "We took four springbok from the quota for this meeting," the same man says. "We're cooking them up with some pap, and everyone will eat later today." He pauses. "We have a lot of problems here, and there are plenty of disagreements," he continues. "But in the end, everybody eats together. We're all in the same community. That won't change."

And that, perhaps, is the best possible coda for conservation efforts in Namibia. No one expects miracles here, but everyone demands progress. And despite personal and tribal differences, progress—real progress—is being made.

CHAPTER 15

Not a Primary Issue of Concern

Alayne Cotterill, the chief field researcher for the Laikipia Predator Project, wants me to meet somebody: her landlord. "He's an incredibly nice guy," she says, as we pull off the main road to a gated driveway. "And a terrific farmer—he really knows what he's doing. We don't always agree on everything, but I have a great deal of respect for him." Stout, electrified fencing surrounds the property, proof against both elephants and Cape buffalo.

Cotterill and her boyfriend, conservation economist Josep Oriol, rent a small house on Mogwooni Ranch, a sixteen-thousand-acre tract owned by Jackie Kenyon and his family. Mogwooni is small as ranches go in Laikipia, but its reputation among Kenyan livestock producers compensates for its modest size. Kenyon is by many accounts the foremost breeder of Boran cattle in Kenya, possibly the whole of East Africa. This is no small thing. Developed in the first decades of the twentieth century by early Kenyan settlers, the Boran is now the preferred breed throughout the arid portions of Africa. Its primary antecedent is the common Zebu, a long-legged, hump-backed, short-haired breed originally from Ethiopia. But at least two other breeds—a Middle Eastern variety and a native Kenyan-Tanzanian bovid—also figure into the Boran's genetics.

Like the Zebu, Borans, in addition to being hump-backed, are relatively large. But they are better at converting the low-quality pasturage of the northern rangelands into meat. They are especially hardy and noted for their ability to walk long distances—a great advantage in Africa, where fodder and water sources are often far from one another. They are disease resistant, and the cows are particularly good mothers, assuring high calf survivability ratios. Their dark skin pigmentation protects them from sunburn.

Finally, Borans are noted for their strong herding instinct. This makes them relatively adept at fending off predators, because the bulls and cows congregate to protect the calves; it also keeps the cattle together in the bush, making them easier to round up and simultaneously minimize stress on the individual animals. In short, the Boran is considered the ideal breed for modern East Africa—an animal that makes efficient use of the range, producing the most meat with the least impact on the landscape. And this, in turn, makes Kenyon something of an agricultural superstar: his Boran bulls are considered among the world's best.

As we drive onto Mogwooni, it rapidly becomes evident that Kenyon is as adept at managing his rangeland as he is at refining bovid bloodlines. Across most of Laikipia and the Northern Frontier, the land looks hard used. Overgrazing is the norm, and erosion is glaringly evident. But Kenyon's property seems positively lush. There is actually standing grass here and an abundance of large trees. It almost looks like primeval savanna, save for the sleek Boran cattle cropping the rich pasturage. "Jackie is a real steward of the land," Cotterill continues. "He's conservative about stocking levels, and he does everything he can to stabilize the soil and improve the range."

But land stewardship and wildlife stewardship are two different things, and in Kenyon's opinion, I find, the second doesn't necessarily jibe with the first. We meet Kenyon at his family compound: a typical low, northern Kenyan ranch house fronted by an open-air pavilion. This latter structure is covered by a peaked thatched roof, and it's obvious that the family spends most of their time here. The furniture is both worn and comfortable, and a refrigerator is stocked with plenty of icecold Tusker lagers. Kenyon is holding two of them as we approach the compound and gives them to us after a hearty handshake. Middle-aged, dark-haired, medium in stature, muscular from a lifetime of ranch work, he is instantly likable; a big smile seems a permanent fixture of his face. This isn't because he's trying to be ingratiating; like most self-sufficient rural people, Kenyon isn't much inclined to expend energy on ingratiation. He simply has a preternaturally sunny disposition. White rural Kenyans tend to be somewhat reserved, guarded, and laconic. Kenyon seems more like a stereotypical Australian: bluff, open, quick with both a laugh and a repartee. We sit down in big chairs and take big swigs of our beer, which is deeply satisfying.

Kenyon has been described to me as something of an outlier among Laikipia's ranch owners: a man who has no great interest in preserving wildlife. In our initial conversation, he acknowledges that wildlife conservation is not his primary goal, but that is not the same, he says, as hostility to the cause of conservation. Rather, the issue is one of priorities.

"I'm in the cattle business, not the wildlife business," he says. "There's wildlife on my land—I'm glad it's there. But I can't have elephants on the property, because they'd destroy the range and my water infrastructure. Buffalo? Forget it—they carry East Coast fever. Here, we have to dip our cattle every two weeks, and that's a major expense and effort. But on Ol Pejeta [a large neighboring ranch that encourages wildlife], they have to dip every five days. That's a burden we can't incur." Nor is Kenyon enthusiastic about zebras: "Ol Pejeta has twenty-five hundred zebra, and they eat forage equivalent to seventy-five hundred cattle. If we had to sacrifice that amount of fodder, we'd quickly be out of business." Nor can Mogwooni tolerate an abundance of lions, leopards, and hyenas, Kenyon observes. "If you're serious about raising cattle in these parts, you have to actively control large predators," he says. "There's no alternative. Once one of them starts keying in on domestic animals, the only way to stop it is through lethal means."

Kenyon reflects a sensibility that is widespread in Kenya. Despite their country's carefully cultivated image as a wildlife haven, most Kenyans are less than obsessed with game, unless it's from a gastronomic perspective. Kenyans are deeply tied to the land but think more like farmers than conservationists. Fully 75 percent of the population is dependent on agriculture. Only one-third of the land is suitable for intensive cropping, with the remaining two-thirds used for grazing. Along with *ugali* (cornmeal), meat and dairy products are the traditional Kenyan staples; they are the food products that the land produces most easily, analogous to rice in tropical Asia. Conservation is a laudable pursuit, Kenyon says, "but the reality is that the average Kenyan man on the street doesn't give a stuff about wildlife. By that I mean 90 percent of the electorate. They only care about wildlife in the sense that they are outraged when someone is killed by a buffalo or elephant. Even on the rangelands, wildlife is not the issue of primary concern. What is the primary concern? Food. People are going hungry in Kenya. A thousand sacks of grain were distributed for famine relief in Nanyuki alone last week, and conditions are much worse to the north."

That enforces, Kenyon says, a certain utilitarian ethic on land use: the greatest possible good for the greatest possible number. And in Laikipia, that doesn't necessarily mean wildlife conservation. It means ranching—a specific kind of ranching.

"Despite our relatively small size, we're making it here at Mogwooni," he says. "Partly it's because we run a tight operation, and partly it's because of our cattle. All the world wants good quality Boran cattle. They're thrifty, they can utilize poor forage efficiently, they can handle a hot climate. If we can produce them we can sell them, and we can make a pretty good business of it."

Implicit in this observation is an opinion of what doesn't work: ranches that rely on ecotourism as their primary means of income and traditional pastoralism. Ol Pejeta, which originally was owned by Kenyon's family, is now managed as a nonprofit conservancy. That justifies the fodder it devotes to its twenty-five hundred zebras and thousands of other herbivorous wild animals, but Ol Pejeta is an impractical model for Laikipia as a whole, Kenyon insists. (Most tourists who come to Kenya stick to the Maasai Mara National Reserve and Tsavo and Amboseli national parks in the southern part of the country; relatively speaking, Laikipia is a minor draw for wildlife enthusiasts.)

"From the point of view of a businessman, the conservancies actually help me," Kenyon says. "They reduce the competition: fewer cattle are produced locally than otherwise would be the case. But we can't afford to turn all the rangeland into conservancies. Even with multiple-use management—cattle production as well as wildlife preservation, as is being done on Ol Pejeta—you simply can't produce enough meat to satisfy domestic needs. Feeding the nation has to be paramount."

Kenyon is also dubious about the methods promoted by groups such as the Laikipia Predator Project and the Laikipia Wildlife Forum. These techniques, he observes, are geared to pastoralists—tribal people who wander across the land in a constant round with their cattle. But pastoralism as it is typically practiced in East Africa is hardly the most efficient method for cattle production, nor is it easy on the land. With the pastoral tribes, the emphasis is on the number of animals in the herd, not their pedigree. Consequently, most pastoralists own scrub cattle. They are small animals, often weak and disease ridden, and poor at converting forage to meat. And because large herds are de rigueur for any tribal livestock owner (cattle, after all, are hard currency in pastoral cultures), the land suffers proportionately; more cattle mean more erosion and an accelerated loss of vegetative cover. You don't need to be an agronomist to notice that Kenya's pastoral commons are far more degraded than private ranches managed under modern techniques, such as Mogwooni.

"It's something of an irony, perhaps, but I have some of the best-looking habitat around here precisely because I manage the way I do," Kenyon says. "Yes, I exclude elephant, buffalo, and zebra, but I also control my stocking levels [for cattle]. I have the biggest thorn trees in Laikipia—it's a mature forest out there. My soils are stable. I have plenty of grass. It's a system that is in natural balance."

To improve the land and habitat on the pastoral holdings, Kenyon insists, it's necessary to reduce stocking levels—to whittle down the number of cattle the tribes herd, to get pastoralists to accept the Kenya shilling (or the Euro, or the American dollar, or gold) as an acceptable substitute for cows. That won't be easy, Kenyon acknowledges.

"Ultimately, the food aid now given to the pastoral communities needs to come with some strings," he says. "As it stands, you have sacks of grain and other commodities given to families who truly are starving, but they're also keeping large herds of cattle and goats. So the message should be, 'Okay, first you have to sell some animals. Say, kill two cows, eat one, and use the money from the other to buy local food.' That would result in better nutrition for the people. It would encourage local food production and trade, and it would improve the land." Kenyon pauses and quaffs from his Tusker. "But the thing is, that message can't come from the government or NGOs," he says. "The government is distrusted, and the NGOs are simply played: they're basically seen as a source of goods and food to be exploited. To get this going as truly effective policy, the word has to come from the tribal elders; those are the only real authorities that the community members respect. The elders are the people you really have to reach, and I don't see that happening."

Finally, Kenyon disparages the "predator friendly" husbandry generally supported by conservationists. "It's terribly inefficient," he says. "It's poor agricultural policy. I'm speaking here mainly of *bomas* (temporary thornwood corrals). Conservationists encourage pastoralists to herd their animals into *bomas* every night to protect them from lions and hyenas. From the standpoint of stock protection, that works pretty good, especially if you have *moran* around or inside the *boma* to increase security. But you can't really be serious about beef production if you're promoting *bomas*. Cattle graze a lot at night, at least where they're allowed to. If we used *bomas,* we'd lose a year on bringing our animals to sale; they'd have to feed for a whole extra year to reach market weight. There's no way a serious rancher can support that."

Still, Kenyon says, African megafauna appeal to ranchers in Laikipia for a number of reasons, and he has no problem with any efforts his neighbors make both to sustain wildlife and to turn a buck off it. He believes in free choice, reflecting one of the basic verities of Kenya's entrepreneurial society. And that's why he finds the country's current wildlife policy lamentable: while it purports to protect the game, he says, it actually does the opposite by stripping wildlife of all possible value. "If you could still crop zebra, you'd see more zebra in Laikipia," he observes. "There was certainly a very good market for the hides [when cropping was legal several years ago] and a pretty good one for the meat as well. Even in Laikipia, where conservation is very much the fashionable thing, the enthusiasm for wildlife relates directly to the profit people can derive from it."

But if he finds the proscription of cropping absurd, he is genuinely upset over the difficulties landowners face in eliminating problem animals. Current Kenyan law makes it virtually impossible for cattle owners to effectively address a lion or hyena that is depredating stock. They can't simply go out and shoot it; rather, they have to jump through a number of legal hoops and plow through windrows of red tape before Kenya Wildlife Service rangers will deign to investigate. More often than not, the KWS will then try to trap the problem animal and transport it to another area, where it will continue its outlaw ways. Nor is it any comfort if the rangers do decide to kill the wayward beast; KWS staffers are notoriously inept at fieldwork and often prove incapable of the efficient elimination of target animals. "The whole theory of 'humane' predator control is flawed," Kenyon continues. "When you stop ranchers or pastoralists from legally killing problem lions, you're not going to save lions. Instead, you're ensuring that every lion in the area will be snared or poisoned. No stockman is going to tolerate a predator that is wiping out his life's work."

Kenyon also disparages programs that compensate livestock owners for cattle, sheep, or goats that are killed by predators. "Even the best compensation plans are completely inadequate," he says. "What people don't realize is that it's not a matter of the one cow you lose to a lion. It's really about the forty kilograms of weight per head that you lose from your herd of one hundred cows that have been panicked and put off their feed by the attack. It will take you months to get that weight back, if ever. Predation doesn't happen in a vacuum; it's not like you lose an animal, you get paid, and everything goes on as before. Every attack has long-term consequences."

Therefore, any legislation that would increase the strictures on wildlife utilization, such as IFAW and other animal rights groups are now pushing, would only exacerbate citizen resistance to conservation, Kenyon insists. "It would just ratchet up the poisoning and snaring to new levels," he says. "It'd be out-and-out war against any wild animal."

Kenyon is in total agreement with conservationists on one thing: ranching offers far more opportunities for wildlife preservation than farming does. Indeed, he observes, intensive farming essentially eliminates wildlife habitat. And farming can also have an impact on ranching, because it changes land use regionally. But more than that, he is concerned about a certain kind of farming. Or rather, he's worried about a practice that isn't farming per se. It's more of a landscape-scale process that involves plants: Kenya's commercial greenhouse flower industry. By any evaluation, Kenya's hothouse flower trade brings significant benefits to the nation. The country accounts for 30 percent of the cut flowers sold in Europe. Kenya's flower production business, mostly long-stemmed roses, employs five hundred thousand people directly and an additional one million in ancillary and support enterprises. In 2009, cut flowers generated forty billion Kenya shillings, or the equivalent of almost five hundred million U.S. dollars.

But if the revenues in hard currency are large, so are the impacts on the environment. Not many years ago, the night in the rural regions was pristine; save for the few towns such as Naivasha, Nyeri, and Nanyuki, the land was dark under a sky blazing with constellations. Today, the greenhouse complexes are effulgent with artificial light, illuminating vast portions of the countryside, confounding migratory birds and terrestrial animals alike, draining the night sky of its beauty, mystery, and sidereal majesty. Driving past the flower operations during the day is a numbing experience: miles upon miles of hothouses—mostly plastic sheeting arrayed over PVC piping—sprawled across the landscape. Wherever water is available in Kenya, the hothouses are going up.

And the greenhouse industry affects more than the vistas, emphasizes Kenyon. He sets down his empty Tusker bottle. "Let's take a walk," he says. "I want to show you something." The night has begun to fall, and the sky is that particular cool, opalescent blue that seems unique to East African twilights. As we walk across a paddock toward a line of large fever trees, bats of various species knife through the air, gleaning the abundant crepuscular insects. Their presence reminds me that despite its profound problems in regard to megafauna preservation, Kenya remains incomparably rich in smaller wildlife species. It is still a birder's paradise; the bird key for the country is as thick as a standard dictionary. And while bats are in dire jeopardy in most parts of the world, here they are thriving.

When we get to the fever trees, I see that they mark the course of a stream: the Nanyuki River, Kenyon tells us. No water is flowing; the bottom of the river is utterly dry, a bed of clean gray cobbles and gravel. Kenyon sighs, and I realize he is deeply distressed. "It wasn't too many years ago when this river flowed year-round," Kenyon says. "The water was cold, crystal clear. The entire river was full of rainbow trout. When I was a kid, we caught them all along here, along the entire river where it flowed through our property." Back then, continues Kenyon, Kenya had two thousand miles of productive trout streams. Mostly these streams originated on Mount Kenya and the Aberdares, and they drew sport anglers from around the world, just as the country's bushlands and savanna drew trophy hunters. Now, says Kenyon, no more than a hundred miles of self-sustaining trout streams are left.

For many conservation biologists, the loss of the trout fishery in and of itself is no great tragedy. Trout are not native to Kenya. They were introduced to the country during the early twentieth century by nostalgic colonialists who wanted to re-create a sport pursued by the privileged classes of Great Britain, continental Europe, and the eastern United States: fly-fishing on private water for wild salmonids. Within the context of preserving Kenya's native wild systems, the rainbow trout has no place; it can even be considered a threat to indigenous fish, amphibians, and invertebrates.

But for Kenyon, the trout—or rather, their absence—are indicators of a system in crisis. Rainbow trout need abundant, clean, cold water to survive, and they no longer have it in Kenya. A deficit of water for the trout corresponds to a lack of water for Laikipia's rangelands, and that *does* affect Kenyon and all the other ranchers of the region, including those who foster wildlife. Where did the water go? To commercial horticulture, says Kenyon. Producing hothouse roses demands a tremendous quantity of water: roughly three-quarters of a ton of water for every ton of flowers produced. The math is implacable: the more flowers that are sent to Europe, the less water there is for the country's rangelands. This, says Kenyon, is the real environmental crisis facing the country, one that transcends wildlife and habitat conservation and animal rights. Without water, everything else is irrelevant.

"Certainly there are economic benefits provided by flower production, but I question that it is in the best interests of the country to favor this industry above all other uses for the land, to allow it to commandeer our most important resource," Kenyon says. "I come right back to my initial point—food. People are starving in Kenya, a lot of them. We have to feed them, and the best way to do that is to encourage farmers and ranchers to produce food. You can't eat roses."

Kenyon is not alone in his condemnation of the cut flower industry. The conservation group Wetlands International also pillories the trade. During the 2009 drought, the organization notes, food production plummeted in Kenya. Cattle and goats died en masse on the pastoral lands, particularly in the north. Prices for food shot up 130 percent—a phenomenon I personally witnessed in Nairobi. According to Kenyan government statistics, about four million people—more than 10 percent of the population—had insufficient food, their conditions ranging from unrelieved hunger to outright starvation. The 2009 drought also had devastating impacts on the country's game, with massive die-offs of grazing and browsing species on both the pastoral lands and the reserves. Scores of elephants died from thirst and insufficient browse in Laikipia, including the Samburu National Reserve, and in Amboseli National Park. Further degrading the protected lands were incursions by pastoralists desperately questing for water and fodder. National Geographic reported thoroughfares of cattle tracks leading into the Maasai Mara and the forced eviction of ten thousand head of cattle and their herders from Tsavo West. Meanwhile, the trade in flowers continued unabated, with a hundred tons of cut blooms a day shuttled via jet to Western markets. In other words, while people starved and wildlife perished wholesale from the drought, the flower sector was getting all the water it needed. Yet the impacts of the flower industry on both agriculture and wildlife have gone largely unremarked.

For the near term, Kenyon favors expanding water storage facilities on the Nanyuki and other rivers. "We need to capture and store every drop of water we can," he says. "Precipitation is always scant in northern Kenya, and it seems to be getting increasingly sporadic. So we need dams—big dams—and we need to build them soon, and we need to avoid the corruption that screws up most public works projects in this country."

That's easier said than done, Kenyon acknowledges. "I belong to an ad hoc group, the Nanyuki River Water Users Association," he says. "We put in a proposal to the Ministry [for the Development of Northern Kenya] for a dam. We found a site, had it surveyed—it looked like things were moving along, that we would actually get somewhere. But then we heard that somebody important wanted to build a hotel there. Now the whole project is stalled. Who knows what will happen? That one dam would've supplied the entire town of Nanyuki and a lot of the surrounding agricultural lands."

But dams alone won't solve Kenya's water problems. To save both the game and livestock, Kenyon insists, the water must be distributed equitably. First and foremost, a comprehensive and accurate inventory must be taken of the country's aqueous resources. Given the shortage of scientists and technicians in the country, Kenyon thinks it's only appropriate that NGOs kick in. It's time, he insists, to quit squabbling over side issues like hunting, to transcend narrow fields of specialized studies, and concentrate on bigger, more important issues.

"Horticulture killed the Nanyuki River," Kenyon observes. "If we want to get it back, everybody around here has to work together—ranchers and tribal elders, conservation NGOs, animal rights groups. I'd like to see [the] Mpala [Research Centre] focus on restoring the Nanyuki River corridor instead of emphasizing Ph.D. studies on the ants and beetles they find under logs. That would actually benefit the people who live in Laikipia instead of academic elites from Princeton and Harvard. If we're going to have conservation programs here, let's actually try to conserve something significant—something that will make a difference."

CHAPTER 16

Hard Choices

Arizona State University in Tempe reminds me of the East African interior in one sense: the heat. It is an extreme heat and an extremely dry heat. As I venture out on the campus, I feel myself wilting like a tender green sprout. The air seems to suck greedily at the pores of my skin, and I feel like red-hot rivets are being driven into my skull by the cruel sun. Still, I've experienced such heat before, from the California desert to the border of Kenya's Northern Frontier District, and I know I'll acclimate. Certainly, everyone else I see here already has: hundreds of students in shorts or cutoffs stroll past me on their way to class, comfortable as chuckwallas basking in the sunshine.

My destination is the Global Institute of Sustainability, an organization housed in a large multistoried building on the northern border of the campus, a couple of blocks from ASU's seventy-five-thousand-seat Sun Devil Stadium. The two constructions speak of very different perspectives. The stadium is built to a scale that dwarfs everything else on campus. It is a modern Colosseum, and like the Colosseum, it is the product of a civilization that acknowledges no boundaries and revels in its might, wealth, and power to consume.

The GIOS headquarters, on the other hand, is all about acknowledging limits. The building has been completely renovated with energy conservation as the goal. All exterior brick has been removed to create breezeways and direct natural light to interior offices. Solar shades on the windows reduce air-conditioning needs, as do the plantings of native vines that entwine the building. The furniture and carpeting are largely made from recycled materials, and specialized low-flow plumbing and irrigation systems have been installed. R-30 insulation is standard throughout, and an energy-efficient roof has been installed. Low-energy bulbs are used in every fixture, and sensors turn off lights in rooms that are not in use. Wind turbines and solar panels located on the roof can generate 1.6 megawatts of electricity, enough to supply 260 Arizona households at full capacity. If the institute looks to the future—and it does—it's a future that is tightly circumscribed, one in which nothing can be taken for granted and resources cannot be wasted.

I'm here to attend a meeting of scientists and scholars associated with Advancing Conservation in a Social Context, a subsidiary project of the institute. As noted earlier in this book, ACSC is predicated to a large degree on a contrarian presumption: win-win conservation scenarios in the developing world are wishful thinking. This is far more radical than it may seem at first take. Since the 1990s, most major conservation initiatives have been driven by the notion that significant economic and social benefits can be folded into them. In the United States, this has been expressed mostly as conservation easements for large private properties in areas with high ecological value. A rancher who owns a property that contains rare endemic plants or rich wetlands or critical migratory routes for mule deer or bighorn sheep might enter into a pact with a private conservation organization or a coalition of private groups and government agencies. In exchange for a sizable cash payout and the right to pursue traditional ranching activities—cattle production, generally—the landowner agrees to development restrictions and certain management regimens. Under such agreements, for example, cattle may be excluded from stream courses, stocking levels may be adjusted, and the restoration of sensitive habitats may be required. Such agreements are heralded as win-win: the rancher receives a big chunk of cash and maintains an established lifestyle on his or her own land, and the essential habitat values of the land are preserved in perpetuity—or at least for a long time.

Easements and similar conservation schemes focused on preserving private equity rather than extending government fiat have been successful across the United States, and the model has also been applied internationally. As Richard Leakey noted to me, Kenya could well benefit from the greater use of easements on both private ranches and communal holdings. Typically in the developing world, win-win conservancies focus on large areas with outstanding habitat values that are either in communal ownership or publicly held but exploited as commons by local residents. A core area that contains the most highly valued assets is identified and declared sacrosanct. Economic activities are then allowed in an expansive buffer zone that surrounds the core preserve. These are usually traditional pursuits, such as grazing, firewood and wild honey collection, and subsistence hunting. Even in the buffer zone, however, such activities are monitored and regulated. To as great a degree as possible, locals are employed by the conservancies as game scouts, rangers, and technicians, the logical theory being that community commitment to a project can be best assured by involving as many people as possible in its implementation.

Such community-based projects are tremendously seductive on paper, particularly for the supporters of the conservation and social justice NGOs that support them. Both traditional conservation organizations such as the Nature Conservancy and newcomer animal rights groups such as IFAW promote them, though their focus is necessarily different. IFAW does not endorse hunting, subsistence or otherwise, as an element of their projects. Their flagship project in Kenya is centered on Tsavo National Park and emphasizes support of Kenya Wildlife Service patrols in and around Tsavo, the removal of livestock illegally grazing in the park, and the improvement of community schools and water systems. Still, the intent is the same: combine wildlife protection with improved community services and economic progress.

But according to ACSC, win-win doesn't live up to expectations. Ultimately, the group posits, there are winners and losers in any conservation project. This isn't to imply that conservation is a zero sum game, but in any so-called win-win situation, some players will come out on top of other players; wildlife, wildlife habitat—indeed, ecological values in general—are more often than not at the bottom of the heap. This is an inconvenient truth that few in the conservation (and wildlife rights) community want to hear. Over the years, their talking points, their funding sources—their very raison d'être—have become inextricably bound to the win-win conceit. And yet, ACSC maintains, win-win must be debunked, or at least whittled down to size, if any real progress in conservation will be made in the future that is bearing down on us—a future that will be increasingly crowded, more environmentally stressed, less politically stable, and increasingly deficient in accessible natural resources.

Tom McShane is the point person for ACSC. He is a man of middle years, trim and athletic, with an affable manner and an easy way of conversation that underlie an incisive and utterly unsentimental intellect. McShane is the coauthor of *The Myth of Wild Africa,* a seminal text that examines the relationship between African conservation initiatives and local communities. The book is an early articulation of the ideas that ultimately manifested as ACSC, and it has driven changes in habitat conservation theory that are still unfolding.

ACSC is somewhat unusual in ad hoc conservation-oriented groups in that it draws people from a wide array of disciplines. Certainly, wildlife biologists and zoologists are well represented in the organization. Prior to the formation of ACSC, McShane was a senior conservation adviser to the World Wildlife Fund International, with responsibility for projects in Africa, Asia, and Latin America. Sheila O'Connor, a biologist and codirector of the program, is also a World Wildlife Fund International associate and currently directs WWFI's conservation measures and audit program. Hoang Van Thang is a Vietnamese conservation biologist, and Alexander Songorwa is a Tanzanian zoologist. But J. Peter Brosius is an anthropology professor at the University of Georgia, specializing in ecological and environmental anthropology. Ann Kinzig, a professor at Arizona State University's School of Life Sciences, is an authority on the interaction of social and ecological systems. Juan Luis Dammert is a Peruvian sociologist. Manuel Pulgar-Vidal is the executive director of the Peruvian Society for Environmental Law, and Bruno Monteferri Siles is a Peruvian lawyer and associate for the same organization. Ugandan David Mutekanga holds a Ph.D. in environmental management and specializes in policy research and advocacy. Paul Hirsch, an assistant professor at Syracuse University's Maxwell School of Citizenship, focuses on the nexus of science and politics.

In short, the purview for ACSC isn't just the preservation of endangered ecosystems, habitats, and species. Rather, it is employment of authorities from a variety of disciplines to deconstruct the conservation ethos and recast it in a way that makes it more resilient, responsive, and—it's hoped—effective. Its central question: *Quo vadis* conservation? Are we headed in the right direction? Are our goals practical? More to the point, given the hard realities of life on planet Earth, are we even asking the right questions?

On that last rhetorical query, ACSC responds with a resounding no. And the organization's primary job, as its members see it, is to get the questions right. After that, perhaps, real progress can be made in conservation, particularly in the places where it is most needed, in the biodiversity hotspots of Africa, Southeast Asia, and the Amazon Basin; it is no coincidence that ACSC maintains research and monitoring projects in Tanzania, Vietnam, and Amazonian Peru. While these areas are appropriate priorities for conservationists, they are also inhabited by poor—in some cases, desperate—people. Ambitious conservation projects in these regions that do not take paramount human needs into account—all too common in NGO strategizing—are thus likely to fail, says McShane. Instead of asking how to achieve ideal goals determined in New York or London, conservationists should be asking how to help local people establish goals that are practical, sustainable—and honestly acknowledge the necessity of trade-offs.

ACSC's principals are academics, and that fact was driven home to me repeatedly during the weeklong conference at ASU. Papers were presented and workshops convened, and the subjects were recondite and technical. The conversation was abstruse and sometime torturous, an intellectual patois that would parboil the frontal lobes of anyone schooled in the *Associated Press Stylebook*. But the discussions were seductive, almost Socratic in nature. The *language* of conservation was the issue here, and the conference was essentially an attempt to forge a new and more effective vocabulary.

I've often noted a profound personality variance between environmental activists and academics involved in conservation issues. The former, even if they have advanced degrees, tend to be committed to a doctrine rather than a process and are often so focused that every aspect of their lives is subsumed by their work, which is to say, their beliefs. They usually don't take a joke very well. Conservation-oriented academics, on the other hand, may be just as enmeshed in the same issues, dire issues that literally concern the fate of the earth. But though they may fight very hard to promote their ideas, they still seem able to maintain an emotional distance from them. They are quick to enjoy a drink and repartee, and they can laugh even as they discuss the unfolding of catastrophic scenarios. This may be due to the perspective conferred by the study of subjects linked to geologic time, an interval in which mass extinctions and ultimately the physical destruction of the very planet are assured. Or maybe it's because intellectual rigor precludes emotional involvement to at least some degree. In any event, McShane is anything but fervent and wide-eyed. There is an easiness to his nature. It is pleasant to discuss even terrible things with him; somehow, they seem more bearable.

That doesn't mean he doesn't take his work and the larger issues of conservation seriously. "We first got started because it was becoming clear that the conservation community needed to improve its understanding of social context, particularly in the developing world," he observed. "Relationships between conservation and development tend to be oversimplified. They're artificially separated into distinct domains, they're naively connected by win-win propositions, or they're presented as fundamentally incompatible."

Win-win viewpoints are rhetorically powerful and thus easy to employ as talking (or shouting) points, McShane allows, but they do not fully represent the complexity of the issues involved. More to the point, the actions that derive from these faulty concepts are invariably unsatisfactory and sometimes disastrous; they simply do not achieve their goals. This creates great disappointment, particularly among local stakeholders, and makes the implementation of subsequent programs all the more difficult.

The situation has worsened as win-win has evolved over the past two decades from an attractive concept to a standard template for conservation projects, observes McShane. "It has reached the point where it is extremely difficult to obtain funding for a project unless you embed multiple goals," he says. "From a practical standpoint—that is, when it gets to actually doing the work on the ground—it may be impossible to reconcile those goals. But that doesn't really matter; more and more, governments and even NGOs are reluctant to commit money unless you claim, for example, you're going to save wildlife *and* improve the local economy."

In McShane's view, things reached something of a nadir in 2000, when the Organisation for Economic Co-operation and Development (OECD) issued the Millennium Development Goals. The overarching point of the program was the reduction of poverty. There were ancillary goals, including environmental improvement, education, HIV-AIDS reduction, and water development and accessibility. But poverty reduction on a global scale was first and foremost. In fact, said McShane, no project would be approved under the program unless it explicitly made poverty reduction paramount. So money that was available under the Millennium Development Goals for watershed protection or antipoaching efforts in Kenya and Tanzania would be released only if poverty reduction was somehow shoehorned into the effort.

"By 2000, win-win was implicitly part of many programs," McShane says. "You had to address local economic issues to at least some degree. But before the Millennium Goals, it had never been so boldly stated. Now it was: 'We will solve poverty *through* conservation.' That's when win-win started falling apart. Because it's not that simple. It glosses over the tremendous challenges and complexities associated with conjoining two goals—goals that may well be disparate."

The real goal, then, shouldn't be tweaking conservation and development programs to dovetail like finely mitered joints, says McShane; by and large, that isn't possible. Development—no matter how progressive in its intent or efficient in implementation—invariably involves environmental impacts. Instead of constructing impractical win-win scenarios, conservationists and social justice advocates should be analyzing the real impacts of their proposals and identifying acceptable trade-offs. The bottom line is utilitarian, in the Benthamian sense: the greatest possible good for the greatest possible number. If a project helps more people than it hurts, if it assures the long-term protection of certain ecological values, even at the expense of some others, then it should probably go forward. If the payoff is all klaxon horns and flashing lights with little verifiable benefit, however, then it shouldn't. All such trade-offs, McShane acknowledges, involve hard choices, and some of them will be very hard indeed.

"Part of this process," he says, "is identifying choices that are too hard, when the prospect of development, no matter how 'green' it is, would be too high. At that point, the choice should be rejection of the project." Examples of such projects are already cropping up in East Africa. Massive biofuel schemes proposed for the Kenyan and Tanzanian coasts could well offset some of the atmospheric carbon loading now imperiling the planet, but they would destroy vast swaths of wetland and coastal forest. Most environmentalists—even those rigorously focused on climate change—would not consider the trade-offs sufficiently worthwhile.

On the other hand, projects that allow local pastoralists to cut firewood and graze livestock in forest reserves could work, provided sufficient capital and political backing are allotted to protect mature woodlands, watersheds, and wildlife. There would still be impacts: a "working" forest likely will support less diversity than a pristine and inviolate forest. But the support of the local people, who might otherwise utterly destroy the forest if they were not allowed regulated use, makes for an acceptable trade-off.

Given ACSC's emphasis on utilitarianism, trade-offs, and the subsequent necessity of making hard choices, some approaches to conservation would be considered inappropriate, even disingenuous, from the outset. Projects centered on animal rights would probably be among these, particularly in Africa. Cases can and should be made for restricting human activities in some areas, if specific species of concern or entire wildlife assemblages are at stake; a large soybean complex in the middle of the Grumeti Corridor, for example, would have to be vigorously resisted, because it could destroy the great wildebeest migration between the Serengeti and the Maasai Mara. But as McShane observed earlier in this book, the "no kill" policy for dangerous megafauna now pursued to greater or lesser degree in Kenya does little more than enrage local communities. Transferring a testy elephant or livestock-killing lion from one district to another fulfills the no-kill mandate, empowers IFAW and allied NGOs operating in the country, and provides good fodder for animal rights Web sites and publications. But as previously noted, there are no empty spots on the Kenyan map, save for some bandit territory in the Northern Frontier District. The animal that caused trouble for people in the area where it is captured will likely cause just as much or more trouble for people in the area where it is released. And even if the animal avoids contact with other humans, it will inevitably run afoul of members of its own species. Lions are highly territorial and will not accept outsiders. Elephant social groups will sometimes accommodate transferees, but the typical problem elephants—old, solitary bulls—are not good candidates for adoption into matriarchal pachyderm family units.

Moreover, the expense and human labor involved in tranquilizing and removing problem animals is considerable, and it sends a less than flattering message to pastoral communities: the individual animal is more important than your family, clan, or village. We are willing to spend money on its welfare but not yours. You don't even get the meat from the problem animal. And certainly, you have no say in animal control policy. The ministers of Parliament and NGOs in Nairobi propose, the Kenya Wildlife Service disposes, and you on the *shambas* and *manyattas* must simply suck it up and accept our beneficent policies.

Ultimately, this gets back to language—or, rather, the disconnect that inevitably occurs when translation between two or more languages is necessary. Conservation invariably involves tropes and concepts developed in Western academic and scientific circles. Translating these concepts among the different players involved in any project is extremely difficult, but that difficulty is seldom acknowledged. Usually, McShane and his colleagues say, Western scientific knowledge is so markedly emphasized in conservation initiatives that local knowledge is marginalized or even ignored; the language that drives any given initiative is typically a language of the developed world, one that accommodates Western scientific and social concepts easily but may be largely incomprehensible to local actors.

Such "language hegemony," say ACSC associates, is counterproductive for two reasons. First, even passive disparagement of community wisdom typically incurs great resentment among locals—the essential linchpins for any successful conservation project. Too, local knowledge of natural processes very often contains embedded data critical to conservation. Community residents, after all, typically accrue their knowledge over centuries or millennia. They may know of areas of particular biological richness, for example, or the location of rare plants, the behavior of specific species during specific seasons, the site of a cryptic water source. So forging a linguistic construct that is accessible and means the same thing to all parties is critically important. Unless everybody shares common definitions and concepts—that is, unless everybody speaks the same language—conservation initiatives can founder.

Another difficulty is that initial success in conservation projects can paradoxically lead to ultimate failure. ACSC researchers point to a prime example of this in the Madre de Dios region of Peruvian Amazonia. This part of the Amazon Basin is almost pristine. A project is under way there to help local settlers harvest and market Brazil nuts from the local *"castaña"* trees, which form a significant percentage of the forest canopy. By any measure, the project has been largely successful: the settlers have enthusiastically responded to the technical help offered in the harvesting, preparation, and sale of the nuts and in the management of the *castaña* forest. The market for Brazil nuts is robust, and the *castañeros* of Madre de Dios have been able to capitalize on the sustainability of their project, adding considerable market value to their product.

The problem is that the program may be too successful to assure continued protection of the forests. As the *castañeros* have improved their incomes, their aspirations have climbed accordingly, particularly for their children. Many *castañero* families use their extra income to send their children to schools in Lima, Cuzco, or other cities to improve their prospects. Others have simply opted to use their savings to open a business elsewhere; life in the rain forest, after all, is hot, dangerous, exhausting, and ultimately affords little security.

In a paper produced under ACSC auspices by Nino Bariola of the Peruvian Society for Environmental Law and Patricia Dunne of the University of Georgia, a *castañero* sums up the situation: "Children do not always want to keep going to the [*castaña* groves]. After studying, they want to go out and do something else. . . . My children are study-ing; one of them has ended his career already and is in Cuzco, and I have two others [who] are studying in Lima. Perhaps it's a mistake to have not identified them to be close to the rainforest. . . . Maybe it is that they have not been identified with it."

With children leaving for the cities, many *castañeros* find they have no progeny to maintain their *castaña* concessions, so they sell them to the highest bidder in the open market, and the buyers usually have no interest in conservation. The groves may be exploited in a less than har-monious fashion or may be logged and the land put to other uses.

On pondering the *castañero* conundrum, I can't help but see paral-lels with the cattle-herding communities of East Africa. I recall Richard Leakey's observation: that it is both preposterous and arrogant to assume a Maasai or Samburu pastoralist does not aspire to another vocation for his children, that he does not want them to be educated, become doctors or lawyers—to have, in short, a "better" life. And that's the problem: without traditional people on the land, how can we hope to conserve? Traditional subsistence communities bring their own suite of problems to wildlife preservation, of course, but their lifestyles are more appropriate to conservation goals than corporate business plans centered on clear-cut logging or sugarcane production. But conservation projects that combine economic development goals may end up so suc-cessful that all incentives to conserve ultimately are lost; replacing the stick with the carrot means nothing if the carrot ultimately disappears.

ACSC is focused on research and not advocacy, so its associates are generally disinclined to comment on the "soundness" of issues such as animal rights. Indeed, any goal theoretically can be justified in the pur-suit of conservation, McShane observes—and that's the problem. The win-win paradigm has allowed the conflation of conservation with any number of ancillary projects, from resort development to rehabilitation centers devoted to saving individual members of certain charismatic species. But when such disparate goals are combined, the research dem-onstrates that true conservation usually is the loser. When IFAW comes into an area, its goals are clear: to make sure elephants are not killed, for example. Either deliberately or inadvertently, its administrators don't adequately take into account the complex relationships between subsistence communities and destructive megafauna. It is normative thinking (i.e., the way things should be rather than the way things are) that makes win-win situations unstable and ultimately unworkable. IFAW brochures are very effective in touching the hearts of First World donors and sympathizers. These promotional materials are not duplicitous: the portrayed baby elephants and their gentle handlers really exist. But they don't tell the whole story, because to do so would undercut the core message. They tell of the baby elephant that was saved in a specific locale, but they don't tell of the scores of other elephants in the region that were killed because of crop depredation or land tenure disputes. IFAW's methods have thus proved effective in saving individual elephants, and for this their strategy is sound. Setting up elephant rescue centers is doable. But the larger mission implied by their work—"saving" Africa's elephants—remains unfulfilled and may in fact be sabotaged by IFAW's own work. The lavishing of hundreds of thousands of dollars on the suckling of baby elephants while locals see their maize crops razed and their cattle stomped flat by irate pachyderms sends the familiar, loud, and dissonant message to rural Africans: too bad about you; this cute little elephant comes first.

Alex Songorwa, an ACSC associate, notes such examples are rife in conservation efforts across Africa. "The fact is that local people are bearing the brunt of the costs in conservation," he says. "No matter what the project, they are the ones who have to deal with the downsides. Meanwhile, the NGOs that are sponsoring the individual projects are reaping the benefits—the publicity, the donor support. To the extent that East Africa and its wildlife are considered global assets, then, it is the world that gets the benefits, while some of the poorest people on the planet are supporting the costs. So if you want conservation to work in Africa, you have to find ways to turn that equation around."

That is proving very hard to do. The reality is that conservation involves hard choices that can run counter to the interests of communities, individual animals, or specific ecosystem goals; disenfranchised groups are inevitable in any "solution" and can ultimately lead to the unraveling of any deal. In Kenya, individual animals may win at the expense of habitat conservation or community prosperity. In Tanzania, this is seldom if ever the case; the lives of specific animals are never accorded much official consideration. Still, the "hard choices" equation remains in play. A highway now planned for the heart of the Serengeti, for example, may improve trade and community well-being, but it threatens to destroy the great wildebeest migration. (The proposed road is especially problematic because a suggested route to the south would achieve most of the same ends without major ecological disruption. The Tanzanian government appears determined to proceed with the original proposal, despite a deeply negative international response. Even the

World Bank has weighed in, offering Tanzania financing for the alternative southern route.)

On the other hand, some trade-offs may favor wild systems at the expense of rural communities. Songorwa cites a trenchant example: the eviction of pastoralists, farmers, and their livestock from the Usangu Basin, an eight-thousand-square-mile tract of wetland and savanna bordering the Great Ruaha River in southern Tanzania. The river supports hydropower projects that supply the capital city of Dar es Salaam with electricity. In recent years, however, the amount of water flowing down the river has decreased dramatically. This is due to water diversions for rice and other crops in the Usangu area as well as the stripping of vegetative cover in the Ruaha watershed; as the trees and forage have disappeared, the land has lost its ability to absorb and retain water.

The lack of sound governance is almost as much a problem in Tanzania as in Kenya, and poor land use rarely goads pointed action from officials. But when the lights in Dar es Salaam started going out, Songorwa drily observes, it was decided that something had to be done. And when it was done, it was done quickly, efficiently—some say brutally. Thousands of people and their livestock were relocated, sometimes forcibly, from the Usangu wetlands. In the eastern portion of the region alone, about ten thousand people, fifty-two thousand head of cattle, eighteen thousand goats, fifteen thousand sheep, and fifteen hundred donkeys were moved to other areas. Nor did the Usangu migrants find life in their new environs agreeable. Generally speaking, says David Mutekanga, the assistant director of the Ruaha Landscape Program for the Wildlife Conservation Society of Tanzania and the coauthor of a report on the relocation, they are worse off. They have not received promised government aid to construct new homes, and they have less access to natural resources: land for their crops, forage, firewood, water.

Still, the benefits of the program are real and significant to the nation—indeed, the world, given that Tanzania is, de facto, a wildlife reserve of global significance. Vast areas of wetlands are now conserved and managed for wildlife as well as watershed protection. The vegetative cover on the upland areas is returning, and soils are stabilizing. The flow down the Ruaha has improved dramatically. And most significantly, power supplies to Dar es Salaam are once again (more or less) reliable. The tragedy of the Usangu diaspora is real, says Mutekanga; several thousand people have been forcibly displaced and have been left largely to their own scant resources. But their unhappiness must be measured against the impacts of power disruption to Dar es Salaam, a city of more than two million people and the economic and political node of the country; and as a lagniappe, the wildlife carrying capacity of the region has been tremendously enhanced.

Was it worth it? Clearly, the residents of Dar es Salaam would say so. And so would advocates for African wildlife; in this one case, at least, members of the World Wildlife Fund, Safari Club International, and the International Fund for Animal Welfare would all find themselves in accord. But for the pastoralists and the small farmers of the Usangu Basin, the decision was an unmitigated catastrophe: they lost almost everything. "Usangu clearly is not win-win," Mutekanga says. "It is not two-dimensional—it has many dimensions. There are multiple benefits, and there are real losers. The project as a whole can be justified. But there can't be any denying the real hardships the program imposed on thousands of people and the broken promises of the government."

This, then, could be the new, grim face of conservation: progress, certainly, but progress that comes with real costs, including human misery. It's not that such trade-offs are new, says McShane: they've always been there. Now, however, "we're finally starting to acknowledge them. And without that acknowledgment, without a means of measuring and evaluating them, we can't really have effective approaches to conservation. We have to be honest about who wins and who loses."

CHAPTER 17

The Nation on a Plate

Radio is a lively affair in Nairobi, a medium that provides a good measure of the national mood. Kenyans have strong and disparate opinions, and they are more than willing to share them in venues where they feel secure and comfortable; these, unfortunately, are few.

Though a nominal democracy, the government is heavy-handed in its attempts to silence critics. In 2006, masked thugs raided the newsroom of Kenya's oldest newspaper, the *Standard,* and the offices of the Kenya Television Network. Several days earlier, the paper and station had run stories on secret meetings between President Mwai Kibaki and his arch foe, the environment minister Kalanzo Musyoka. Both men were deeply displeased by the coverage; neither acknowledged instigating the attacks, but it was widely believed they were involved. Certainly, government interference in the media—as well as extrajudicial killings by the country's police, malfeasance in any kind of bureaucratic dealings, and general disregard by authorities for the citizenry—constitutes business as usual in Kenya. One sticks one's neck out at great risk of having one's head chopped off.

Radio, particularly talk radio, provides a much-needed antidote to the lamentable malaise infecting the body politic. Protected by the anonymity of the airwaves, callers are free to express their opinion in no uncertain terms. While some shows promote the interests of specific tribes or political coalitions, others are more catholic, offering a platform for unexpurgated screeds on the problems facing the nation.

During a stay in Nairobi in March 2009, I tuned as usual to the talk shows to find out what people were thinking. That, as it turned out, wasn't particularly difficult: they were thinking about a book. Specifically, they were thinking about *It's Our Turn to Eat*, written by Michela Wrong, a British journalist who has covered Africa for the *Financial Times*, Slate.com, and the *New Statesman*. Wrong's book was nominally about John Githongo, a young Kenyan apparatchik appointed by Kibaki as an anti-corruption czar. Kibaki and Githongo are both Kikuyu. Apparently, Kibaki thought that their tribal ties were sufficient to insulate his administration from any serious inquiry.

He was wrong; Githongo is an anomaly in East Africa, a technocrat from a privileged family who holds dual citizenship in Kenya and Great Britain. His allegiance transcended his tribal ties, indeed, was supra-national; he was driven not so much by Kenyan nationalism as by an innate sense of probity and devotion to fair play. In short, Githongo did his job so well that he implicated every significant player in the administration, including Kibaki himself. Ultimately, Githongo had to flee to Britain to ensure his safety.

But Wrong's book was no simple yarn about a doughty whistle-blower. It was an indictment of Kenyan politics in general, a lament that the country once promoted as the great economic and social hope for Black Africa had fallen so far and landed in the muck so hard. And everyone who was calling in to the talk shows that week I was in Nairobi wanted to talk about the book, Githongo, and, most pointedly, about the disgraceful state of the government. They talked about the book, but few had actually read it. That's because it wasn't available anywhere in the country. Kibaki was too shrewd, apparently, to declare an outright ban on *It's Our Turn to Eat*. But with the memory of the raids on the *Standard* and Kenya Television still fresh, booksellers nevertheless got the message and refused to stock the book. Still, boot-legged copies and unauthorized transcriptions began circulating widely throughout the country, confirming what most people already knew or suspected: their country was for sale, with all proceeds going to the men and women at the top.

As Wrong describes it, the Kenyan political system is resolutely fixed to tribal affiliations and obligations. Unlike Julius Nyerere in Tanzania, Jomo Kenyatta (who died in 1978) made no serious effort to forge a national identity and quash tribal impulses. On the contrary: Kenyatta was a Kikuyu. To a large degree, the country's independence emerged from the resistance of the Kikuyu and allied tribes, the Embu and Meru, to white rule. When Kenyatta assumed power, the Kikuyu, a populous agricultural tribe from the Mount Kenya area, were the primary beneficiaries. All the choice positions in government went to Kikuyus and their allies. Government, in short, quickly evolved into a patronage system: Kenyans call it "eating."

When Kenyatta died, his vice president, Daniel arap Moi, took over. Moi was a member of the Kalenjin tribe, and it was now the Kalenjins' turn to "eat." And eat they did, to a surfeit, while the other tribes got scraps. Kibaki was elected president in 2002 on a reform platform, and hope ran high in Kenya that the country was finally going to achieve a degree of good governance. Not so: the Kikuyu once again sat down at the trough and began eating with a vengeance. The situation worsened during the 2007 elections, which were characterized by widespread fraud and resulted in the dubious reelection of Kibaki over Raila Odinga, a Luo. The Luo are a Nilotic people, mostly fishers by trade, who live along the shores of Lake Victoria. (The tribe gained some international recognition with the election to the U.S. presidency of Barack Obama, whose lineage is Luo.) Though the Luo are Kenya's third most populous tribe, they have long felt disenfranchised, and they did not take Kibaki's clumsy power grab lightly; 2007 was going to be their turn to eat.

Kenya dissolved into factional violence, and for two months the country was in a state of chaos. At least twelve hundred Kenyans were killed, and uncounted thousands were injured. More than forty thousand homes, business enterprises, and farms were looted or burned. At least three hundred thousand people were displaced, with members of specific tribes moving back to their ancestral homelands; all sense of intertribal comity was lost. Tourism, one of the cornerstones of the Kenyan economy, tanked, and it has yet to fully recover. The situation was mitigated only by an agreement between Kibaki and Odinga to preside over a coalition government: Kibaki would remain as president, while Odinga would serve as prime minister. While this accommodation has quelled most of the overt violence, it has done nothing to remedy the underlying tensions, the sense of betrayal Kenyans feel at the aborted reforms, or the basic problem of "eating."

Moreover, Kenya's corrupt governance presents a special set of embarrassing problems to conservationists. That's because all conservation must be implemented through the government or at least with its imprimatur. And in Kenya, government participation invariably means payoffs to government officials. True, it's seldom if ever as crass as conservation NGO staffers handing authorities envelopes stuffed with wads of shillings or dollars. But any money that is directed through any of the ministries, including those responsible for wildlife and the environment, is skimmed, with the proceeds divvied up among political beneficiaries. Sometimes it's more than skimmed: it's largely diverted, and the people (and animals) on the ground end up with little or nothing.

I interviewed Wrong by phone, and she observed that the culture of corruption has changed little since the publication of *It's Our Turn to Eat*. In her book, Wrong noted Githongo was responsible for exposing the Anglo Leasing and Finance Company, a shell company that diverted about a billion dollars in public funds to the pockets of Kibaki cronies. Githongo and his allies hoped the sunlight he shed on the scam would yield real results, sufficient citizen outrage to instigate real changes. And indeed, average Kenyans were apoplectic at the revelations. The Kibaki administration vowed action; the heads of a few minor officials rolled, and some monies were returned to the exchequer. But the Big Men in the administration suffered little inconvenience, and the gluttony never stopped.

"It's really quite appalling," said Wrong. "Since my book, there has been scandal after scandal—huge ones involving the diversion of maize and oil worth millions and millions of dollars. If anything, the rate of looting has accelerated. You have this sense that everyone is stealing as much as they can as fast as they can, in preparation for the next election, because, of course, you'll lose your place at the table if your party loses."

In such a kleptocracy, NGOs and donor organizations, including those involved with wildlife, must be complicit, Wrong says. As noted, it's not a matter of NGOs actively fostering corruption; it's more a case of corruption tainting every aspect of the country's political and economic life. It is ubiquitous; it cannot be avoided. And yet, Wrong notes, NGOs and bilateral donors should at least *make* the effort to avoid it. They should not yield so readily to it, not so willingly embrace the familiar and cynical acronym, TIA: This Is Africa.

"It is just so pervasive, and it's especially discouraging when you see the really large players go along with it," Wrong says. "Under Moi, the International Monetary Fund lavished funds on Kenya, despite their knowledge that most of it was being stolen. They knew Moi couldn't be trusted, and they occasionally suspended their disbursements when things got ridiculously blatant, but they always resumed them." Despite their good intentions, observes Wrong, the NGOs undermine sound governance in Kenya. That's because they are, paradoxically, *too* successful: too well-funded, too effective, too equitable in distributing their largesse to their staffers. By being so "fair" in paying their Kenyan employees salaries commensurate to those they'd earn in the developed world, they create an *über*class of professionals whose raison d'être isn't so much promoting the ideals or agenda of the NGO as hanging on to position.

"By Kenyan standards, the salaries [paid to NGO staffers] are beyond generous: they represent true wealth," says Wrong. "And then there are the perquisites and benefits—the car that comes with the position, the health coverage, the prestige, the fact that you travel in elite circles and get to speak the language of human rights and social and environmental justice. Contrast that with the business or government sectors. If you go into business, you're hobbled at every step by corruption; you have to pay a massive bribe just to get a phone hookup. In government, the salaries and status are low and nepotism is rife. So if you're a young Kenyan with a good degree, where are you going to go? The NGOs are soaking up the best and the brightest, leaving only the stupid and sleazy for government."

As a result, Wrong continues, the NGOs are now the sector Kenyans reflexively turn to for accountability, aid, succor, or justice. "It's gotten to the point that they now hold the NGOs responsible for dealing with any problem," Wrong says. "If cholera is running rampant or people are starving, they get mad at the NGOs, not the government. It's assumed the government will be inept and corrupt, that they'll be unable to mount an effective response. They expect the NGOs to step up."

These rising expectations for NGOs both marginalize the role of the national government and invest aid organizations with powers that serve the interests of foreign constituencies—specific religions, animal rights, conservation, what have you—rather than the needs and aspirations of Kenyan citizens.

Moreover, Kenyan power brokers have realized that the NGO model is in itself an opportunity for plunder. "Many of them have set up their own NGOs," she says. Sometimes, she continues, this is a good thing: John Githongo, for example, founded the Kenyan chapter of Transparency International, an organization that tracks government corruption. But more often, the NGOs established by Kenyan politicians and businesspeople are shell entities designed to seize and hide public or donor funds. "The sad fact is that corruption is deeply entrenched in the NGO sector," Wrong says. "The people who run the [corrupt NGOs] are very sophisticated, very skilled at playing the game. They know how to get money from donor organizations, and they skim half or more off the top. Githongo, in fact, first blew the whistle on an NGO that stole money from the Ford Foundation."

That incident marked the beginning of Githongo's career as a champion of good governance. In 1998, he agreed to edit an economic magazine for the Series for Alternative Research in East Africa, an NGO directed by political science scholar Mutahi Ngunyi. In the course of his work, Githongo discovered that Jonathan Mayo, a Ford Foundation staffer in charge of NGO disbursements in Kenya, was working with Ngunyi to divert money from Ford to their private accounts. Githongo was a prosecution witness in the case against Ngunyi and Mayo that followed.

Something else militates against good governance—and indirectly, wildlife conservation—in Kenya, observes Wrong. It isn't illegal or even inappropriate, in that it speaks directly to basic human yearnings for security and stability. But it still bodes ill for ambitious and effective conservation programs in the country. "Kenyans are really smitten by land lust," Wrong observes. "Every Kenyan wants a plot, and it's putting tremendous pressure on the nation." I thought of Richard Leakey's observations on the same issue: how Kenya's embrace of an entrepreneurial economic model has had the unfortunate consequence of breaking up group ranches and other commonly held tribal holdings, leading to widespread habitat fragmentation, haphazard development, deforestation, and soil erosion.

"As the population grows and the demands for land increase, the plots keep getting smaller and smaller," Wrong says. "This creates a good many problems, foremost among them the fact that much of the land in Kenya cannot provide proper returns if it is managed in small plots. Over much of the country, the soils are too thin and the water supplies too arid for farming. Also, most the country is still rural with poor infrastructure; commercial opportunities are extremely limited. So really, ranching, for either livestock or wildlife, is the only practical way to go. But a successful ranching operation in Kenya demands thousands and thousands of hectares. You can't make it on smallholdings."

The impracticality of small-scale farming in arid ranching country hasn't stopped the demands for reforms to break up large holdings, most particularly those belonging to white Kenyans in and around the Great Rift Valley. The specter of a Zimbabwe-style "liberation" of non-tribal land is causing deep anxiety among the country's white and foreign ranchers. The situation was exacerbated in 2006, when Thomas

Cholmondeley, a scion of a venerable white Kenyan family with aris-
tocratic antecedents, shot and killed a black poacher on his fifty-five-
thousand-acre ranch near Lake Naivasha. It was the second time Cholmondeley had killed a black intruder on his property, and his arrest and
trial were front-page news in the Nairobi newspapers day after day. So
was his release three years later for "good behavior," which was seen by
average Kenyans as another sign of money and influence compromising
the country's judiciary. Moreover, the Cholmondeley case focused the
spotlight on Kenya's remaining thirty thousand white citizens, particularly those owning large tracts of land. The calls for reform—for breaking up the big white-owned ranches—increased dramatically.

"Black Kenyans see it as a matter of fairness," says Wrong. "They see
the ranchers as a white spoiled elite who control vast areas of land. Why
should that guy have so much land while I have none? That's a legitimate issue, but so is the fact that the land can't be managed in an economically and environmentally sound way if it is broken up into small
parcels." For conservationists, this presents a tremendous dilemma.
Large ranches can be managed for wildlife through conservation easements, but the same is not true for small farms. Promoting habitat protection without seeming to suck up to the landowning elite—in many
cases, the "white elite"—is a task of consummate difficulty.

Parenthetically, it should be noted that IFAW and other animal rights
groups do not share the same problem; IFAW, in fact, supports the burgeoning reform movement that could put more property in the hands
of landless people (e.g., "indigenous communities") and, by implication,
break up large holdings. The activities of animal rights groups in Kenya
are largely concentrated in the national parks and animal rescue centers. (The latter, obviously, don't require large acreages.) Because private
ranchers typically want the consumptive use of wildlife linked to conservation efforts on their lands, they are seen more as adversaries than
as potential allies by animal rights NGOs.

Land reform, then, could well obstruct megafauna and habitat conservation in Kenya; this cuts against the conventional wisdom that social
justice and environmental equity go hand in hand. Too, the country's
morally bankrupt government means that even the best land reform
scheme will be undermined. Since independence, a number of progressive laws have been passed in Kenya, laws couched in high-flown language, laws embodying the most laudable of ideals. But they have been
largely ignored, except where their ad hoc application has benefited one
Big Man or another. Even if a forward-looking, fair-minded land reform

bill is passed, the chances of it translating into land allotments for the country's disenfranchised masses are poor: the eaters will keep eating, the hungry will get hungrier.

Moreover, says Wrong, Kenya's broad-based collective obsession with land threatens to hobble the country's economy as well as its environment. In a very real way, it simply reflects the population's traditional views on wealth—views that are very old, very conservative, and rooted in the region's pastoralist and farming traditions. To agricultural tribes such as the Kikuyu, tillable land is the only store of wealth that is reliable. The same can be said for pastoral tribes such as the Maasai and access to grazing land.

"I read a very interesting article [in a Kenyan journal] recently," Wrong tells me. "The writer was alarmed with predictions that more than 20 percent of Kenyans will end up owning no land. This was framed as a disaster, as a sign that millions of people will be destitute, that the national economy was at grave risk. Contrast that with Britain. Despite some current problems, the economy is pretty sound, and most people are far from destitute. Yet most of us don't own land. We have more diverse, more sophisticated stores of wealth—bank accounts, stock and bond investments, trust funds. That gives us greater economic and social resiliency. Relying on land as the primary store of wealth hobbles a country, prevents it from fully participating in the global economy. And for a country with an exploding birth rate such as Kenya, it also implies some very real and frightening limits: there is only so much usable land to go around."

Further, land lust runs directly counter to the country's "wildlife paradise" brand: in the long run, you can't simultaneously chop up large swaths of habitat into small plots and maintain healthy populations of megafauna. But while this is a serious issue for conservationists, it has no bearing on government policy. The eaters will have it both ways. They'll continue to flog the country as Africa's premier ecotourist destination—a destination where wildlife is so esteemed that a hunting ban has been maintained valiantly for two decades, despite calls for a reversal from cruel, wealthy trophy hunters; at the same time, they'll promote land conversion policies that enrich them personally and benefit their tribes.

As Wrong intimates, virtually every Kenyan ministry and agency is compromised. The Kenya Wildlife Service—the agency directly responsible for the nation's parks, reserves, and game—is no exception. As noted, it was fairly effective when Leakey ran it, but even then it was hardly considered squeaky clean. "Leakey was by no means popular," says Wrong. "There were numerous scandals during his tenure, mostly involving recruitment; it wasn't clear where he was getting [his subordinates] or why they were hired."

That was twenty years ago, and the service's reputation has steadily declined since. In 2004, when John Githongo was hard at work rooting out corruption, the NGO he founded, Transparency International Kenya, reported that 520 of the 1,000 KWS ranger trainees inducted that year were patronage beneficiaries, people with direct connections to powerful politicians. In a 2010 analysis by Transparency International, the Kenyan Ministry of Forestry and Wildlife (which oversees the KWS) was ranked as the tenth most corrupt institution in the country, following the Kenya National Police, the Nairobi City Council, the Ministry of Defense, the national judiciary, the Ministry of Lands, the Department of Registration of Persons, the Kenyan Prisons Service, the Kenyan Ports Authority, and the Ministry of Immigration.

The vast majority of people I've talked to who have had any direct dealings with the KWS have found their experiences unsatisfactory at best; many have described both managers and staffers as inept, poorly trained, venal, or grossly corrupt. Not everyone who works with Kenya's wildlife sector has such low opinions of the agency, however. In general, the animal rights groups active in the country seem to have better relationships with the KWS than organizations strictly concerned with conservation. Will Travers, the executive director of Born Free, generally is positive about the efforts of KWS; Born Free contributes a good deal of money to the service, much of it to support anti-poaching efforts and other field activities.

"I have worked with the senior people at KWS since 1989," Travers wrote in an e-mailed response to queries on the agency. "I think that [covers] seven different directors. While I have [noticed] a difference in levels of experience, I have never had my efforts or that of Born Free hampered, derailed or compromised by corruption. We have never paid a bribe and have never been asked for one. We maintain strict financial controls and are open and transparent—there is no room for corruption to hide."

Still, the problems at KWS point to a broader malaise, one that transcends simple inefficiency and corruption: citizen indifference. Kenyans are having a difficult enough time making government responsive in the areas they care about—the police, the courts, the bureaucracies concerned with agriculture and land distribution. Its reputation as a wildlife haven notwithstanding, Kenya is not Namibia; game is not an integral part of most people's lives; it is not generally viewed as a resource worthy of husbandry. When it is considered at all, it is as a hindrance or a threat. Outrage over government malfeasance in the wildlife sector, then, ranges from scant to nil.

"I've been to the parks and reserves, and I don't ever recall seeing a middle-class black Kenyan," says Wrong. "And I don't think it's really a matter of expense; Kenyan citizens only pay one-fifth the rates of foreign tourists. It's more that wildlife-related tourism is considered a white indulgence—a folly, even." These attitudes tend to harden if there is any intimation from outsiders, particularly white outsiders, that Kenyans are mismanaging the game. Again, this is partly due to differing priorities. "Many Kenyans feel [visitors from Europe and North America] care more about wildlife than people—their fellow human beings, in other words, who are destitute or even starving," Wrong says. "They find that astounding."

And then there is the residuum of colonialism. Older Kenyans, particularly older Kenyans in power, tend to bristle at any criticism that originates from Europe or North America. "I remember one time I was interviewing this older [politician]," says Wrong, "and the issue of wildlife conservation came up. He got very angry at the direction of my questioning. His attitude was, 'How dare you say we don't care about our heritage! You can't tell us what to do!' Then he stalked out. You just get this sense that many older people would rather live with sleaze than accommodate any discourse from outsiders, which they associate with the colonial yoke."

At the time of this writing, much ado was being made in the international press of the passage of a new Kenyan constitution. Newspaper articles and blogs described citizen jubilation, and wire photos showed celebrants dancing in the streets of Nairobi. The new document, approved by almost 70 percent of the voters in a national referendum and signed into law by Kibaki, is roughly constructed along the lines of the American constitution, providing a system of governmental checks and balances. Most significantly, it greatly diminishes the power of the presidency, technically making patronage—and, by implication, corruption—less of a factor in political life. The passage of the constitution added considerable luster to Kibaki's sullied reputation, boosted support for the Kibaki-Odinga coalition government, and allayed some of the bitterness left over from the violence following the 2008 election.

But will it really change Kenya's "eating" culture? Wrong doesn't think so. Talking to her, one gets the sense that the TIA acronym colors her perspective on the continent—on Kenya in particular—to an indelible degree. She considers the breathlessly optimistic coverage that followed the adoption of the new constitution inexcusably naive—reporting of the shallowest, sloppiest sort. "Full adoption of the constitution will take five years, and a lot can happen—or not happen—in that time," she observes. "Also, every section of the constitution must be formally implemented by special committee, and there's a huge wrangle under way on who will sit. It is clear that powerful people will have a great deal of say on committee members and that, as a consequence, their influence will be felt in the final implementation of the constitution."

Also, says Wrong, a close reading of the constitution reveals that much power remains invested, however obliquely, in the presidency. She attended a meeting of former diplomats and legal pundits who had gone over the document in detail, "and they agreed that it's not going to make a great deal of difference. A very big issue is that the power of district officials remains intact, and district officials are the president's secret hand. He has direct authority over them, and they do his bidding. Also, the president retains control of the security forces, and they are hardly subtle about enforcing the president's will on the people. Finally, the constitution is supposed to provide for devolution of funds from the central government to the provinces. But very little funding is actually earmarked for the provinces—around 15 percent. And how much of even that small amount of money will actually get beyond Nairobi remains very open to debate."

The depressing conclusion, then, is that things are unlikely to change at Kenya's banquet table. The queue to the feast may change on occasion, depending on tribal influence. But seating will perforce remain limited: a few will eat to excess, and everyone else will starve. And the wildlife, it seems, will either sit with the hungry or end up on the menu.

CHAPTER 18

Topsoil and Condoms

Sometimes the white-hot disputes between animal rights advocates and traditional conservationists—between people who consider every wild animal's life sacred and those who feel it may be necessary to kill some game in order to preserve functioning ecosystems—seem ridiculous, lunatic even, comparable to fighting over the number of angels that can dance on the head of a pin. I was struck with such a sense of the absurd while looking at a World Bank graph on Kenya's population growth.

The line was clean and almost straight, rising at an initial angle of perhaps 20 degrees in 1960, when the country had eight million inhabitants, then climbing at close to 35 degrees by 2008—the last year of available statistics—when the population stood at almost thirty-nine million. There was great upward force implicit in that line, a sense that the angle would increase inexorably, driving human numbers to unsustainable limits—and soon. Given current trends, the population should hit sixty-five million by 2050.

Though it is relatively small as African countries go, Kenya nevertheless encompasses a sizable chunk of real estate. At roughly 225,000 square miles, it is significantly larger than California, which has 164,000 square miles. Given that California has a population only slightly smaller than Kenya's, it might seem that there should be plenty of land for both people and game. After all, despite its huge human population, California still has vast areas of forest and desert and relatively abundant wildlife. Even apex predators are doing well; it's estimated that at least twenty thousand black bears and five thousand cougars reside in the state. Charismatic herbivores, such as desert bighorn sheep, tule elk, and pronghorn, are holding their own, and the wetlands and seasonally flooded ricelands of California's Central Valley are a wintering ground for the millions of waterfowl and shorebirds that ply the Pacific Flyway.

But California is wealthy. It has a highly developed infrastructure and an urbanized population. Most people live in a few intensely developed metropolitan areas along the coast and in the Central Valley. Agriculture is completely mechanized; even though the state's croplands produce billions of dollars in food and fiber, only a small percentage of people actually work the land. True, there are great stresses on California's environment and its diverse biomes. Wholesale water diversions from north state rivers to San Joaquin Valley agribusiness, for example, have devastated the state's once mighty salmon runs. But considering the great demands that have been placed on its land and resources, California is more remarkable for what it has preserved than for what it has lost.

Kenya, however, must be viewed through an entirely different lens. California's population is close to 95 percent urbanized, while fewer than 40 percent of Kenya's people live in cities. Most people in Kenya, in other words, are forced to wrest subsistence from the land. And farming and ranching on East Africa's tribal lands are very different from farming and ranching in the United States. Soil cultivation relies on the grub hoe, not the tractor. Cattle culture consists of moving as many animals as possible across the land, with little if any regard given to stocking levels or selective breeding. There is little or no money for fertilizers, highly productive seed strains, or livestock vaccines and medicines. There are no effective government programs to deal with deforestation, erosion, or watershed degradation. In short, the stresses put on rural land are much greater in Kenya than in California.

And those stresses will increase in lockstep with population growth. Kenya's ecosystems already are fraying, and its wildlife populations crashing. What will happen when another fifteen million hungry people are added to its population? Such a rhetorical question prompts an altogether too easy answer: nothing good. Nairobi and Mombasa will absorb some of these newcomers, but a good many of them will stay in the hinterlands. They will have no choice, because their opportunities for upward mobility, for a chance at participating in a modern society and economy, will be nil. It is unlikely they will receive the education necessary for even a menial job in Nairobi, nor will they have the money for transportation and shelter. They will remain tied to the land, herd-

ing cattle and goats or cultivating maize and beans. But the land will not
be able to meet the increasing demands placed on it: it will become less
productive as more and more people attempt to derive their livelihoods
from it. The soils, currently poor throughout much of the country, will
continue to diminish in fertility. Charcoal burning, a practice already
driving deforestation, will expand. And as the forests shrink and people
teem across the landscape, there will be fewer and fewer places for the
wildlife to go.

This process is under way as I write, and it is accelerating. Wherever
I travel across Laikipia or south toward the Mara, east to the coast, the
charcoal burning is ubiquitous. Wherever there is woodland or bushveldt, plumes of smoke spiral skyward. Charcoal, either bagged or in
piles, is cached at every roadside turnout, either for sale to passing
motorists or awaiting truck transport to the cities. There are few trees,
even scrubby acacias, along the highways—just hacked trunks to mark
the relentless quest for fuel. Cattle and goats, all stunted and scrawny,
are ubiquitous. In the farmlands of the country's western and central
regions, every square meter of land, it seems, is growing maize and other
subsistence crops for local consumers, hothouse flowers for foreign capital, or khat to satisfy the habits of the region's millions of aficionados.

There is a graph line that is relevant here as well, the one that
tracks agricultural commodity prices in East Africa. According to the
Population Reference Bureau, the price for wheat climbed from $152 a
metric ton in 2005 to $347 in 2008; in the same period, maize jumped
from $98 to $259, and rice rose from $288 to $953. This price inflation
is insupportable for Kenya's poor, who constitute most of the country's
population. Ultimately it means that a great many people will go hungry, some of them will starve, and the pressures on natural resources
will only increase.

At a certain point in my research, I find myself on the verandah of the
Fairview Hotel in Nairobi. The Fairview is one of the city's older hotels.
It is surrounded by gardens and at one time afforded the lovely prospects
of open countryside that its name alludes to. Even now, it is exceedingly
pleasant to sit in the shade of a pergola overgrown with bougainvillea,
sipping gin and tonics. I share my table with the predator researcher
Laurence Frank and one of his old friends, Lyman McDonald.

McDonald is a University of Wyoming statistician and biometrician,
specializing in the modeling and monitoring of biological communities. Africa is not his specialty; much of his work centers on marine and
riparian environments and the terrestrial ecosystems of the American

intermontane West and Great Plains. Still, Africa interests him deeply, and he is visiting at the behest of Frank. Nor does he see the continent through the eyes of a tourist; he cannot help observe and analyze it as a scientist. And what he sees isn't just "shifting megafaunal biomass," as Ian Parker might put it. It's not just a matter of the biomass transforming from a diversified foundation of different types of big animals to a greatly simplified base: human beings and their livestock. The changes are deeper than that. The wholesale transformation of the bush into charcoal is just the most obvious aspect of this shift; other manifestations are not nearly as apparent. Indeed, they are deceptive; they convey a sense of a healthy system, masking the true and dire malady.

A prime example of this is the issue of "increasers and decreasers" on the rangelands, says McDonald. He is talking about plants: herbaceous plants, annuals and nonwoody perennials. "It is a matter of grazing or, rather, overgrazing," McDonald says as we sip our drinks and watch the weaver birds flit among the trees on the Fairview's grounds. "Especially [in and around the Maasai Mara], it is apparent that the resilient species—the increasers—are taking over."

In other words, says McDonald, as cattle graze they select nutritious, palatable plants: bunch grasses and succulent forbs. Not coincidentally, these are the same plants favored by wild ruminants. Normally, the land and the herbivores living on it establish equipoise. The animals eat the most nutritious plants and move on. The plants regenerate. But overgrazing upsets this cycle, observes McDonald, and the more intensive the grazing, the more violent the disequilibrium. In the most extreme examples, of course, the grazing can continue down to mineral earth; the soils erode from wind and water, and ultimately desertification ensues. But things don't have to get so extreme before the impacts are both profound and detrimental. Shortly before this writing, a particularly vicious drought ended in Kenya. Before it was broken by the much-delayed Long Rains, much of the country's wildlife and livestock had perished; in the southern provinces, the forage had been grazed down to red laterite. The land seemed terminally barren, incapable of ever producing anything of use to beast or human.

But the rains caused a great greening-up across the region, and McDonald witnessed it. This would seem cause for optimism, but the plants that were sprouting had little value as forage. They were "increasers," selected for survival by the relentless gnawing of cattle and goats over the past few decades. All that remained, all that was growing, were plants that were noxious—or even toxic. "All the palatable plants had been targeted by livestock to the point that the more resilient, unpalatable species had completely taken over," says McDonald. "In some areas, the only thing growing was morning glory. It's pretty, it has beautiful blooms, but virtually all livestock and wild animals find it inedible."

There were some exceptions to this rule, says McDonald: areas where villagers had agreed to restrict grazing to preserve local habitat and wildlife, thus attracting ecotourists. "This was near the Maasai Mara, close to the Mara River where the wildebeest typically cross during the migration from the Serengeti," says McDonald. "The villagers had done a very good job in managing their livestock. The habitat was in very good shape, and the forage was abundant; the seed heads on the grasses reached the top of the zebras' backs."

That provides at least a modicum of hope for the effective management of Kenya's rangelands, and it would seem to bolster IFAW's contention that ecotourism is an effective mechanism for addressing the needs of both people and wildlife. But the Mara is unique. It is a nexus for the world's most famous wildlife migration, a region that functions as its own international brand. It draws tourists reliably, more in good times than bad, but they will always come in numbers, because the Mara is famous; the images it provides of wildebeest surging across the Mara River, feeding scores of hungry crocodiles in the process, are almost as well-known as those of the Eiffel Tower, the Statue of Liberty, the Tower of London, and Red Square. The incentive for preserving habitat is significant and immediate: the villagers get *paid*. By all accounts, they are ripped off to a significant degree by the shadier tour operators, but they still get some money, and any money is a lot of money in the Kenyan countryside.

The situation is far different in other parts of the region, off the migration route, or in the north or west around Lake Naivasha. Wildlife exists there, and more would exist if the land were better managed, but no matter how much grazing is restricted, the concentrations of game will never match those portions of the Mara in the path of the wildebeest migration. Ecotourists will never flock in droves to a tribal homeland at the end of a rutted track supporting a small and Spartan lodge in deep bush, where the game concentrations are relatively thin and very hard to see—a description that applies to most of the private holdings in Kenya.

And more often than not, says McDonald, ecotourism exacerbates habitat problems; the villages that are able to enhance local habitat for the tourist trade are the exceptions. "More often a lodge gets established, and a borehole is drilled to provide water for the community and draw wildlife," McDonald says. "Initially, it seems like a good deal all around. The water benefits the villagers, livestock, and wild animals. The habitat is good; it's generally ungrazed, except during the dry season. There's plenty of forage, the soils are stable. There's lots of wildlife. Money is coming in for the locals; they get jobs with the lodge and have a ready market for their cattle, so there's an incentive for preserving the game."

The sticking point, says McDonald, is that such ventures can become too successful, exceeding the carrying capacity of the land. People settle around the lodge in greater and greater numbers, because it is a node of employment, of cash and other resources. And in Africa, rural people do not come alone; they bring their livestock with them. So more and more domestic animals forage around the lodge's environs, and now they are grazing year-round, not seasonally. And the newcomers also put in crops, which require fencing and water, thus fragmenting habitat and exerting an impact on water supplies. In short, the "ecolodge" ends up causing far more damage to habitat and wildlife than a hunting concession. Big game hunting, after all, typically involves relatively brief forays into wild country and temporary camps rather than permanent lodges. Established villages, livestock, gardening, and farming—all are anathema to robust populations of game. "It's an irony," observes McDonald. "Often, an ecotourism lodge ends up in a situation where the surrounding habitat is severely degraded and the reason for the whole enterprise is lost."

This dynamic has hardly gone unnoticed by Kenyans. During my last visit to the country, I read an opinion piece in a Nairobi newspaper decrying the fraying of the Maasai Mara and pegging the decline specifically on the ecotourism trade. The writer, a Kenyan national, noted the explosive growth of grain-based agriculture in the region, the sprawling and ill-planned support infrastructure, and the vanishing game. The op-ed reflected the essential pragmatism of the Kenyan ethos: though the writer noted the unraveling of the Mara ecosystem is tragic for environmental and cultural reasons, his primary concern was rooted in economics. The helter-skelter development, he noted, is killing the goose that has laid the golden eggs of ecotourism. The visitors will stop coming if the charismatic animals disappear; Kenya, he observed, cannot afford to lose its greatest franchise.

For McDonald, a scientist accustomed to thinking on a landscape scale, Kenya's conservation priorities can be summed up succinctly. "The best thing that can be done here," he says, "is to distribute condoms generously and do everything possible to conserve topsoil." In other words, the usual conservation methods—creating pastoral conservancies, funding programs with regulated hunting or ecotourism, establishing rehabilitation centers for injured and orphaned wildlife—are doomed to failure unless Kenya gets a handle on its exploding birth rate.

This will be difficult. There is a perception among Westerners that old mores and traditions are falling away in Africa, and this is true in the sense that higher education is vigorously pursued, that modern technology—from the assault rifle to the smart phone—is valued, and that relatively few people affect traditional dress except during ceremonial events. But many of the basic constructs of traditional culture remain in place. You can see it, for example, in Nairobi and the central highlands in the rise of the Mungiki. On the one hand, the Mungiki are a kind of domestic mafia, controlling the *matatu* (microbus) routes in Nairobi and reaching into other areas of commerce. On the other, they are a Kikuyu fraternal organization, seeing themselves as guardians of tribal values and traditions. According to breathless and sensationalistic stories in the national press, they have revived the old "oathing" ceremonies of the Mau-Mau.

More pertinent where wildlife is concerned are views on family planning. In the rural areas, particularly, the emphasis remains resolutely on "family," with overt resistance to, or at least deep suspicion of, "planning." Wherever I met pastoralists pursuing traditional lifestyles, one of the first questions I was invariably asked was about my family—specifically, the number of children I had. When I answered that I had a single child, there was typically an incredulous pause, and I then would be peppered with follow-up questions: Only one? Was my wife (or wives) barren? Was I sick? Impotent? How was I handling this great personal tragedy?

Their confusion over my situation was understandable, given their own metrics for wealth and status. Livestock isn't the only store of value among the Maasai, Samburu, and other pastoral tribes; so are children, who are needed to herd and tend the cattle. And children have always been hard to rear to maturity in the rangelands. Historical studies indicate fertility rates among pastoral women in East Africa are lower than those for women from farming tribes. In the late 1980s, the Maasai had a birth rate of 2.2 percent compared to 4.4 percent for agricultural tribes. Fertility among the pastoral tribes has long been depressed because of STDs, poor nutrition, rudimentary sanitation, and the practice of female genital mutilation. And yet, other factors weigh against this trend. Infant mortality, once as high as 50 percent among the Maasai, has decreased as a result of the availability of modern medicine, however limited. Moreover, prominent Maasai elders may have eight or more wives, each of whom may have several children—up to eight over the course of each woman's life, according to a study by A.H. Jacobs in the 1970s. Even with a high child mortality rate, the end result is a population that grows robustly, and that is certainly the case on the Serengit today.

To control human population on the rangelands, where conservation is most practical, then, may require significantly altering, even destroying, pastoral culture. While that supreme pragmatist Richard Leakey considers this a likely scenario—indeed, an inevitable one, given that most people, Maasai and Samburu included, aspire to a better life for their children—it will meet with resistance. Indeed, it already has. The Maasai, greatly upset at past land grabs and agendas that differ from their own, including conservation and wildlife protection, are fairly well organized these days. The Maasai Association, which lobbies for tribal interests in Kenya, Tanzania, and abroad, has a well-designed Web site. It both promotes Maasai culture and solicits help and support; sympathetic Web surfers can even donate a cow or goat to a tribal member with a click of the mouse, an option that must make old school conservationists shudder. The tribe is producing a sizable cadre of attorneys and other professionals, and they are aggressive and competent in the promotion of tribal interests. If pastoralism is weakening, there is little sign of it in Maasailand—quite the opposite, in fact.

So capping the surging birth rate of Kenya's pastoral communities will remain a challenge for decades to come. In the interim, says McDonald, the focus shouldn't be on preserving individual animals or suites of species—or even "habitat" in the sense of well-vegetated, diverse biomes. Most East African habitats are fairly resilient, able to revive if provided with some precipitation and protected from relentless grazing and browsing. "But if you don't have the topsoil, you won't have anything," observes McDonald. "Without topsoil, nothing grows; you don't get habitat back. We're seeing that play out all across this region."

Erosion is thus among the most pernicious of Kenya's ecological problems, the issue that underlies many other issues: habitat loss, wildlife loss, scant water resources, poor water quality, sedimentation of waterways and marine reefs. It is a sad fact that the area best suited for agriculture—the central region, which includes Mount Kenya and the Aberdares—is also most susceptible to erosion. This zone has sufficient water and soils rich enough to grow maize, the preferred Kenyan staple. But maize is hard on the land. It requires large infusions of fertilizer, and it tends to deplete soil. Also, it is not conducive to the minimal-till strategies that reduce erosion so effectively on modern maize farms in North America and Europe. Such approaches require expensive equipment, copious quantities of herbicide, and large fields to be economically viable. Kenyan corn typically is grown on small plots, often on steep slopes; clean tillage is the rule, and there is seldom any vegetative matter left on the ground to protect it from water erosion. Thus, the best farm lands in Kenya are being eroded away as demand for commodity crops spirals.

Still, farmland loss isn't necessarily germane to wildlife conservation; in Kenya, land suitable for farming typically was stripped of habitat long ago and is isolated from significant reservoirs of game. The real opportunities for conservation remain in the vast arid and semiarid areas that are too dry for the cultivation of maize, which constitute 70 percent of the country. But simply because more than two-thirds of the country is too dry to grow corn, people are not deterred from trying to grow it; in fact, crop failures in Kenya's breadbasket lead to more, not fewer, stresses on the land. Plantings expand to marginal areas, firewood gathering and charcoal burning increase, wildlife is poached. And typically, families tend to hold on to their cows ever more tightly in times of drought, social upheaval, or resource shortages rather than selling them to improve nutrition and financial liquidity and reduce impacts on the grazing commons.

Thus, Kenya's relatively small agricultural areas shouldn't even be considered in any conservation scheme. They are too valuable for food production. It is essential that erosion-reduction plans are implemented for the central corn belt, however; to do otherwise will only guarantee even more hungry people in the future and make it even more difficult to establish conservation-based management plans for the rangelands.

So again: it is on the semiarid to arid rangelands that Kenya's wildlife has the best long-term chance. To save the rangelands—for wildlife, cattle, or people—the topsoil must be conserved. And the most effective way to save topsoil in the vast nonagricultural areas, observes McDonald, is to reduce grazing; in other words, restrict the number of cattle out on the range.

This calls to mind my conversation with Leakey about the necessity of getting pastoralists to eat more beef (or sell it) and horde it less—to shift the primary store of value in the Kenyan hinterlands from the cow to the shilling. Dire as the situation is currently, it is positively benign compared to all likely futures if rural birth rates stay high. As it stands, the land serves as the reserve on which pastoralist "savings" accounts are based, and it is a reserve teetering on bankruptcy. When the land is finally stripped of its topsoil—when it yields to terminal desertification—then there is no possible future, for either pastoralism or conservation. There is only a new arm of the Sahara, an occasional nomad with a camel and a goat or two, a scattering of *shifta*, the extremely rare oryx, gazelle, or fennec.

From this perspective, there is a possible upside to Kenya's rapid and messy urbanization: consumerism as a social priority. You can't buy the latest cell phone with a cow; you have to sell the cow and then use the shillings to buy the cell phone. This, then, could be the engine that drives Kenya's pastoralists away from the cow and toward hard currency. And as I saw on the Serengeti among the Maasai—by any account, the most culturally conservative people in East Africa—this already is happening.

Moreover, urbanization generally has the side effect of emptying the countryside. As more people move to the cities to seek employment opportunities and goods, the rural areas tend to depopulate. Theoretically, this could create, as Leakey noted, opportunities for community conservancies and other conservation schemes. But will it be enough? Frankly, the odds aren't good, particularly for those areas where the soils are relatively rich and the precipitation relatively generous; the Mara again comes to mind. Even with the dramatic, ongoing expansion of Nairobi and Mombasa, demand for rural land among Kenyans remains high in general and particularly for those areas where you can actually grow something.

Too, it's not simply an issue of exploding numbers of people and cows or even land lust. The lack of central planning—of any planning—is a salient characteristic of Kenyan society. Endemic corruption, of course, is part of the story. But with or without corruption, life is hard in Kenya; for most people, survival is a daily struggle. When the opportunity is presented for anything—an antelope, some forage by the side of the road, a load of firewood—it will be taken. That ethos continues right up the chain to the Big Men, who see nothing inconsistent in trumpeting the wonders of the Mara even as they destroy its signature wildlife populations with ill-planned "ecolodges," helter-skelter infrastructure, and sprawling agricultural projects.

In the end, Kenya may well be left with lovely lodges, good roads connecting them, some sizable populations of semitame game behind wire, and a network of animal rehabilitation centers, where visitors can pet a baby rhino or give an orphan elephant a giant bottle of formula to suckle. But there will be nothing wild. It will be Kenya-as-Potemkin-village, a simulacrum.

CHAPTER 19

Summing Up in Diani

Field research is difficult in Kenya with its particular physical and emotional demands. For me, this especially applies to extended sojourns in Nairobi. Getting around the rural areas of the country can be grueling, even dangerous, but the effort is counterbalanced by the inspiration I always find in the East African landscape and sky. It is the cities—Nairobi in particular—that wring me out like a dishrag.

At one point toward the end of my research, I was required to stay in Nairobi for more than a week. It was a particularly frustrating period, coming at the end of a long trip. I had several interviews to conduct, and some of my subjects were less than diligent in keeping appointments. I had to reschedule them multiple times, and some I had to abort completely. Lodging in Nairobi is always tight, and anything tolerable in terms of hygiene and safety is expensive. I typically stay at one of the few exceptions to this rule: a small lodge near the Israeli Embassy that is modestly priced by local standards and immaculate. It also serves an excellent free breakfast and has good Internet connections. On this particular trip, however, the lodge was fully booked. I had to take a room at one of the monolithic high-rise hotels that dominate the Nairobi skyline. I couldn't really afford the top-end places, and the hotel I chose had a reputation for stolid mediocrity. The room was cramped and shabby, the air conditioning inadequate, and the Internet connection was poor. After I'd banged around the hot, polluted city all day chasing interviews, it was small comfort to come back to the hotel; I found myself at the bar too often, drinking too many beers and complaining too much. In short, I was just like every other person who comes to Kenya on business and ends up stymied, tired, feckless, and carping.

As is my usual habit in the large cities of developing countries, I had sought out and found a fixer: in this case, Alex Nyoike, a cabbie who habitually wore a soft slouch hat and mirror sunglasses. A Luo, he had a respectable paunch, a lazy and infectious grin, and an amiable disposition. His intelligence, competence, and companionability were an anodyne to the harsh realities of getting around and getting things done in Nairobi. Alex met me every morning at the hotel and shuttled me about on my usually fruitless missions. I made sure he was handsomely compensated, and he reciprocated by smoothing my path in countless ways: finding the moneychanger with the best exchange rates, the restaurants that served the best food at the most reasonable prices, a cobbler to fix a sole on a hiking boot. He found a cell phone for me at a good price and a competent doctor to attend to a gastrointestinal problem. When I wanted to idly shop and roam around, he took me to the safe part of town, then called me periodically on my cell to make sure I was okay. On more than one occasion, he chased away intimidating persons who were importunate in making my acquaintance. Ultimately, he became a friend.

We talked at great length of our respective lives as he negotiated the hellish traffic. I told him of my life, and he told me of his. He was married, with a couple of children. His wife owned a small grocery. They were devout Christians but by no means religious zealots. They worked hard and, by Kenyan standards, were doing relatively well. They ate regularly, had a good roof over their heads, and occasionally had money for small amenities. Their children were excelling in school, and he was cautiously optimistic about their prospects.

I questioned him about conservation, about its importance to his country and its significance to his own life. He was fastidiously politic at first, responding with sunny bromides. But I gently prodded him over our week together, and he finally spoke freely. Basically, his position was this: wild animals are fine, but they can't be a priority when people are starving. "We're running out of water and food," he said. "People are dying in the north by the thousands. You're not going to find any Kenyan feeling sorry for an elephant when he doesn't have *ugali* for his children or fodder for his cattle. That's the reality, my good friend. And I think it'd be the same in America."

If conservation was a less than pressing priority with Alex, he found animal rights an altogether lunatic philosophy. He was aware that IFAW had considerable influence with the central government ("I've seen the posters at the airport"), but that didn't make the idea any less repugnant. Like most Kenyans, he assumes government policy is dictated by the amount of money funneled into the pockets of Parliament's ministers. "What the government says and what the people think are two different things," he observed. "I don't know anybody who thinks that a wild animal in the bush has rights." He laughed. "That's just crazy. I worry about my rights, about human rights, not animal rights."

By the time I wrapped up my obligations in Nairobi, I still had a few days to cool my heels before I left the country—not enough to get any real work done in Laikipia or the Mara, but too long to stay sweltering and hacking up phlegm in the hot, smoggy air of the capital. I'd never been to the coast, and I decided to go. The idea of fresh seafood, white sand beaches, and warm water was suddenly irresistible. Excellent resorts were reputedly located in Malindi and Diani, small towns near Mombasa. I researched them one evening and found the prices daunting. I mentioned this to Alex the next morning, and he waved his hand dismissively. "No problem," he said. "I know a travel agent who can arrange things."

We drove to a small building in the city center, and I followed Alex to a travel agency located in a basement office. There the proprietress, a comely Hindu woman in a brightly colored sari, sat pecking away at her computer and sipping tea. She greeted Alex warmly in English, and they began conversing in Swahili. She tapped a pen on the desk as she talked, punctuating her conversation regularly with "Okay. Okay. Okay." Finally, they reached some resolution. She turned to me. "I think we'll be able to help you," she said. She took out a large binder and turned to a page that contained promotional materials for the Leopard Beach Resort in Diani, about an hour's drive south of Mombasa. "Very nice," she said. "Upscale really, with excellent service and a large private beach. I send a lot of business their way; I'll be able to get you good rates."

This turned out to be one-fourth of the standard tariff, and I accepted gratefully. The next day I flew a Kenya Airways jet to Mombasa. As the plane cruised eastward at thirty thousand feet, I watched the country scroll out beneath me. The land was utterly parched and seemed visibly inflamed, febrile: a vast mottled map of red, ocher, and brown. Vegetation was scant. We flew over Tsavo National Park, which seemed particularly desiccated. The panorama filled me with a dire foreboding.

I recalled Leakey's predictions on the impacts of global warming and the fate implied for the rangelands of East Africa. If southern Kenya, where rainfall is relatively generous, was so dry, conditions in the Northern Frontier District would be positively hellish. No wonder people and livestock were perishing wholesale. And what succor could there be for wildlife when the entire nation seemed in a state of terminal dehydration? The controversy over animal rights and science-based conservation seemed bootless, a bagatelle, a matter of no consequence. From my seat I could look north, where the land was lost in a camel-colored haze. I had a sense that I could actually see the Sahara encroaching, crawling south in perceptible increments, gathering the rangelands, pastoralists, cattle, wildlife, everything, in its arid and fatal embrace.

The captain came on the loudspeaker right about then and announced that Kilimanjaro was visible to the south. I walked to the tail of the plane and looked out an available window. I was shocked by the mountain's mass. Even at this altitude and distance, it seemed to fill the sky. I stared at Kilimanjaro for a long time; it made me feel better. There was snow near the summit, and the air was clearer, the sky bluer, to the south. I knew that the Serengeti unspools in its vastness at the foot of the mountain and that the Long Rains had recently begun, however fitfully, in the region. It seemed that the land was beginning to green up over there, but that could have been an optical illusion generated by wishful thinking. Still, conditions were obviously better to the south. The land was not so hard used; there were fewer people, more game. Kilimanjaro said: there is still reason for hope. I wanted to believe it.

The plane descended into Mombasa. Located on an island in a complex of river channels, bayous, and sloughs that drain into the Indian Ocean, it is the second largest city in Kenya, but with fewer than a million people, it does not evoke the same metastatic aggressiveness as Nairobi. Founded as a port for the gold and ivory trade in the twelfth century, it is one of the oldest cities in Africa. A famous landmark of four fabricated elephant tusks in the city center is a testament to Mombasa's historic significance in the ivory business, and a good deal of illegal ivory is still smuggled through the port.

Many of the wetlands surrounding the city are lined with mangroves, which seemed relatively healthy; as we approached the airport, I could see fishermen in small dugouts working the waterways. The temperature was hot, hotter even than Nairobi, and heavy with water vapor. It didn't feel oppressive, though. After the polluted dry air of the capital city, Mombasa's atmosphere was a welcome change. My skin was hydrated and soothed, and the wet, warm air blowing in from the sea felt good in my lungs. I caught a cab for the hour drive to Diani. Our route took us through the heart of Mombasa, a district in genteel decay. At one point, we had to take a ferry across Kilindini Harbor, a mile-wide channel that debouches directly into the ocean; the water looked clear and clean. On the south terminus, boys and young men fished the heavily surging tide with hand lines and had strings of big fish of various species to show for their efforts. Their catch and the clarity of the water were encouraging. The marine environment, at least, seemed to be relatively healthy here.

The road to Diani passes through small towns, villages, and agricultural lands, with stretches of bush and coastal forest. After about forty-five minutes we turned east, drove a couple of kilometers past shops and small business centers that became increasingly upscale, then struck north through high bush along a coastal frontage road. The gate to Leopard Beach is imposing, heavy ironwork affixed to stone posts. A country club with one of the better golf courses on the East African coast is located directly across the road. Two burly guards scowled menacingly at the cab, until they saw my white face, which instantly translated as "guest." Their smiles were reflexive and ingratiating. We drove through manicured grounds to the resort entrance, where a tall and imperious majordomo in sultan's regalia welcomed me and handed me a chilled glass of fruit juice. The resort's main complex is mostly open to the air, a series of gardens, pavilions, restaurants, and shops that step down in levels to the sea. Small artificial streams course through the property, the water stocked with various species of cichlids, the predacious, stunningly diverse family of fishes native to the Rift Valley lakes. Shade trees and flowers rustled in a salt-scented breeze from the ocean. Birds and butterflies flitted around the blooms, and a family of black-and-white colobus monkeys looked down lugubriously from the canopy of a fever tree. The resort seemed half-full at best, and that was fine by me; I came for peace and quiet. As I followed my bags across the grounds to my room, I recalled a passage from one of Paul Theroux's travel books about an interlude of wallowing in "sluttish luxury" at a high-end Hawaiian resort. I was ready for some of that myself.

I quickly established a routine that I followed for my week at Leopard Beach: up before dawn and a walk along the beach that I deliberately kept brief—my reasons for this later. Then breakfast in the main restaurant, followed by a couple hours of work in my room. Then a swim in the ocean and a session with the weight machines in the resort's small gym. After my shower, I'd walk up the main road to Diani, where I'd lunch in a small, somewhat shabby bistro that served superb Italian fare. Back to the resort for a nap, another swim, another work session, perhaps a sundowner at one of the bars. Then back up to Diani for dinner. I'd read for a few hours on returning to my room and go to bed early.

Like many travelers, I generally take a great deal of pleasure from observing and interacting with my fellow wayfarers. But at Leopard Beach, the emphasis was on observation; interaction was minimal. Aside from a few Germans and a white Kenyan couple with their kids, all the other guests were Italian. I learned that the Kenya coast has long been a destination for Italian tourists, a kind of alternate Riviera. The entire coastline from Malindi through Mombasa to Diani is, in fact, occupied year-round by both Italian expatriates and successive waves of visitors from the homeland. On the beach, I was not difficult to identify as a North American: I don't smoke, I'm anything but pretty, and I was the only male wearing baggy camouflage shorts, a baseball cap, and a T-shirt. Most of the other men chain-smoked; wore Speedos, gold jewelry, and bespoke short-sleeved shirts; had expensive and impeccable coifs; and seemed uncommonly handsome. I essayed conversations a time or two in the bars but was pointedly snubbed. This may have been due to my terrible Italian, but if I'm the typical doltish monolingual American, my fellow guests were certainly good Europeans in terms of their facility with languages; judging from the peremptory way they ordered the staff around, most had a working knowledge of English, so language was clearly not a barrier. I simply had to come to terms with the fact that Americans are not well loved, particularly by Europeans. Also, my pariah status may have been buttressed by timing; my visit came shortly after the egress of the Bush administration, and the wars in Iraq and Afghanistan were considered stains on the American escutcheon.

Still, my time at the beach was an idyll, which isn't to say life at the coast is idyllic. The lives of the tourist and the local, of course, are separated by a tremendous economic gulf. It is thus only fair that the tourist serves as a resource for the local—a fact that isn't necessarily pleasant for the tourist. Walks along the beach were difficult. The sand swarmed with "beach boys"—young aggressive men anxious to make some shillings. They hawked shells from threatened mollusks directly under signs warning that the sale or purchase of such items was a serious crime; they sold ganja and cocaine to young hipsters fresh off the plane; they peddled "genuine" Maasai spears and *rungus,* arranged camel rides, diving trips, safaris to Tsavo, dinner in a bistro where a cousin waited tables. Though they generally were able to conduct their business successfully, they were closely watched by tall, tough guards armed with truncheons, who patrolled the hotel grounds and beach. If any beach boy became threatening or even overbearing, he would quickly be confronted by one or more of the *askaris*. On one occasion, I was enjoying a beer at a seaside table when I saw a beach boy and a guard engaged in a heated argument by the water. Suddenly, the guard drew his nightstick and thumped the beach boy on his elbow. The beach boy turned and ran, the guard at his heels, swinging his stick and occasionally making contact. In another incident, I was accosted while walking to my favorite restaurant in Diani by a tall, blade-thin man with Bob Marley dreads and cicatrices on his cheeks. "Hello, my good friend," he said. "You are interested in young girls? I know some very nice ones, very pretty."

"Sorry. Not interested."

I kept walking, picking up the pace, eyes straight ahead. I'm normally at ease in my travels even in relatively dicey environments, but my radar was up this time. Dusk was falling, we were alone on a mostly deserted road fronted on both sides by high bush, and my interlocutor carried a gnarled acacia *rungu* that could've split my skull like a casaba.

"Very pretty," he persisted.

I said nothing, kept walking; a few hundred yards ahead, I could see the lights of my restaurant glowing in the blue twilight. The man fell silent as we drew closer, then almost growled out of frustration. "So okay. Not today. But listen, my good friend, I must make a living. We all do here, and you must understand that. We'll meet again." He fell behind, and I kept my eyes straight ahead, focused on my destination. I could almost feel the *rungu* exploding at the back of my neck. Luckily, I never saw him again.

But for me, that encounter definitively exposed the illusion of the Kenyan coast as a happy and prosperous place. Outside the tall stone walls of the resorts, it is as desperate as any other region in Kenya. True, there is an economic base of sorts: tourism. But tourism in Kenya is an extractive industry, just like ivory, gold, bush meat, and any of the other resources exploited in Africa; there is nothing "sustainable" about it. On the coast as in Nairobi, lip service is paid to the country's commitment to conservation, to its nonconsumptive approach to wildlife management. Diani is not terribly far from Tsavo, and the shingles of safari companies are everywhere along the main coastal road, offering "green" tours to the hinterlands to view the nation's dwindling populations of wild animals. But tourism, whether it's based on game viewing or sun bathing, is proving as subject to booms and busts as any other economic sector. The tourists come when the political condition seems stable and stay away at all other times. That means that they've been staying away in droves in recent years. And when they are absent, the coastal people go hungry. Even when visitors are present, the locals get crumbs; the real money goes to the resort owners and the politicians who are their allies.

Meanwhile, the coastal forest and wetlands continue to disappear under the onslaught of resorts, golf courses, squatter settlements, and subsistence *shambas*. Most of the wildlife has disappeared. There are no elephants, large antelope, giraffes, lions. Although some leopards no doubt remain, providing a legitimate eponym to my resort, that in itself hardly constitutes a conservation success story, given the ability of the spotted cats to adapt to suburban settings and a prey base consisting of rats, cats, and dogs.

But some wild species are surviving, even thriving, on the coast. These are creatures that have been able to adapt to, even exploit, the human presence. Avian life is abundant. Weaver birds of various species are ubiquitous and find the elaborate landscaping of the resorts particularly attractive for their communal nest complexes. Invasive birds have taken to the coast with enthusiasm, particularly the bane of Ian Parker's career, the Indian house crow. And a few primate species have adapted particularly well to the changing environment. I would not include black-and-white colobus monkeys in this category, though they are still fairly common. A local conservation organization is dedicated to their preservation, and residents seem genuinely devoted to their welfare. Far more successful are vervet monkeys and baboons. Both species are extremely common along the coast, squatting by the side of the road for mutual grooming sessions, foraging through the bush, and, in the case of the vervets, scampering along the phone lines that cross the main highway. The resorts have made some effort to exclude baboons from their grounds, a wise policy considering they are potentially dangerous, particularly for unwitting tourists who may attempt to interact with them.

Nothing, however, could keep the vervets out of any place or anything. They were always thrashing around in the treetops, loping down the pathways, stampeding across the lawns during my visit. I admired their resiliency and boldness, and they amused me greatly with their antics. Not everyone shared my enthusiasm, however. The staff was generally wearied by them, and some of the guests were intimidated. One morning, I entered the resort's main restaurant and queued up at the lavish breakfast buffet. Suddenly there was commotion at a far group of tables. Several vervets had invaded the restaurant and were running across the tabletops, grabbing rolls and fistfuls of eggs and fruit, knocking over coffee cups, and condiments and scaring the tourists witless. The waiters and cooks, apparently experienced with such forays, promptly took up brooms and mops and set off in hot pursuit, finally driving the monkeys into the rafters, where they leaped about screeching wildly before bailing out through openings near the eves.

I also was somewhat heartened by the condition of the local fisheries. True, large portions of the coral reef are dead, a result of an extended influx of excessively warm water a couple of years prior. Some old-timers told me such "bleaching" incidents had long been a sporadic phenomenon along the East African coast, but they had become far more common during the past two decades; I could marshal no supporting evidence on the spot, of course, but it seemed clear to me that climate change has to be playing a role.

If the area's near-shore reef ecosystems are having troubles, however, the same cannot be said of the offshore fisheries. They are robust. Big pelagic fish—tuna, marlin, mahi-mahi, wahoo, barracuda, snapper—are extremely abundant and available in every market and restaurant at reasonable prices. The waters off Kenya, Tanzania, and Mozambique, I was told by both resident fishermen and visiting blue water anglers, positively teem with sailfish, making the region perhaps the best big game fishing destination in the world. But the abundance of these top-of-the-food-web predatory fish is not due to any conservation initiative or rigorously enforced quota. Rather, the fisheries are thriving as an indirect result of maritime lawlessness.

Early in 2010, reports circulated in the international press of a tremendous boom in fish stocks due to the absence of the international fishing fleet—gigantic trawlers, drift netters, and long-liners from Europe, Russia, and elsewhere in Asia that had been stripping the Indian Ocean off the African coast for decades. They have disappeared in recent years, of course, because of the spike in Somali piracy. As the pirates have extended their reach hundreds of miles into the Indian Ocean, the international commercial fishing fleet has retreated accordingly. Relieved of the intense exploitation, the fish have rebounded in spectacular fashion. The irony of this situation is profound and has been widely noted. Clive Schofield, a research fellow with the Australian Centre for Ocean Resources and Security at the University of Wollongong, authored a paper noting that foreign vessels' annual illegal catch from Somalia's maritime jurisdiction had been between ninety million and three hundred million dollars annually. That catch has now been eliminated. In other words, Schofield observes, Somalia's pirates have neutralized an outlaw fishing fleet, allowing them to style themselves as "coast guards" and describe their ransom demands as "fines" for the theft of their fisheries.

But if the rebound of East Africa's pelagic fisheries is good news, the implications of the phenomenon are not. The fish have returned not because of law and security; they have returned because there is no law, there is no security. Policy, it is clear, means nothing in Somalia or, increasingly, in Kenya. Fish are wildlife—marine wildlife, to be sure, but wildlife nevertheless. When their recovery off East Africa is linked to the complete breakdown of civil authority, the implications for Africa's terrestrial wildlife are anything but heartening. Kenya is still the poster child for a no-hunt conservation policy. IFAW and its philosophy are ascendant here. Support for animal rights is strong in Parliament and seems to be spreading to government bodies in adjacent nations, particularly Botswana. You can't legally bag a trophy in Kenya if you're an American or a European hunter, nor can you legally kill an eland for the pot if you're a Pokot or a Maasai pastoralist. But that doesn't mean a thing. The wildlife continues to dwindle to the poacher's spear, poison, and snare. Meanwhile, off the coast, where brigands keep the fishing fleet of the "civilized" nations at bay, the fish are returning.

Something is very wrong with this picture. Can any conservation policy actually succeed in Kenya? Certainly, IFAW is getting a good name globally for its work, but the results of the hunting ban have been completely underwhelming. More of the same effort is good for IFAW, for People for the Ethical Treatment of Animals (who, among their other causes, want the media to call fish "sea kittens" to discourage their consumption), for the Humane Society International, but it must be noted that the payoff for wildlife has been nil. Nor is there any guarantee that regulated wildlife consumption will be uniformly successful. In Namibia it seems to be working, but the success of Tanzania's pro-hunt policy has been spotty at best. Maybe, as Lyman McDonald says, it all must come down to the distribution of condoms and the preservation of topsoil; maybe everything else is a sideshow.

At my favorite bistro in Diani the night before I left the coast, I ordered a fillet of red snapper. It was grilled with olive oil, capers, and shallots and was complete perfection. I was aware that I was able to savor this choice cut from a "sea kitten" largely because Somali pirates were operating not far from where I sat, but I must admit this knowledge did not detract from my enjoyment of my meal.

I had been in Africa long enough to understand the wisdom of the old saw: whatever works.

Recommended Reading

Adams, Jonathan, and Thomas O. McShane. *The Myth of Wild Africa*. University of California Press, 1992.

Adamson, George. *My Pride and Joy* (including a series of taped interviews between Bill Travers and Adamson). Collins Harvill, 1986; reprints, Fontana Paperbacks, 1988, 1990.

Adamson, Joy. *Born Free: A Lioness of Two Worlds*. 1960; reprint, Pantheon, 2000.

———. *Living Free: The Story of Elsa and Her Cubs*. 1961; reprint, Fontana Press, 1991.

Aggarwal, Safia, and Chris Thouless. *Land Tenure and Property Rights Assessment: The Northern Rangeland and Coastal Conservation Programs of USAID/Kenya*. USAID, 2008.

Beers, Diane L. *For the Prevention of Cruelty: The History and Legacy of Animal Rights Activism in the United States*. Swallow Press, 2006.

Bentsen, Cheryl. *Maasai Days*. Summit Books, 1989.

Biesele, Megan, and Robert K. Hitchcock. *The Ju/'Hoan San of Nyae Nyae and Namibian Independence: Development, Democracy and Indigenous Voices in Southern Africa*. Berghahn Books, 2010.

Bonner, Raymond. *At the Hand of Man*. University of California Press, 1993.

Bowen-Jones, E., and S. Pendry. "The Threats to Primates and Other Mammals from the Bushmeat Trade in Africa and How This Could Be Diminished." *Oryx* 33, no. 3 (July 1999).

Capstick, Peter Hathway. *Death in the Long Grass*. St. Martin's Press, 1977.

Cohen, Adam. "Can Animal Rights Go Too Far?" *Time*, July 14, 2010.

Crandall, David P. *The Place of the Stunted Ironwood Trees* (a study of Namibia's Himba pastoralists). Continuum, 2000.

Cunliffe, Stephen. "Hot Tropics" (an article on the parks of Namibia's Caprivi Strip). *Africa Geographic,* April 2010.

———. "Tuskers' Last Stand" (an examination of the Phirilongwe-Majete elephant transfer conflict). *Africa Geographic,* September 2010.

Davis, Anna, Chris Weaver, et al. *Namibia's Communal Conservancies.* Namibian Association of CBNRM support Organisations, 2007.

Derman, Bill, Rie Odgaard, and Espen Sjaastad. *Conflicts over Land and Water in Africa.* Michigan State University Press, 2008.

De Waal, Frans. *The Age of Empathy: Nature's Lessons for a Kinder Society.* Crown, 2009.

Douglas-Hamilton, Iain. *Among the Elephants.* 1975; reprint, Penguin, 1978.

———. *Battle for the Elephants.* Viking, 1992.

Duffy, Rosaleen. *Nature Crime: How We're Getting Conservation Wrong.* Yale University Press, 2010.

Frank, Laurence. "Hey Presto! We Made the Lions Disappear!" *Swara,* April 2010.

Goldberg, Jeffrey. "The Hunted: Did American Conservationists in Africa Go Too Far?" *New Yorker,* April 6, 2010.

Gourevitch, Philip. "The Monkey and the Fish: Can Greg Carr Save an African Ecosystem?" *New Yorker,* December 21, 2009.

Graham, Max, et al. *The Darwin Initiative—Final Report* (a report on a University of Cambridge–United Kingdom effort to resolve elephant-human conflicts in Laikipia, Kenya). University of Cambridge, 2009.

Guither, Harold D. *Animal Rights: History and Scope of a Radical Social Movement.* Southern Illinois University Press, 1998.

Hartley, Aidan. "When Elephants Fight, the Grass Suffers" (a meditation on the Samburu-Pokot "war"). *The Spectator,* January 12, 2008.

Hasselback, Drew. "South Africa Court Slams Canned Lion Hunting." *FP Legal Post,* June 12, 2009.

Hirsch, Paul, William Adams, et al. *Acknowledging Trade-Offs, Embracing Complexity: A Challenge for Conservation.* Conservation Biology, 2010.

Honey, Marsha. *Ecotourism and Sustainable Development: Who Owns Paradise?* Island Press, 1998.

Jacobson, Peter, Kathryn N. Jacobson, and Mary Seely. *Ephemeral Rivers and Their Catchments—Sustaining People and Development in Western Namibia.* Desert Research Foundation of Namibia, 1995.

Joy, Melanie. *Why We Love Dogs, Eat Pigs and Wear Cows.* Conari Press, 2009.

Kelly, Nora. "In Wildest Africa: The Preservation of Game in Kenya 1895–1933." PhD dissertation, Simon Fraser University, 1978.

Lawyers' Environmental Action Team (Tanzania). *Regulating the Hunting Industry in Tanzania: Reflections on the Legislative, Institutional and Policy-Making Frameworks* (white paper). 2003.

League against Cruel Sports. *The Myth of Trophy Hunting as Conservation* (a submission to British environment minister Elliot Morley, MP). 2004.

Leakey, Richard E. *Wildlife Wars: My Battle to Save Kenya's Elephants.* Macmillan, 2001.

Lucheli, Isaiah. "Thirteen Commandments to Fight Cattle Rustling Set Up." *Kenyan Standard,* March 25, 2011.

Manly, Bryan F., Lyman McDonald, and Dana L. Thomas. *Resource Selection by Animals: Statistical Design and Analysis for Field Studies.* Springer, 2002.

Marlowe, Frank. *The Hadza: Hunter-Gatherers of Tanzania.* University of California Press, 2010.

Matahiko, M.G.G., E. Gereta, et al. *Towards an Ecohydrology-Based Restoration of the Usangu Wetlands and the Great Ruaha River, Tanzania.* James Cook University, Queensland, 2006.

Matthiessen, Peter. *Sand Rivers.* Viking, 1981.

Mbaria, John. "New Bill Opens up Cropping of Wildlife as KWS Role Is Split Up." *East African,* February 23–March 1, 2009.

McKenna, Virginia, et al. *Born Free at 21.* Born Free Foundation, 2005.

McShane, Thomas, Paul Hirsch, et al. *Hard Choices: Making Trade-Offs between Biodiversity Conservation and Human Well-Being.* Biological Conservation, 2010.

Mugo, Micere Githae. *Muthoni Wa Kirima, Mau Mau Woman Field Marshal.* Sapes Trust Books, 2004.

Mwai, Muthui. "What Makes Mungiki Tick." *Daily Nation,* October 23, 2000.

Naess, Arne. *The Ecology of Wisdom.* Counterpoint, 2008.

Norton-Griffiths, Michael. Norton-Griffiths's Web site contains a number of papers—some published elsewhere—on the economics of conservation in Africa. These include "How Many Wildebeest Do You Need?" "The Case for Private Sector Investment in Conservation," "An East African Trust Fund for Conservation? What Will They Think of Next?" "Wildlife Losses in Kenya—an Analysis of Conservation Policy," "The Economics of Wildlife Conservation Policy in Kenya," "The Kiss of Death—or Does Conservation Work?" "Property Rights and the Marginal Wildebeest," and "Godzilla vs. King Kong—East African Style." www.mng5.com.

Nyasa Times. "Malawi Elephants: People Opposing Relocation Receive Death Threats" (an unbylined article noting local opposition to the International Fund for Animal Welfare's influence in Malawi's elephant policies). June 22, 2009.

Nzioka, Patrick, and John Njagi. "Mungiki Kill Villagers in Night Raids." *Daily Nation,* April 21, 2009.

Onjala, Joseph Oginga. "Managing Water Scarcity in Kenya: Industrial Response to Tariffs and Regulatory Enforcement." PhD dissertation, Roskilde University, Copenhagen, 2002.

Packer, Craig. "Rational Fear" (a study of lion predation on humans). *Natural History Magazine,* May 2009.

———. *Savannas Forever: A Certification Program for Lion Trophy Hunting.* African Conservation Foundation, March 2006.

Packer, Craig, et al. *Proceedings of the First Tanzania Lion and Leopard Conservation Plan Workshop.* Tanzania Wildlife Research Institute, February 2006.

Park, Mungo. *Travels into the Interior of Africa.* 1799; reprint, Eland Books, 2004.

Parker, Ian. *What I Tell You Three Times Is True: Conservation, Ivory, History and Politics.* Librario, 2004.

Peterson, Dale, and Karl Ammann. *Eating Apes.* University of California Press, 2003.

Petrides, George A., and Wendell G. Swank. "The Status of Wildlife and Wilderness Areas in East Africa." *Oryx, the International Journal of Conservation* 5, no. 4–5 (1960). (Included in the study is an examination of the Galana Scheme.)

Poole, Robert M. "Heartbreak on the Serengeti." *National Geographic,* February 2006.

Rewe, Thomas O. "Breeding Objectives and Selection Schemes for Boran Cattle in Kenya." PhD dissertation, University of Stuttgart–Hohenheim, 2009.

Ross, Mark C. *Dangerous Beauty—Life and Death in Africa: True Stories from a Safari Guide.* Miramax, 2003.

Ruark, Robert. *Something of Value.* 1955; reprint, Safari Press, 2009.

Salt, Henry S. *Animals' Rights: Considered in Relation to Social Progress.* Macmillan and Co., 1894.

Schaller, George B. *The Serengeti Lion: A Study of Predator-Prey Relations.* University of Chicago Press, 1972.

Schofield, Clive. "The Floating Treasure" (a report on the origins of Somali piracy). www.pya.org/wp-includes/pdf/floating-treasure-pya-news-17-full-version.pdf, accessed July 8, 2011.

Sheldrick, Daphne. *The Tsavo Story.* Collins and Harvill, 1973.

Sillet, Mary. "Why the International Fund for Animal Welfare Does Not Meet the Requirements for Membership of the IUCN" (letter from the Inuit Tapirisat to the IUCN). www.highnorth.no/library/movements/IFAW/wh-th-if.htm, October 15, 1996.

Singer, Peter. *Animal Liberation.* Harper Perennial, 2009.

Thomson, Ron. "Kruger National Park's New Elephant Management Plan." www.safarinewsreel.com/blog/?p=560 (a Web site featuring Thomson's blogs on game management), April 26, 2010.

Vasagar, Jeevan. "Joy Shot Me in the Leg So I Gunned Her Down" (a reconsideration of the Joy Adamson murder case). *The Observer,* February 8, 2004.

Walters, Barbara. "Smoke Alarm" (a treatise on charcoal burning). *Africa Geographic.* April 2010.

Wambuguh, Oscar. *Conservation of Biological Diversity in Developing Countries: The Issues Challenges and Possible Solutions—a Case Study in the Laikipia District of Kenya.* Lambert Academic Publishing, 2010.

Wasser, Samuel K., Bill Clark, and Cathy Laurie. "Forensic Tools Battle Ivory Poachers." *Scientific American,* July 2009.

Waugh, Evelyn. *Black Mischief.* 1932; reprint, Back Bay Books, 2002.

Woodroffe, Rosie, Simon Thirgood, and Alan Rabinowitz, eds. *People and Wildlife—Conflict or Co-Existence?* Cambridge University Press, 2005.

Wrong, Michela. *It's Our Turn to Eat: The Story of a Kenyan Whistleblower.* HarperCollins, 2009.

Acknowledgments

Feeling proprietary about Africa is a mistake, particularly for the visitor. Knowing this full well, I still succumbed. To spend any significant time among the game and the people assures a deep and violent romance, one marked by unreasoning passion, self-doubt, jealousy—and, ultimately, despair over separation. Authorities far more qualified than I have parsed all that is wrong with Africa, and I cannot dispute them. That doesn't mean I don't yearn to go back. I don't know how many visitors have looked out on the Serengeti or the bushlands of Laikipia and thought, "I am home," but I must add myself to that legion. It is an arrogant thought, of course: these are *not* our places, at least in terms of current tenure. But I suspect our love, our desire to possess, is rooted in our DNA. Our predecessors were hunting-and-gathering hominids who evolved here. How could we not recognize and covet the landscapes that sustained them?

But it is unproductive—dangerous, even—to become bedazzled and besotted by the subject of one's reporting. I am therefore indebted to the many people who helped me with my research and kept me on track. They gave unstintingly of their time, their wisdom, and their resources. They guided me, advised me, corrected and chided me, and sometimes held my hand, literally.

I would especially like to thank Laurence Frank, who introduced me to the residents and rangelands of Laikipia; Rian and Lorna Labuschagne and their associates, who provided much needed context on continental conservation issues and arranged for critical interviews; Ian Parker, whose modesty, wry humor, devoted service to the game, and ongoing joie de vivre still fill me with admiration; Will Travers of Born Free, whose insights on the personality and philosophy of George Adamson helped anchor this book; Tom McShane of the Global Institute of Sustainability at Arizona State University, whose work is providing a new set of metrics for judging the relative success of conservation projects; and Greenwell Matongo and Chris Weaver of the World Wildlife Fund, who made my reporting in Namibia possible.

Finally, I'd like to thank Alex Nyoike, in my opinion the hardest-working cabbie in Nairobi. His indefatigable good humor, patience, personal courage, insights, and connections made the many days I spent in Kenya's capital productive, secure, and ultimately enjoyable.

These good people and everyone else I encountered in my reporting contributed to anything that is valuable in this book. The errors are my own.

Index

West Africa, IFAW in, 91–92
wetlands: coastal, 228, 232; Usangu Basin, 201
Wetlands International, 188
What I Tell You Three Times Is True (Parker), 23
white-winged bat, 52
wildebeest: Loita Plains, 33; Mara-Serengeti
  herd, 70–72, 103, 115–16, 117, 123, 200, 218;
  Namibia, 167–69, 174; Singita Grumeti
  Reserves, 117, 123
wilderness, conceptions of, 8–9; Eden myth,
  9, 67
Wildlife Conservation and Management
  Department (Kenya), 30
Wildlife Conservation Society, 20, 21
Wildlife Conservation Society of Tanzania, 201
wildlife diseases, 3, 56, 176, 182
Wildlife Laikipia Forum, 155. *See also* King,
  Anthony
wildlife policy: animalism and, 20; Namibia,
  164–67; need for flexibility, 135, 153; South
  Africa, 97; unexpected consequences, 43.
  See also Kenyan wildlife policy; *specific policy issues*
wildlife populations: audits of, 94; California,
  214–15; in countries that allow hunting, 93–
  94, 97–98; Kenya coast, 232–33; Kenya, generally, 7, 9, 32–33, 67, 79, 94, 215; Namibia,
  166, 174, 177; Singita Grumeti Reserves, 117–

18, 119*fig.*, 121*fig.*; Tanzania, 93–94, 102–3,
  111. *See also specific animals and locations*
wildlife products and trade, 34, 74–75; harp seal
  hunt, 49, 90, 92–93; lion bone, 56; rhino
  horn, 30, 33, 44. *See also* cropping; ivory
  trade
wildlife rehabilitation, 13, 224; Adamsons' work,
  12–13, 16–17, 21–23; IFAW's support for, 91
Windhoek, Namibia, 162
win-win thinking, 72–73, 191, 194, 195–96, 199–
  200, 202; acknowledging trade-offs, 72–73,
  191, 194–202
wolves, 43
Woodroffe, Rosie, 18
World Bank, 200–201
World Organization for Animal Health, 40, 193
World Wildlife Fund (WWF), 19, 66, 161, 165,
  167
Wrong, Michela, 204–13

Yellowstone National Park, 43

Zebra Book, 151
zebras, 28, 88, 117, 125; cropping of, 135, 161, 185;
  impact on rangelands, 182, 183; Namibia,
  161, 167
Zebu cattle, 180
zoning, for wildlife uses, 103–4

TEXT	10/13 Sabon
DISPLAY	Sabon
COMPOSITOR	BookMatters, Berkeley
INDEXER	Thérèse Shere
CARTOGRAPHER	Bill Nelson
PRINTER AND BINDER	Maple-Vail Book Manufacturing Group